Four Waifs on Our Doorstep

Four Waifs on Our Doorstep

Trisha Merry

with Jacquie Buttriss

**SIMON &
SCHUSTER**

London · New York · Sydney · Toronto · New Delhi

A CBS COMPANY

First published in Great Britain by Simon & Schuster UK Ltd, 2015
This paperback edition published by Simon & Schuster UK Ltd, 2018
A CBS COMPANY

While this book gives a faithful account of the author's experiences, some names
and details have been changed to protect the privacy of the individuals involved.
Trisha Merry is a pseudonym.

1 3 5 7 9 10 8 6 4 2

Simon & Schuster UK Ltd
1st Floor
222 Gray's Inn Road
London WC1X 8HB

www.simonandschuster.co.uk
www.simonandschuster.com.au
www.simonandschuster.co.in

Simon & Schuster Australia, Sydney
Simon & Schuster India, New Delhi

The author and publishers have made all reasonable efforts
to contact copyright-holders for permission, and apologise
for any omissions or errors in the form of credits given.
Corrections may be made to future printings.

A CIP catalogue record for this book is available from the British Library

Paperback ISBN: 978-1-4711-7707-1
eBook ISBN: 978-1-4711-3846-1

Typeset in the UK by Hewer Text UK Ltd, Edinburgh
Printed and bound by CPI Group (UK) Ltd, Croydon, CR0 4YY

To my amazing family. Every day I thank my lucky stars that I have you in my life. I love you all very much.

Contents

I

Four Hungry Waifs

'6 March 1997 – Children taken into police protection.
7 March 1997 – Emergency Protection Order made in respect
of all four children, who are taken to foster carers.'

Social worker's case notes

It was eleven o'clock at night when we heard a vehicle pull up outside our house. I peeked out through the curtains and saw a white minibus parked under the street lamp. Two women got out and came up the path.

'They're here!' I called to Mike, and he joined me in the hallway as they knocked on the door. I immediately opened it.

'Hello,' said one of the women. 'Mr and Mrs Merry?'

'Yes, that's right.'

They introduced themselves – a social worker and a support worker. 'I believe you are expecting us?'

'Yes, do you have the children with you?'

'We do. We've just woken them up, so they're still a bit sleepy I'm afraid,' said one.

'They've had a difficult day and a long journey, but they slept most of the way,' added the other.

We stood out on the doorstep, ready to welcome them, as the support worker carried the youngest and the social worker ushered the other three up our path towards us. I can remember my shock, even after all those years, and the hundreds of children we'd cared for.

As the eldest, a boy with a shaven head, approached, I noticed the big wet patch down the front of his light-coloured trousers. He looked petrified. They all did. In all my years of fostering, I had never seen children look more frightened than these four. If I could have taken a photo of them that evening, it would have been just like those sepia prints I'd seen of Dr Barnardo's urchins, taken off the streets of London in Victorian times.

They trembled in their thin, shabby clothes, much too light for the cold of the night, the younger two in T-shirts and nappies, the elder boy's jumper torn and half unravelled up one sleeve. Then there was the obvious bruising on their pinched faces and bony hands . . . I dreaded to think what other unseen injuries they might have.

Both the boys' heads were shaved; the older girl's hair looked as if it had been badly cut with blunt scissors, all jagged and tufty, and the younger girl had bald patches where her hair had apparently been pulled out in clumps. This child also had her arm plastered and in a sling, a swollen lip and a black eye. She looked very frail. The other girl had a black eye too. The baby was lethargic and seemed to have some sort of skin condition. He turned his head away when I looked at his face.

The eldest of the four was almost rigid with anxiety, his

expression darting from one sibling to another, as if checking they were all right.

We were experienced – we knew we had to keep our faces right, our expressions smiling, but in that brief moment when I took in that sight of the four of them, I thought: *Oh my God!* Then my brain went into overdrive, imagining the lives these poor waifs must have led, and wondering how we were going to cope with their various needs.

As the children came nearer, we could smell them. When you look at a healthy baby's skin it has a bloom on it – a shine, doesn't it? But when you see children that aren't washed, their skin is dull and textured, like suede. These four were grubby all right, very grubby, and all scratching their heads and bodies like crazy.

Steeling ourselves and still smiling, we took a few steps towards them and gave them all hugs. That was the most important thing. I remember the three older children's faces, their looks of astonishment, mixed with acute apprehension.

'Welcome to our home. Come on in – we've got hot chocolate and bickies for you,' I said as I ushered them into the hall. 'This will be your home too for as long as you stay. We've been really looking forward to seeing you.'

As Mike took the two social workers and the children into the sitting room, I dashed upstairs and found a pair of my grandson Brett's trousers for the elder boy to change into. Fortunately they fitted well enough, with a belt round the waist and the bottoms turned up. He looked relieved to get rid of his wet trousers, out in the hallway, though he trembled with fear.

'I couldn't help it,' he wailed, unable to stop the tears. 'I told them I needed to go. I asked them to stop, but they wouldn't. I knew you would be very cross with me.'

'No, I'm not. It wasn't your fault, so there's no reason for me to be cross.' I gave his unyielding body another hug. 'You don't need to be worried about anything in this house,' I tried to reassure him.

'But I do. I have to worry about the others,' he replied with a quiver in his voice, as he wiped away his tears with his shabby sleeve, leaving a smear across his cheek.

I wanted to take him out of all his clothes and put on clean ones, but realised that would be too traumatic for him so soon.

'Simon needs to have his nappies changed,' he said as he zipped up his trousers. I remember being quite surprised by this remark. Young children don't usually notice such things.

'Do you know when he was last changed?' I asked him.

'When the social workers came this morning. One of them did it.' That would have been more than twelve hours before. 'I usually have to try to do it,' he added.

'Well, I have lots of nappies, so I'll change him straight away.'

'Caroline too?'

'Yes, Caroline too.' I grabbed the nappy bag from the downstairs cloakroom and we went back to join the others.

'What's your name?' I asked him.

'Hamish,' he said.

'And how old are you, Hamish?'

'Seven.'

I had to pick up my jaw. He didn't look any older than four or five, his body so bony and his face very thin. To be honest, I thought he looked half starved, so perhaps that was why he was so small for his age.

'Can you introduce me to your sisters and brother?'

'Yes, this is Anita,' he said, pointing at the girl with tufty hair. Then he turned to the younger girl. 'Caroline has a broken arm.' Finally he pointed at the baby, now plonked onto the floor and making no effort to move. 'And this is Simon.' As he spoke, I noticed there was something odd about Hamish's speech. Perhaps a slight impediment of some kind.

'I'm Trisha and this is Mike.' I smiled my warmest smile to them all.

'What does it say on your top?' asked Anita with a cheeky grin.

'I straightened my T-shirt and pointed out the words to her, one at a time. '"I'm the boss."'

'What does that mean?' she asked, tilting her head to one side.

'It means I'm the one that organises things in the house. Like cooking, for instance.' The three older children's faces lit up. 'Now, I expect you're tired, after your long journey.'

I could not fail to notice the girls' dismay, and Hamish's look of alarm. Panic more like. His eyes darted to the hall-way. Did he want to leave? Was it something I'd said? . . . or maybe something I hadn't said? At that moment, I realised.

'. . . and I expect you're hungry. Let's get you something to eat.' As I said this, his expression immediately switched to one of immense relief.

'For all of us?' asked Hamish. 'We're all very hungry.'

'Yes, for all of you. What would you like?'

'Can we have pasta?' asked Anita.

'Yes, of course you can.'

Just then, the two women stood up.

'I'm afraid we have to leave now, if that's all right with you,' said the social worker. 'We have a long drive back.'

I showed them out to the front door. 'Did the children bring anything with them, any clothes or wash things, or anything?'

'No,' answered the social worker. 'Nothing but what they are wearing.'

It must have been an urgent case then, I thought, as most children bring something with them, whatever their circumstances. I remembered Caroline's arm being in a sling when I opened the door.

'The agency told me Caroline was in hospital,' I said. 'Was that because of her arm . . . or something else?'

'Yes, she has a broken arm,' said the support worker. 'She's had the injury for several days, but it's only been treated today.'

I shuddered at the thought of the pain she must have been in.

'Can you tell me anything else about the children?'

'I'm afraid not, Mrs Merry.'

As I closed the door, I knew these women weren't

allowed to say anything. After all, it was an emergency care order and we would probably only have the children with us for a week or two, so what did we need to know? As usual, we foster parents were left in the dark, to work things out for ourselves.

Of course, to be fair, it was sometimes possible that a family had not been known to the authorities until something traumatic happened, such as a parent's serious injury or death.

But I had developed an instinct over the years, and straight away, looking at these children, there was no way they wouldn't have been known to Social Services. Absolutely no way. For a start, we only had to look at them to see how underfed they were, not to mention the injuries, or anything unseen.

'Come on, kids,' I called. 'Come to the kitchen and tell me what you want to eat.'

Well, it was a stampede!

I opened the fridge door. We had a big, American-style fridge, packed from top to bottom with food.

They were transfixed. Caroline was actually trembling when she looked at all the food.

'You can have cereals, or fruit, or eggs, or baked beans on toast . . .' Usually, newly arrived foster children would happily choose something from what I had suggested. But I felt as if I was going about it all wrong with these four, as the older three all rushed at the fridge, with Hamish pulling things out and handing them to his siblings. The girls fought to grab their own food too. Meanwhile, Simon, the placid baby, seemed almost unaware of what was going on.

'OK, OK. There's no need to rush. We have plenty enough for all of you, so let's take everything through to the dining room.'

So we carried all the food we could from the kitchen to the dining room, setting it all out on our long dining table until it was almost fully covered. The children stood and looked at it all in stunned silence. The sight of so much food seemed to overwhelm them.

Normally, I would have made sure they all washed their grubby hands but, for once, I realised that the most important thing was to feed them.

Suddenly I remembered what one of the girls had asked for earlier. 'You can all choose anything you like to start with, then sit down at the table to eat, and I'll quickly cook some pasta for you as well.'

Hamish went forward first and picked up various things with his hands to give to the others, then took some for himself. This started a feeding frenzy as they grabbed everything they could, snatching from each other. They crammed their food straight into their mouths and wolfed it all down, still standing up, while clutching at more in case it disappeared.

'You can sit down to eat,' I repeated, but that seemed to confuse them, so I decided to leave table manners to the next day. I filled some bowls with cereals of their choice – we had lots to choose from.

As soon as they realised that if they finished this, they

could have something else, they began to calm down and just concentrated on eating. But Hamish was still shaking as he ate, turning this way and that to make sure his siblings were all right.

I brought in a big tureen of pasta in tomato sauce, and they all wanted some. I filled up big bowls to the brim for each child and watched them ladle it into their mouths with their hands, making a terrible mess, which satisfied them no end. I had put out cutlery for them, but they seemed to have no concept of eating with a knife and fork.

For somebody so tiny, Caroline could certainly put her food away. She managed to eat three full bowls of pasta before she finally had to give in. Anita's eyes darted across the table as she ate.

'I can do with some more,' she announced with her cheeky grin.

Hamish fed himself and Simon by turns.

I watched them as they finally began to flag. The difficult bit, I thought, is that we're looking at four filthy children, and I could almost see their hair and clothing move with lice, but they must be so tired and so anxious. I can't bath them tonight – they can barely stay awake, now that they've filled their tummies.

So, catering for the children's evident insecurities, Mike and I committed the sin of turning one double bed around, so that the side was up against the wall. Then we took the children to the bathroom for a quick wash – not a popular move, especially as they didn't seem to be familiar with soap. Caroline held back, outside the door, so I didn't insist. We would have to leave a more thorough wash until the morning.

We only had one pair of pyjamas that weren't too big. They were my grandson Brett's. The legs were too long for Hamish, but at least he could tie the waist so they didn't fall off. The other three had to go to bed that first night in what they had on, minus their ill-fitting footwear – quite an assortment. Hamish had his feet crammed into a cracked pair of plastic sandals, Anita wore floppy wellington boots and Caroline was in threadbare slippers. None of them wore socks, except for Simon, and when I took his off, I was shocked to see what looked like a deep cigarette burn on his grubby ankle.

Hamish's face lit up – a picture of wonder – at the sight of a thick, clean duvet covering the soft, springy mattress. He kept touching it all as if it was a new experience. We laid all the children side by side across the bed. This way, if they woke in the night, anxious or confused, they would have the security of each other nearby.

That first night, and every night after, we left their bedroom door open, with their light and the landing light on. Our bedroom was directly opposite theirs, across the corridor, so we could see into their room and all the way to the bed.

When Mike and I had finished cleaning up the mess we were worn out. We sat down with a hot drink before bed and just looked at each other. I think we were both shell-shocked.

'I hope we haven't bitten off more than we can chew,' I sighed.

Mike remained very quiet. He just gave me a look that was supposed to be encouraging. He's always so positive, but I knew he was really thinking: Mmm, have we done the right thing?

We were both feeling very apprehensive. Seeing those poor waifs arriving on our doorstep in that state and watching their behaviour with the food and everything . . . it had all been quite upsetting. I knew we were both quiet because I was thinking and Mike was thinking, and neither of us wanted to voice those thoughts. Not yet anyway.

As I lay in bed, mulling it all over in my mind while Mike slept, I could see across the landing how restless the children were and how fitfully they slept. Every now and then one of them would moan or cry out, especially Anita who wailed the loudest, and the first few times I got up to go and comfort them, only to find they were crying in their sleep. Back to bed I went, wondering about their nightmares.

Had we taken on too much? It had all happened so quickly – just a few weeks from being a retired couple moving house, to taking on this new little family, perhaps the most challenging we have ever had. My thoughts went back to the events leading up to the children's arrival on our doorstep . . .

2

Change of Plans

'Trisha Merry, who found room in her heart to foster hundreds of children, has been named "Mum in a Million" . . . At one time, when she had twenty children staying with her, she took them all on holiday to Bournemouth.

Nowadays though, she has a quieter life . . .'

Evening News, 1994

'This place is like a 1960s timewarp!' I said to Mike when we first viewed the house in Church Road. 'I'm going to do it all up and only have the grandchildren at weekends. I know just how I want it.'

'We'd better buy it then!' He grinned.

In the first few weeks of 1997 we moved in and started decorating. This was going to be my dream home, with Laura Ashley wallpaper throughout.

'Why not paint?' asked Mike.

'We've had washable walls in every house we've lived in, since we took in our first children all those years ago,' I sighed. 'Nearly seven hundred children later, this house is going to be just for us, to enjoy our retirement.'

By the end of February, we had decorated all the upstairs, and we'd just started on the hall and study when I heard a knock on the door.

I was surprised to see John there on our doorstep. He used to be a social worker, so I knew him from my fostering days.

'Can I come in?' he asked.

'Yes, of course.' I showed him into the sitting room. 'Is this a social visit?'

'I've been thinking about you and Mike. You see, there's a new way of fostering now,' he explained. 'It's through an agency, so it's more care-focused.'

'About time somebody focused on care, instead of the money side of it!'

'I've just opened up a fostering agency in this area. It's called the ODFA, which stands for the Open Door Fostering Agency. Local authorities ask us to place their difficult cases. We have our own list of the best foster carers . . . and that's why I've come to you. We do training sessions, and get all our foster parents together to share their experiences and tips.'

'That would have appealed to us twenty years ago,' I said. 'We would have liked that idea, but we've moved on since then. We've retired.'

'Yes, I remember. You used to have emergency cases, mums with babies, large sibling groups or difficult children, didn't you?'

'That's right.' By now, I was feeling even more curious. *What is he doing here?*

'Don't you miss having a houseful?'

'Well, no, not really. I think we've earned a rest! I'm fifty-five you know, and Mike's sixty-two.'

'But you don't seem it, and you were such great foster parents, you and Mike. Wouldn't you like to foster again?'

'No. No, we wouldn't. No-no-no-no-no. No. Definitely not!'

'Well, maybe you might reconsider?'

'I don't think so!'

We talked a bit about some of the children we remembered. Then he stood up to leave.

'So you'll think about it . . .'

He looked so hopeful that I didn't like to say no outright.

'Well, maybe.' I paused. 'I'll mention it to Mike and see what he thinks.'

I didn't expect to give fostering another thought that day, but I was wrong. As I painted the skirting boards, I found myself harking back to the antics we'd had with so many foster children, some just staying for one night; others for weeks, months, or even years.

Of course, I knew what Mike would think, but I asked him anyway.

'Do you remember John, who used to be a social worker? Well, he came round this morning, while you were taking the car to the garage.'

'What did he want?'

'He was telling me all about his fostering agency, and the way they offer training and invite their carers to meetings together.'

'Oh yes,' he said, absent-mindedly.

'So what do you think?'

'About what?'

'He wants us to consider going onto his list of the best foster carers. I felt mean to keep saying no, so I said I'd ask you about it.'

He was silent for only a moment or two. 'No, we're too old.' He picked up his newspaper to read, so we just left it at that.

The next day I was about to call John to give him our verdict, when he rang me.

'I've been telling my partner Suzy all about you,' he began. 'We run the agency together and she would like to come and meet you. Could we come round this afternoon, at about fourish?'

'Well, yes . . . but . . .'

'Great. See you then.' And he put the phone down, before I could tell him we weren't interested.

So, I made some scones, put the kettle on and they arrived at a few minutes past four.

After the introductions, as I was pouring out the tea, John's partner began to tell me about her role in the agency.

'Oh, it's so exciting now,' she said. 'We can offer loads of support to our foster carers and pay them well too. We invite them to regular meetings where we can sit round and chat about all their problems. People find that so helpful.'

'Yes, I'm sure they do . . .'

'And that's not all,' she cut in, brimming over with

enthusiasm. 'We have some brilliant trainers to help you consider different approaches to some of your problems . . .'

'Wait a minute.' It was my turn to interrupt. 'We're not foster carers any more. We're enjoying our retirement.'

'I know. But if you're good at something, why waste it?'

I sat silently for a moment and thought about that. There's not a lot I've excelled at. I'm good at cooking. I'm good at coming in under budget when I'm doing up houses . . .

'Don't you agree?'

'Well, yes,' I hesitated. 'I did a fair job on fostering. We both did.'

'John told me you won the "Mum in a Million" title a few years ago. Isn't that marvellous?'

'Well, it was only the Midland region,' I explained. 'I was just runner-up in the national awards. But Mike once won a Tommy Steele lookalike competition . . . and a bar of soap for his knobbly knees.'

They looked confused. They probably had no idea who Tommy Steele was, and knobbly knees contests had passed them by.

'We'd really love to add you to our list of top foster parents,' said John. 'Did you talk to Mike about it?'

'Yes, I'm sorry he couldn't be here this afternoon. I did ask him what he thought, and he said, "We're too old for all that."'

'I bet you don't feel old?' suggested Suzy. 'You don't seem it at all.'

'And you have so much to offer,' said John. 'Both of you. We have a lot of urgent cases these days, which means they're with you before you know it, and you get very involved in it all.'

'And with emergency placements they don't usually stay long,' added Suzy. 'So you could have plenty of rest days in between.'

'Please don't say no,' continued John, 'without considering how different and how much better it would be this time around. We'd love you to join us.'

'Well . . .'

'Good.' He stood up. 'It's time we left. Thanks very much for the tea.'

'And the delicious scones.' Suzy smiled.

'And promise me you and Mike will reconsider?' pleaded John. 'I'll call you at the end of the week and you can tell me then.'

'I'm keeping everything crossed!' Suzy called back as they walked down our path to their car.

The next day, I was putting up some pretty, blue-diamond-patterned wallpaper in the bathroom and thinking: No, I don't think I want any more foster children, thank you! We'd just bought a beautiful cream suite. I'd waited all my married life for a cream suite and finally, after thirty-six years, I'd got one. And it was quite a large house, so I had in my mind that I was going to do bed and breakfast for Americans. I would be able to do nice, grown-up cooking, and the house would be clean and tidy.

All my decorating was nearly done and I thought: Yes, this is going to be really lovely.

But, much as I wanted this new, carefree life for our retirement, there was still a niggle in my mind. We'd helped so many damaged children over the years, and the more I thought about it, the less I remembered the horrible bits. I just thought about all the fun, you know? And I thought . . . Yeah. We could enjoy some more of that.

'What do you think, love?' I said to Mike that evening, trying to sound undecided.

He gave me a look. I think he knew I'd already made up my mind.

'Well . . .' He broke into a wide smile. 'We've got a five-bedroom house and there's only the two of us . . .'

So that was it.

'I suppose we ought to tell the children?'

'Yes, but I can just imagine what they'll say!' he laughed.

'You're mad!' exclaimed Sally, the eldest of our three adopted children. 'Why do you want to work that hard again, Mum?'

Daniel was away in Russia at the time, so I couldn't tell him till much later. But when I rang the youngest, Jane, it was like déjà vu.

'Mum, you must be crazy! Absolutely bonkers.'

Finally I spoke to Anna, our teenage foster child who was only with us at weekends now.

'Yes, I can understand why you want to go back to it,' she said, without a glimmer of surprise.

* * *

Social Services knew us well and had a lot of information about us already, but they needed to do a new assessment, to make sure we were still suitable. We should be too old really, but we knew they had very few people willing to take sibling groups and the most difficult children. We went to meet a panel of professionals who consider: Are you experienced enough? Yes – tick. Have you enough space? Yes – tick. And are you young enough? No – a big cross! Would that be a barrier? Apparently not.

'Yes, you can have sibling groups up to four children,' they said.

It had all happened very quickly, but I assumed it would be some time before a family group would come up.

First thing the next morning, the phone rang. 'Hello, Mrs Merry, it's the ODFA, the fostering agency,' said a young voice at the other end. 'We've got this sibling group of four children arriving today, on an emergency protection order. Will you take them?'

'Yes, all right,' I gulped, stunned that it was all happening so quickly. We hadn't even thought about getting the house ready for fostering.

'They should be with you this afternoon.'

Well, I prepared as best I could, not knowing anything about these children, their ages or their needs. I just remember thinking, we don't have cereal and we don't have nappies or babies' milk. How old are they? Will they come with any clothes? So many questions . . . and not one answer. We'd soon find out.

I did some food shopping, put it all away, then wondered again about clothes. I had some of my grandchildren Brett and Laura's things, which they kept here for weekends, and I found a bag of young children's clothing – bits and pieces left over from our fostering days.

I made the beds and put some cuddly toys out in their rooms.

Our house and our lives were about to be taken over but, not knowing anything about these children, it was impossible to have a foolproof plan. We just had to be ready for anything. That's how Mike and I had always approached it, with an open mind and a warm heart . . . and more than a little apprehension.

As four o'clock approached and I sat down for a break, my thoughts went right back to the days before all this began. I'd been a nanny when I left school, which I loved, looking after a baby boy called George. But his parents went bankrupt, so that ended sooner than expected. Next I went to work in a shop, but that definitely wasn't for me!

Neither was my next job in Kay's catalogue office. It was very regimented there. The supervisor walked up and down between the desks and you couldn't look up, you couldn't stop writing. Definitely the wrong job for me. After six weeks I moved to the office of a factory making metal boxes. Why I thought I could cope with that any better I don't know.

'I don't like this job,' I moaned when I got home from work that first evening.

'Well, first day. You know . . .' said Mike. 'You've got to give it a go.'

'No, I'm giving in my notice,' I said.

He sighed and went to do the washing up.

The next day, when I walked into town, I saw a big poster, advertising for childminders. My eyes lit up as I stopped to read it. I asked around and it seemed the Council were desperate to have more day-care provision.

Well, I thought, let's weigh this up. Childminding or sitting in an office? No contest!

'Would you mind if I worked from home?' I asked Mike that evening. Poor man. We had only been married for a year and he was still adjusting to my wacky ideas.

'Doing office work?'

'No, childminding.'

He paused, with a quizzical look on his face, which turned into a long-suffering smile. 'If that's what you want to do,' he replied. 'Why not? Give it a go if you think you're up for it. We've got the space.'

That was true, with the two of us rattling around in a four-bedroom house, so that was it. We changed the living room into a playroom and jiggled everything about. Then I put out some adverts and within days I had all these children in.

In my last proper job I had earned £3 and 10 shillings a week, for work I hated. Now people were paying me £2 a week for each child and I had ten children – £20 a week for staying at home and playing, which I loved. I could barely believe it! I started at seven and finished at seven, washing nappies, making breakfast, dinner and tea, having fun and finally I put them into their pyjamas to be collected. I was never without children and I loved it.

One day a social worker came and looked around. Then she sat down for a cup of tea with me, in the middle of the playroom.

'We need to place two children with you to look after daily,' she said. 'But these siblings may have to come into overnight care as well for a short while. Do you think you could manage that?'

'Right,' I gulped. 'OK.'

'Their mother is expecting another baby,' she added. 'And she has toxaemia.'

'Oh dear. Yes, we can do that.'

'But the thing is, you'll have to become foster parents.'

'That's fine,' I replied. 'I love looking after little ones.'

These two became our first foster children. Next came a newborn baby girl, then more babies, followed by several sibling groups. I've loved every day of it . . . well, nearly every day. I've played and played. All my life I've played. And the best bit is when you have young children who understand what you are telling them – about all the things that are on offer for them, all the opportunities ahead of them. I used to think: I want a bit of that. I loved being able to open their doors to life.

Now, here we were, hundreds of foster children later, recently retired, only to start all over again, waiting for our next big challenge. A family of four on an emergency order.

Over all those years, I had learned the hard way. Don't leave any jewellery about. Don't leave the car keys and definitely don't leave any drink out. I found out by trial and error what worked for foster children and what didn't, but I could never be sure if I was right. I never had the chance to go and see what other carers did, or talk about different ways of dealing with things. That's why John's idea of foster carers' meetings sounded so appealing.

As the afternoon wore on, I was beginning to get a bit edgy, for the children's sake. What had resulted in their emergency removal? I could only imagine the terrible impact their circumstances might have had on them, especially if they were very young and nobody explained anything to them, as often happens.

At about four o'clock, the phone rang.

'It's the ODFA here, Mrs Merry. I'm afraid it's going to be a bit later than we thought.'

'Right. Any idea why?'

'All we know is that one of the children was in hospital, and it's a full care order.'

I went and told Mike. 'They've been delayed. They'll be here this evening, and it's a full care order.'

'So that means there are problems!'

'Yes, it's usually major problems with the parents, isn't it?'

And of course the children finally arrived, late that night, looking like workhouse paupers. As I lay in bed, with their occasional wails and moans echoing in the darkness, I felt so helpless. Yes, major problems seemed an accurate judgement. I wondered what tomorrow would bring.

3

Bedlam

'A mad, mad day.'

My diary entry, Saturday, 8 March 1997

It was about half-past seven when the children woke each other up, and right from the start it was bedlam. Absolute bedlam. There was nothing, and I do mean nothing, stopping them — no boundaries at all. Hamish looked shell-shocked. The clues from last night suggested he was used to being in charge of his younger siblings' welfare, but in our house he felt lost. He didn't know whether he was in control, or not, yet he couldn't let go. He didn't quite know what to do.

Their bed was soaking wet and soiled. Nobody had warned me that neither Hamish nor Anita were dry at night. There was going to be a lot of washing in this house!

I took them all into the downstairs bathroom, almost dragging Caroline in behind the others.

'No, I not want to.' She stamped her little foot. 'I not.'

'Everyone has to wash their hands before breakfast,' I said. 'Here's the soap and there's the towel.' Blank faces, so I washed my hands to show them. 'It won't take you long, and when you've finished you can come and have some breakfast.'

I changed Simon and Caroline's nappies and washed their hands for them. As I was getting out the cereals, Hamish came in.

I sniffed . . . twice. 'Have you had an accident, love?' I asked him quietly.

He gave me a puzzled look, and I realised he probably didn't know what I was talking about.

'Have you done a pooh?'

'Yes.'

'Did you wash your hands?'

'No.'

'Right, come on then, because we have to wash our hands after going to the toilet.'

'Why?'

'Well, because pooh has germs in it, and you don't want to eat with dirty hands or you'll have germs in your tummy.'

Just then, Anita joined us and the same smell wafted from her.

So I took them both into the bathroom. Sure enough, the toilet wasn't flushed and there was no paper down there. Just as I was flushing the loo and wondering about no paper, I turned around to see brown handprints all over my beautiful new Laura Ashley wallpaper.

I confess I had a despondent moment, then a sigh and a shrug to remember how pretty my blue diamond-patterned walls had looked. But it was no good reacting negatively, because the children wouldn't have understood. They clearly didn't know about using toilet paper. After all, if a family doesn't have enough food to eat, do you think they're going to go and buy toilet paper?

Well, I didn't know whether to wipe the wall or wash the children first. Of course, it had to be the children . . . and that was a horrible job.

OK, I thought, this might be harder than I expected, but I can do it – yes! (I did try to get the marks off later, and bleached them out in the end, along with some of the pattern.)

What we need is a chart, I decided, with columns for teeth, face, hands, toilet paper – a star in the column and two pence in the jam jar. Four pence out if they forget. I'd get that started as soon as possible, then once they had settled in we could start another column for not swearing – another two pence in the jar. I laughed to myself, guessing it would be a while before we could put a star in that column!

The four waifs had a huge breakfast, three or four helpings, spreading chaos across the table. After that, I took them back up to the bathroom. Caroline hung back.

'Here's a toothbrush each.' They looked puzzled. 'This is how I clean my teeth,' I said, showing them. They seemed to find it quite amusing.

'Why do you do that?' asked Anita.

'To keep my teeth clean so that they don't get decayed and fall out.'

They all looked surprised.

'We never had a toothbrush,' explained Hamish.

'And here's a flannel for each of you, and a hairbrush.'

Finally, we took them down to the playroom we had created in our basement. You should have seen Anita's face when she first caught sight of all the toys. She just stood there for a second or two, transfixed. Within less than a minute though, the three older children had pulled everything off the shelves. They were treading on the toys in their rush, and the whole room was in turmoil. Their short attention spans and complete lack of restraint created pandemonium.

Meanwhile, Simon sat silently where I had put him down, on the carpet amongst some cushions in one corner of the room. The only movement he made was to turn himself round to face the wall. I put a toy in his hand and he looked at it with vague interest, but seemed unsure what to do with it. Had he ever seen toys before? It seemed unnatural to see a baby sitting up and not taking any interest in the people and things around him.

But how old was he? And the others too? They were all so small and painfully thin. As the room warmed up, the children peeled off their shabby tops. I looked at what labels I could find. Hamish had told me he was seven, but I was not surprised to learn that he was wearing clothes for a four- to five-year-old. Anita was in clothes for a three- to four-year-old.

'How old are you, Anita?' I asked her.

'Six,' she replied as she grabbed a 'My Little Pony' from Caroline, who then pulled a tuft of her older sister's hair as she tried in vain to regain it. 'I'll be seven in December,' she added, pushing Caroline down onto the floor. I distracted the younger girl with a baby doll. I was beginning to have concerns about their development, so I was relieved that at least Anita knew her birthday.

'What about Caroline and Simon?' I asked. 'How old are they?'

'Caroline is coming up to five,' said Hamish. 'And Simon is two and a half.'

When I looked at their labels, I found that Caroline was in clothes for a child of eighteen months and Simon in clothes for a child of twelve months.

So the 'baby' wasn't a baby at all. That was the biggest shock. Why wasn't he up and running around like two-year-olds should? Why were the two younger ones so tiny? Had they been premature? Was there a history of poor weight-gain? I would probably never know, but at least I could feed them up now, while they were with us.

I picked up a ball, sat where Simon could see me, cleared a space on the floor and rolled the ball towards him. He watched out of the corner of his eye as it approached and stopped, but he made no move to reach out and pick it up. This didn't seem right to me. Was he traumatised by the situation – by fear? Or was there something else? Did he have learning difficulties, perhaps? Did he have health issues, or maybe it was down to a problem at birth?

I started watching the others. Caroline's movements were immature for her age, and her speech was mostly

grunts, very difficult to understand. Had she been referred
for speech therapy? She seemed to have almost a split
personality. On the one hand, she was fearful of everything,
but on the other she had a fierce temper and she dug her
heels in. 'I will not,' she said whenever she was asked to do
something.

Anita, well, she appeared to be quite bright and bubbly
on the surface, like most six-year-olds. But, watching her
exaggerated poses, her distinctive movements and expressions, and the way she seemed to crave our attention,
especially Mike's, my first instinct was sexualised behaviour. Then I thought, no, surely not . . . this is just a little
girl who hasn't been cuddled or loved. That's all she's looking for.

Hamish was on edge all the time, looking out for his
siblings, checking on their welfare. He seemed almost
resentful of us and the opportunities we were giving the
children. It was as if he couldn't let go of his responsibilities
towards them. In between looking out for them and remind-
ing me to change the younger ones' nappies, he kept
nervously gazing up the stairs. I guessed that perhaps he
was thinking of food.

'Are you hungry again, Hamish?'

'Yes. And we need to get more food,' he answered.

'We've still got plenty left,' I said in a gentle voice.

'No, but we need more cereals and more milk and more
pasta and . . .'

'We can go later on this afternoon.'

'No!' He was shaking. 'We have to go now.'

'Come with me,' I said. I took him up to the kitchen and opened the fridge, and all the food cupboards. 'Look, Hamish. We have loads of food – much more than any of us can eat in a week.'

'But we might run out of bread, or cornflakes, or . . .'

'It's OK,' I said, putting my arm round his reluctant, bony body, trying to soothe him. I wanted to tell him that if we ran out of cornflakes, we could have Rice Krispies, but I thought it was too early to suggest such a thing. 'We won't run out of anything before this afternoon. I promise you we will go to the big supermarket at teatime and stock up on everything . . . as much as you like.'

He looked at me with amazement. 'Anything?'

'Yes, whatever you think we might need.'

'But we have to go every day,' he insisted, anxiety creasing his face. I always had to go every day to get food.'

'If that's what you want, Hamish, then that's what we will do.'

'Yes, because we mustn't run out of food.'

'No, we will never let that happen in this house,' I assured him. 'Did you sometimes run out of food before you came here?' I asked gently. It was too early really to be probing for information of that kind, but he was so panicky I thought it might help him to talk about it.

'We didn't really have food,' he said. 'The social workers used to bring us nappies and money for food, but Mum sold some of the nappies and I don't know what she did with the money . . . Dad was always being arrested, and he left when I was about four.'

'Did anybody bring you food?'

'No. We used to be left alone a lot, and if we had a bit of bread, I made the younger ones toast. Sometimes I found a potato or two and I used to cut them up and heat some oil to cook them in. But mostly there was nothing for us to eat, so I went out in the evenings.'

'On your own?'

'Yes.'

'How did you get out of the house without anyone noticing?'

'I just opened the door.'

'Didn't anyone realise?'

'No. Most evenings we were on our own anyway.'

'So you let yourself out of the door?'

'Yes. I went to Tesco's, round to the back, and got food out of their bins. I always took it straight home for Anita and Caroline to eat.'

'And for you too?'

'Yes.' He nodded. 'Other days I used to rob some Pringles and stuff like that from a local shop, and take them back to the house to feed Anita and Caroline. Once we were so hungry that we sat down outside the shop and ate them all straight away. But the shopkeeper must have called the police.'

'Did they catch you?'

'No. We ran away, down the alleyways.'

'How old were you when you first had to go and find food?'

'I don't know. As long ago as I can remember,' he said.

'We were always hungry, Anita, Caroline and me, so I had to find us food.'

'And what about Simon?'

'I had to tell Mum to feed Simon.' He hesitated. 'Have we had breakfast?'

'Yes, when you got up.' I smiled gently. 'Are you hungry again?'

He nodded.

'OK, we'll take some fruit juice and biscuits down to the playroom to keep you all going. Will that be OK for now?'

'Yes.' As we went back down to join the others, there was a knock at the door and it was Jane, our adopted daughter who lived nearby.

'How's it going?' she asked, making a funny face.

'Bedlam!'

We followed Hamish and the biscuit tin down to the playroom. The noise was almost deafening and the scene was chaos. Anita and Caroline were fighting each other for the same toys, arguing, shouting and pulling each other's hair.

'I'm having it.'

'Mine!' grunted Caroline.

'I saw it first.'

'No.'

'But I picked it up.'

'Give me.'

And all this was littered with words and expressions they shouldn't have known.

'Stop it!' shouted seven-year-old Hamish . . . and they did.

Well, for a few seconds at least. He was the one who looked after them, and he was the one they respected. He was in charge, but I could see that mentally he was desperate to be a little boy and to play with all these wonderful toys.

'I hungry!' wailed Caroline.

'Can we have breakfast?' pleaded Anita.

'You've had breakfast,' I said, 'but Hamish has brought you some biscuits.'

The toys were thrown to the floor and forgotten as the girls rushed to the biscuit tin. That left Simon still sitting where I had put him, and facing the corner. He seemed oblivious to everything.

'Come on, sunshine,' I said as I picked him up and gave him a biscuit. 'We need to feed you up, so that you can play with the others.' He didn't fight me, but he was completely unyielding. There was definitely something not right with this child.

Just then, the doorbell rang. I went upstairs carrying Simon. It was my old friend Marion popping in.

'How are you getting on?' she asked. 'Do you want me to go to the shops for you?'

'You're an angel.' I smiled. 'This is Simon. Come down and meet the other three.'

'Simon – that's a nice name,' she said, lifting her hand to stroke his cheek. He flinched and pulled away. I shifted him to the other arm, to help him to feel safer.

We all sat in the playroom, watching the children and planning out what we needed to do that day.

'Those clothes they've got on are filthy, Mum,' whispered Jane. 'And the kids desperately need a good scrub!'

'Yes, I decided not to bath them until they've calmed down a bit and we've got some nice, new, clean clothes and pyjamas for them to put on afterwards. I was going to take them clothes shopping, but I don't think that would be a good plan when they're all so hyper.'

'No,' she smiled. 'And they'll look like they live in *Little House on the Prairie* if you go shopping for them, Mum. Why don't you leave that side of things to me. I can see roughly what sizes they need.'

'Thanks, love, that would be a great help. They are all older than they look, so get what you think will be best – they need one or two of everything, just to tide them over for a few days. We can go and buy some more things for them when they've settled in . . .' – I lowered my voice – '. . . if we need to. They might not be staying for very long.'

While Jane and Marion were at the shops, the children gradually began to wear themselves out a bit, and their high-spirited fighting turned into a mixture of manipulation and attention-seeking. If Caroline came towards me, Anita pushed her away; if Hamish wanted to tell me something, the girls shouted over him. Hamish hovered on the edge, between boy and surrogate parent.

When Mike came back into the room, Anita and Caroline rushed towards him to vie for his attention.

It was time for more food – almost a continuous feast. Jane and Marion got back at around lunchtime, along with Brett and Laura, and Marion's girls, all laden with carrier bags.

'We've spent about three hundred pounds,' said Jane anxiously. 'Is that all right? We did manage to get a lot of clothes.'

'Of course,' I laughed. 'That's not bad at all . . . as long as they fit!'

'We've kept all the receipts,' said Marion. 'Just in case.'

Hamish, Anita and Caroline were very excited to see other children arriving, but when we started to pull all the new things out of the bags, their excitement turned to frenzy as they held their new clothes up against themselves, like a speed-fashion show. They tossed one item aside to look at the next, and got everyone's things muddled up in the process.

'Look at me,' demanded Anita, strutting about between the toys to show off a new outfit with a suggestive pose. 'I'm a princess.'

'No!' Caroline cried. 'Me princess.'

'You can't be. I'm the prettiest.'

'No, me!'

'You're an ugly cunt.'

'You a cunt,' Caroline wailed, lunging at her sister.

We had to separate them before they damaged each other, or their new clothes. It was bedlam all over again, with fists and swear words flying – no control unless we stepped in, and this carried on through the afternoon.

'My God,' grimaced Marion at one point. 'This day will

live with me forever!' That broke the tension as we shared a laugh.

Meanwhile, despite all our efforts to help him join in, Simon continued to sit on his own, detached and silent. I had to find a way to reach him.

4

Bath-time Blues

'Caroline has sustained a recent fracture, about two weeks old, which has not been reported or treated and must have been very painful . . . On examination, she was also found to have multiple bruises of different ages over her trunk, scalp, arms and upper legs. Over forty bruises and injuries were documented. The consultant declared that the pattern of these bruises as well as the number are in keeping with non-accidental injury.'

Social worker's notes while in A & E, 6 March 1997

'You said we can go and get some food,' Hamish said, tugging at my sleeve, as they all stuffed jam sandwiches into their mouths in their umpteenth mini-meal break, halfway through the afternoon.

'Yes,' I said. 'You can help me to clear this lot up and then we'll go.'

He immediately picked up the plates, carrying them at an angle back to the kitchen and dropping crumbs all the way – very Hansel and Gretel.

All our visitors left and off we went on our first expedition together, the four children, Mike and me, all squashed into our ordinary car. (If the children were staying, we would definitely have to change that.)

'What do we need?' asked Mike.

'Everything,' said Hamish.

'Well, not the whole supermarket,' I added. 'We need to leave a few things for other customers. But if you see anything that you want, you can just tell me.'

'Anything?' repeated Hamish, with a look of wonder.

'Yes, any food.'

As we piled out of the car and went into the front entrance of the supermarket, Hamish's face was a picture of wonder.

'Bloody hell!' He had never gone into a large supermarket like this through the front entrance, like normal people. For him it was always round the back to the bins.

Mike took one trolley and I took another. I popped Simon into mine, while Hamish, Anita and Caroline ran off in all directions. It was like emptying a bag of ferrets – they went wild. I had to leave Mike with both the trolleys while I ran after them, trying to keep them in sight – an impossible task. It was bedlam, and of course you know what people are like. There were tut-tuts from some, and out-loud complaints from others.

The children's faces were alight, looking at all the food – rows and rows of wonderful things to eat. They all ran down the aisles, grabbing anything that appealed to them. Hamish went straight for the cornflakes – box after box of them. I had to stop him putting any more in the trolley after the fifth box.

'We can come back and buy some more tomorrow if we need them,' I said.

We put huge tubs of ice cream into the trolleys, and all the other bits they wanted.

'You can go and choose some new biscuits for the biscuit tin, if you like,' I suggested. You would think I had offered them the moon.

They raced off to find the right aisle and scrambled their way along, ransacking the biscuit shelves and leaving a trail of chaos in their wake.

'Give me those, you cunt!' yelled Anita, snatching her favourite chocolate bars out of Caroline's grasp.

'Fucking hell!' shouted Caroline, the words coming out clearer than usual, as she aimed a kick at Anita, who managed to dodge, just in time.

'Belt up, you bitches,' ordered Hamish.

More disapproving looks and tut-tutting from other customers, but apart from the swearing they didn't get up to anything particularly bad that first time, thank goodness.

I made a mental note to talk to them about choosing which words to use where, but I knew this wasn't the time. Swearing must have been the language they were used to hearing every day in their house, so it was normal to them. They didn't know they were saying anything wrong. These children's feelings were more important to Mike and me than any embarrassment they caused us, or the disapproval of strangers who didn't understand.

As we queued up to pay at the checkout, Hamish looked uncomfortable.

'What's the matter, love?' I asked.

'What are we doing?'

'We're queuing up. This is the checkout, where we have to pay.'

'Why?'

'Because that's what we have to do.'

'Well, if you go round to the back, the manager lets you have food. You don't have to pay because it's free.'

'No, I don't think so,' I said.

'Yes, it is. That's what I used to do. If there was nothing in the bins, I used to knock at the back door at Tesco's. The manager always gave me some food to take home for the others.'

'Really?' I was surprised at this revelation, and pleased that Hamish had found a kind friend to help them. We had a lot to learn.

It was quite a relief to get them all back home again. After unpacking all the shopping and having another chaotic meal, it was early evening and the children began to flag, especially the two younger ones. I don't know who was more tired, them or me.

'Right, it's time for a bath,' I said, and we all clambered up the stairs. I went into the bathroom, ran the water and put lots of bubbles in. Of course, 'safe caring' means you're not supposed to put all the kids in together and I can remember undressing Simon and putting him in first, lowering him into the warm water. He sat there like a lump of dough – no response. Usually, when you put little ones into a bath and you gently splash them, and play peek-a-boo with them, there would be great hilarity. But there was none of that with Simon. Not with any of them it seemed, as I broke rule number two and decided to put them all into the bath together, to make it more fun, and so that I could make sure they all had a good soak.

Hamish and Anita had shed their clothes all over the landing, where there was more space. Now the two of them ran into the bathroom and climbed straight into the bath, splashing water everywhere in a wild water-fight, with Simon at one end, ignoring them both. But no Caroline.

While Mike kept an eye on the others, I went to the doorway and looked out to see this forlorn waif standing against the landing wall, fully dressed and trembling so much that her clumps of wispy hair shook.

'Come on, Caroline,' I said, beckoning her gently. 'Come and have a bubble bath.'

'No,' she wailed. 'No bath.'

'Don't worry,' I said. 'You'll be fine.' I knew I had to be matter-of-fact. I couldn't tell her it didn't matter and she needn't have a bath. It had to be done. So I picked her up and carried her, struggling, into the bathroom, where she fiercely resisted me taking anything off her. I hated to force her like this, but she was filthy and in desperate need of a soak. I wondered why the hospital hadn't cleaned her up a bit, but perhaps she put up a fight there too and they had to give up.

After a bit of a struggle, I got her nappy off and the stench was horrendous. She was rigid with fear, so we had some cuddles as we sat on the bathroom floor, with me gradually taking her clothes off her and trying to pick the lice off her body, one by one. As I revealed her skin, I gulped with dismay. I'm not easily shocked, but I was that day. It was the first time I had seen her completely naked and I had to try not to show my horror at her thin, bony body, covered with bruises of various ages and colours. They were everywhere from the top of her scalp down to her thighs. Many more than I could count. How could this be?

I gave her a big, gentle cuddle as we sat together on the bathroom floor, watching the others having fun in the bath. With Caroline on my knee, I gave Simon a gentle wash. This didn't seem to faze him as he sat still and accepted my using the flannel and the sponge, as long as my hands didn't touch him. All the while, I continued to talk and encouraged them all to play with the plastic ducks and the bubbles, hoping this would help calm Caroline's irrational fear, although by now I was beginning to wonder if perhaps it wasn't irrational.

Finally I had calmed her down enough to lift her into the bath, where she sat trembling between Hamish and Anita, her plaster-casted arm sticking up over the edge. It was quite a squash, and despite the others' fun, Caroline screwed up her face and flinched every time I made a move towards her or the others splashed her. If my hand or arm strayed too close, she pinched and bit me, desperate to get out. She clearly didn't like this ordeal one bit.

Gradually, I washed them all, their skins changing colour from grey to cream, though I had a job scrubbing the thick grime off their feet.

It was time give the children's hair and scalps a thorough wash. I reached for the spray attachment and began with the boys, whose heads had been shaved, with just a short stubble coming through, so didn't take long.

'Your turn next, young lady,' I said to Anita.

'No, I don't want my hair washed,' she protested.

'But I've got some special princess shampoo for you.' I reached to show her the pink bottle with its silver lid. 'Look at that princess in the picture.'

'She's got long hair,' Anita said with a smile.

'Well . . .' I nodded, 'this shampoo will make your hair grow like hers.'

That worked and Anita allowed me to massage and rinse her head. Now I got out the nit comb. I could see this was going to be a challenge.

'No!' she wailed. 'You can't do that.' She looked with horror at the metal comb. 'It will break my hair.'

'I'll be as gentle as I can be,' I reassured her. 'But I must get all those nasty lice out, so you don't have to scratch your head any longer. Then your hair can grow faster.'

'Really?' She looked uncertain, but she allowed me to drag the comb through her newly clean hair, a few strands at a time. I deposited the lice and nits in a deep tin, along with the body lice I had picked off them all earlier. Eugh!

Caroline looked on with increasing discomfort. Finally it was her turn. As I aimed the light spray over her bruised and filthy scalp, gently wetting the clumped wisps of thin hair between her bald patches, her horror overcame her. She screamed and screamed. Anyone would have thought I was trying to murder her. I had to hold her steady as I perse-vered, stroking the baby shampoo all over her head to calm her. When I started to use the spray again, she freaked out and struggled to get out of the bath, splashing us all, and half the bathroom too. Finally I applied the conditioner and combed through her tufts of hair, extricating what lice I could before giving in.

Now that they were all clean, I could see that they each had a few bruises, but none of them as many as Caroline. Both the girls had black eyes, though Caroline's was going yellow now. As I picked Simon up out of the water, I noticed again the deep cigarette burn on his ankle.

I lifted them all out of the bath, one by one, wrapping a huge, fluffy towel round each of them. Anita beamed with pleasure at having such a large, clean towel, all to herself, against her skin. She was in heaven.

'What's this, Hamish?' I asked as he dried himself. 'This big mark on your hand?' It was quite an extensive scar across the back of his hand and wrist.

'That's where I got burnt by a kettle when I was a baby. They used to put me up on the worktops and I played with the wires.'

'Was it just the kettle? It looks as if it was quite a nasty burn.'

'I think there might have been some boiling water as well.'

'It must have hurt a lot.'

'I was too young to remember. But I know somebody took me to the hospital to get it treated.'

When they were all dried and clean and sweet-smelling, perhaps for the first time since they were born, I got them into their new pyjamas and said, 'Come on. Let's go and have a story.' They looked puzzled. I realise now they didn't know what I was talking about.

We all went through to their big bedroom opposite ours, where I thought it best to let them sleep together again, until they had properly settled in.

'Would you like *Goldilocks* or *Cinderella*?'

They all looked at me with blank faces, unable to answer.

At that moment I felt enormous sadness as I realised that nobody had ever read them a bedtime story, and they were unfamiliar with even these popular childhood tales. Perhaps the younger ones had never seen or handled a book. So I explained what reading a story meant and they seemed quite interested in the idea.

'Let's start with *Cinderella*,' I said. 'Now we all need to sit together on the bed.'

I sat down and the older three clambered around me, competing fiercely to climb onto my lap – another rule broken. Meanwhile, Simon sat where I'd put him, on one side of me, but not touching, as I realised that was uncomfortable for him. It was something to work on, but it would take time. He made no eye contact, and did not show any interest in the book at first, though he did begin to look at it as I did the voices and turned the pages.

Finally the house went quiet and the children were all asleep.

'Why do you think Caroline was like that at bath time?' asked Mike as we put the plates away. 'The others were all fine.'

'Yes, something must have happened to her in a bath-room . . . something that frightened her.'

As we finished clearing up, I looked at the clock – half-past nine. I remember thinking: My God, I've got to go to bed. This whole day was a mad jungle. I know I'm not a drinker, but I could drink tonight. It has to get better than this!

5

Revelations

'Mrs Merry reports that the children have begun talking to her about events at their mother's home, indicating some worrying child-care practices.'

Social work notes, mid-March 1997

'Where are the cornflakes?' wailed Hamish. He had looked in one cupboard, then another, and was staring into a third, trembling with anxiety.

'Don't worry,' I said, opening the pantry door to show him all the boxes he had put into the supermarket trolley the previous afternoon.

Breakfast passed in a mad blur, spreading food everywhere, and the children were now creating World War Three in the playroom.

'Shall I take the troops across to the park?' asked Mike with a smile. 'That way you can get on with cooking Sunday lunch.' Mike always enjoyed his Sunday roast.

'Yes please! But watch how you get them across the road.'

The park was opposite our house, so there was just our road to cross. It's a busy road now, but it wasn't so bad then.

'Right, kids,' I said to them as they were clamouring to

be first out of the front door. 'You all have to hold hands to cross the road.'

'I'm good at that,' boasted Hamish. 'I taught myself.' I dreaded to think how.

'Good, you can help Mike look after the younger ones if you all hold hands.'

'We're back,' the two older ones yelled as they ran into the kitchen an hour and a half later.

'We're starving,' said Hamish with a hopeful look on his face. 'Is lunch ready?'

'Nearly ready. Go and wash your hands.'

They scampered off as Mike came into the kitchen.

'Phew,' he smiled, wiping his brow to emphasise his relief at getting them all home safely. 'That was the longest, maddest morning I've ever had!'

'What were they like crossing the road?'

'Like walking ten puppies without a lead,' he laughed. 'Uncontrollable!'

Lunch was another scramble, with the children snatching morsels from each other's plates. Caroline got into a real paddy, trying to guard her food from Anita sitting next to her.

'Get off!' she yelled. 'Mine!' she screeched. I was beginning to understand her words better now, including the frequent expletives, which I could have done without! She had a fiery temper and a lot of spunk, despite her babyish ways. Or maybe that was why. Was she going through the 'terrible twos' at nearly five? When I thought about it later that day, I wondered whether her temper had been suppressed until now. As if she was letting herself express her feelings for the first time. I have noticed it before with other children. Sometimes, when they are away from the source of their fears, it's as if they can find their own voice and express their anger at last.

There was some more shouting and swearing, and their behaviour went downhill from there, throwing food about and making an awful mess of the dining room, where we always ate Sunday lunch. Maybe we'd have to eat in the kitchen until things improved. I'd have to try to get them eating with a knife and fork instead of their hands. And sometime I'd have to start a discussion about inappropriate words, but not yet . . .

The younger three went off to play downstairs after lunch and Hamish helped to clear up the worst of the mess. Then he stood in the kitchen and watched me stack the dishwasher, looking unsure, as if thinking about telling me something. I waited, then out it came.

'I like it here.'

'Good. Why's that?'

'Because you have food.'

'That's good. Is there anything you don't like, Hamish?'

'I don't think so.'

'Well, what do you like best?'

'Chips . . . and cornflakes . . . and pasta. I like the pasta you gave us the night we came.'

'Yes, that was fresh pasta. I'll cook some of that for you tonight if you like.'

His eyes lit up. 'Yes, please. Can you cook lots of it, because Caroline and Anita like pasta too?'

'Yes, of course.' I paused. 'When Mummy gives you food, what does she give you?' I asked.

'Nothing. She doesn't cook, so we don't have anything most days.'

'Oh, so that's why you go to the bins?'

'Yes. And we don't have a table.'

'So where do you eat?'

'Off the top of the washing machine.'

'What about your mum?'

'She has a lot of her mates round.'

'Women friends?'

'No. They're all men.' He hesitated. 'Different men in and out. They babysit us sometimes.' Another pause. 'Anita and Caroline are very frightened of some of them, especially Wayne.'

'Oh, really?' I tried to keep my expression the same and not show the shock I felt at these revelations.

Over the years, whenever I've been training couples to become foster parents, I've always said to them: 'Keep your fostering diaries handy. You never know where you might be, or what you might be doing. You could be chopping carrots when children suddenly tell you something. You just have to keep chopping the carrots and keep a straight face, while you try to remember the name, so that you can write it down in your diary as soon as you can.'

'Is that how Caroline got her broken arm?' I asked.

'Yes, that was Wayne.'

He stopped for several seconds.

'He put a cupboard in front of the door of the bedroom and Caroline started screaming. That's when he broke her arm.' Hamish sniffed. 'I think he must have been hitting her. I tried to open the door, but I couldn't.' He wiped the tears from his cheeks with his sleeve. 'And she kept on screaming, so I kept trying the door, and sent Anita to get the big man over the road to help us. He was very strong and got the door open.' He dissolved into tears. 'I couldn't stop him,' he sobbed. 'I couldn't protect her.'

'But it wasn't your fault, love.' I gave him a cuddle. 'You did the best you could.'

'Wayne's the one who sexed Anita,' he said in a matter-of-fact voice. 'He's been bad to all of us.'

'Well, he can't hurt you here,' I reassured him.

Just then there was a shriek from the cellar playroom and Hamish dashed off down the stairs, with me following behind.

I can't remember the rest of that day. It was a chaotic blur. Somehow, after putting them all to bed, I fought my own fatigue to sort the fast-growing pile of washing and put some in the machine, before going up.

'I'm shattered,' I said to Mike.

'That bad?'

'Yes, anyone would think I'd never looked after a family before. The food is colossal, the washing is huge, and everything is a mammoth task. Even trying to get the kids ready to go to the supermarket, let alone when we get there! It's full on. Do you think I'm getting too old for all this?'

'Of course not. You'll get back into the swing again – you always do!'

'Well,' I yawned. 'I hope you're right.'

Monday morning is another blur. I know it was frenetic, but I don't remember most of the details, except for one thing. I had been worrying about Simon since he arrived. He was immobile for the first couple of days. But once or twice that morning, down in the playroom, he started to crawl a bit. Not very far, but at least he was moving.

'Well done, Simon,' I encouraged him, against the background melee of scrapping children with short attention spans and the growing pile of broken toys, as the older three just trampled over them.

Up to now, I could put him down somewhere and know that if I didn't move him myself, he would be in the same place two hours later. I went over, picked him up and took him to a clean area of carpet, near the door. Then I held him up so that he let his legs down, lowered him to the floor and gently let go. I sat back three or four feet to see what he would do. Simon stood, with his arms outstretched at each side, as if about to hold on to something, although there was nothing there. Then he took a few steps forward, into the room. His legs were very unsteady, as if the ground was moving. I feared he would fall, but he kept going another step or two. It was a very odd and ungainly walk.

'Hamish,' I said.

'Yes?'

'Does Simon always walk like this?'

'He doesn't usually walk. Mum carries him everywhere. He's her favourite. When she isn't carrying him she puts him in his cot.'

'Where is the cot?'

'In the lounge,' said Hamish, reaching for a large ball. 'Can I go outside and play football?'

'Not now, love. But maybe later.'

The social worker from the agency was due to come round that afternoon, so we had an early lunch, giving me time to tidy up before she came. We had stacker boxes full of toys in the kitchen, so I put various toys, puzzles, modelling dough and colouring books out on our long kitchen table, and the children sat on the old church pews at one end. I sat with them to get them started and for the first few minutes, with their tummies full, they all chose something to do without squabbling. That was an achievement.

Then the doorbell rang.

Carol introduced herself and I took her through to join the children at the kitchen table.

I think she wanted to have a chat with them to start with, but by now they were too busy trying to take the puzzles and colouring books away from each other.

'Let go, you wanker!'

'Fuck off!'

Carol raised her eyebrows.

'Let's just talk here,' I suggested, pulling out a couple of chairs. 'I'm sure Hamish and Anita will chip in if they feel like it.'

'Well, the first thing to tell you,' she said, 'is that it's now a full care order, so that means you can do all the normal things that need doing, but you must not cut the children's hair, or take them away overnight, without permission through the fostering agency.'

'I don't think the boys will need their hair cut for quite a while!' I smiled, looking at their shaven heads. 'And Anita says she wants to grow her hair.'

'It's going to be blonde,' Anita added.

Carol looked at her black, tufty hair and smiled.

'Anita's very girly,' I explained.

'What time did they finally arrive on Friday?'

'About eleven o'clock at night. They were in such a state when they got here – tired, starving hungry . . .'

'I believe there were some delays at the other end.'

'Yes, what happened? I did ask Hamish, but he seemed a bit vague about it all. I don't suppose the children were told what was going on.'

'I don't know much more than you do, I'm afraid. All we've been told so far is that Caroline's arm was broken, several days before, and it was a social worker who took her to the doctor and he called an ambulance. I'm afraid it's all quite fuzzy apart from that. It seems they were all at the hospital with the social workers, but it's not been explained what happened to break her arm . . .'

'Wayne,' interrupted Caroline. 'Wayne broke my arm.' I repeated this more clearly for Carol.

'He pulled a cupboard across to block the door and attacked her,' explained Hamish.

'And she screamed,' added Anita.

'Really?' Carol paused and waited, but the children said nothing more. 'I don't know what happened after that,' she continued. 'There seemed to be a gap, till the next day I think, and then they came to you.'

'So why didn't they come here earlier, instead of that awful, long drive late at night?'

'It might have been something to do with the courts.'

Hamish had been half-listening to our conversation. 'Me, Anita and Simon, we went to a foster home for the night, but we didn't like it there.'

'What do you know about the children's family?' I asked Carol, hopeful that she could fill me in.

'Very little, I'm afraid.'

That might have been true, with an emergency care order like this. But if she had known, she probably couldn't have told me anything anyway. The agency is in a difficult situation. They can't slag off the local authority who are responsible for the children, because they are the people taking the children from that local authority.

'All I can tell you is that all four children were on the at-risk register. That's the only information they've sent us so far.'

'I do have a lot of concerns over these children, so I was hoping you could give me some answers,' I said. 'For a start, there seems to be a lot of gaps in their education.'

'You mean their schooling?'

'No, I mean eating, language and social skills – all that sort of thing.'

'Yes, I can see that,' she said with a smile, as Caroline chose this moment to grab a doll from Anita.

'Give me that back, you cunt!' yelled Anita, pulling it back from her.

Caroline immediately burst into tears and banged the table with her uninjured fist. 'I fucking hate you!' she yelled, though it was difficult to understand and I don't think Carol realised what she had said.

'I tell you what,' continued Carol. 'I'll arrange for a support-worker to come and help you. It looks like you might need it!'

'Could you? That would be a great help.'

'It will only be for a few hours a week.'

'Yes, I know. But it will allow me to nip out and get the main supermarket shopping done.' I told her about our chaotic experience, shopping with them all the night before and we had a good laugh. 'They're like over-enthusiastic puppies, you know, so excited they're running everywhere, leaving havoc behind them. You should have seen Mike and me, trying to control the trolleys and run after them at the same time!'

I suddenly noticed the look of alarm on Hamish's face. 'If I can do the big shop on my own once a week,' I continued, 'then I can take the children on a smaller trip every day for their things.' Hamish relaxed again.

'Every day?' asked Carol in surprise.

'Yes, they were starving when they arrived on Friday,

and they're all desperate for food. Hamish panics if he thinks we might run out of anything.'

'Did we get enough cornflakes?' he asked, as he went over to the pantry.

I waited while he checked. 'How many packets, Hamish?'

He counted them. '. . . five, six . . . seven packets,' he announced with a smile.

Carol raised one eyebrow.

'Hamish was in charge of food before they came here. I don't think any of them would have survived without him,' I explained, then turned to him. 'Tell Carol what you told me.'

'About the bins?'

'Yes.'

'Well, we were always hungry, so I had to go out at night to get some food for us.'

'On your own?' asked Carol, shocked by this news. 'Every day?'

'Yes, I used to unlock the door and let myself out when it was dark. Then I went round the back of Tesco's every night to get food out of their bins. If they were empty, I knocked at the door and a man gave me food, so I could take it back for Anita and the others.' He sounded so matter-of-fact. 'We had to eat.'

'Yes, of course you did, Hamish,' Carol reassured him, trying her best to hide her dismay. 'You were a brave boy to do that for your sisters and brother.'

'Give me that fucking pen!' screeched Anita, snatching it from Caroline, who promptly pinched her arm.

'I think it's time for a runaround in the garden,' I suggested. 'Hamish, please can you take Simon out with you and let him play on the grass. Then, go to the shed and get out some garden toys for you all to play with. I'm sure there's a football out there too if you want.'

'OK.' Hamish picked up his little brother. 'Can we come in again when we are hungry?' he asked, his face almost lined with anxiety.

'Yes, of course you can. We'll never be short of food here.'

'Ooh, isn't it quiet?' sighed Carol when they had all gone out.

'Yes,' I said with a grin. 'Great, isn't it? Mike's taken a couple of days off and he's out there gardening, so he'll keep an eye on them.'

'Are you serious about going shopping every day, Trisha?'

'If I don't, Hamish will be permanently panic-stricken, and they all eat like horses, so we would soon start running out of things.'

'Aren't you making a rod for your own backs?'

I shrugged and changed the subject. 'Nappies are a problem. None of them are dry at night. I always put a waterproof cover on the mattress, but the bedding was soaked through and soiled. You should see the mound of washing in the bath!' I laughed. 'But when I looked for nappies for them at the supermarket, there weren't any big enough. I managed to get some trainer pants to squeeze Hamish into and the largest available size of nappies for Anita, but they are too small. Caroline too. It's a good thing they're so thin, or I don't know what I would do!'

'I can help you with that,' said Carol. 'We have a special supplier for all that kind of thing.'

'The girls were both covered in bruises when they arrived. Especially Caroline. She had more bruises than I could count. Simon had a cigarette burn on his ankle and they were all thick with grime and alive with head and body lice.'

'Eugh!' shuddered Carol.

I told her my concerns about Caroline's fear of the bath.

'I wonder why,' she said.

'There's a huge difference between someone who is frightened of water, and the fear caused by something that has happened.'

She gave me a look. I'm sure she knew what I meant.

'Simon worries me too,' I told her. 'The older three are quite wild, almost feral in some ways, but Simon just sits and does nothing.'

'Remind me, how old is he?'

'Nearly three. The strangest thing is that I didn't think he could walk at first, but when I stood him up and let go, he did sort of stagger a few paces, very unsteady on his feet, with his hands held out to the sides like this.' I showed her what it looked like. 'It reminded me of a documentary I saw a few years ago about a Romanian orphanage, where children his age were left in iron cots all day. Some of them stood up and tried to walk in their cots, but the mattresses were so wobbly on the springs, they walked with their hands out, ready to catch the sides. Simon walks just like that, as if he learned to walk in his cot.'

'Where is the father?'

'I don't know. The children never mention him. But I do wonder whether there was more than one father.'

Carol watched the children playing outside while I made a pot of tea.

'I can see what you mean about them being quite wild.' She raised an eyebrow. 'I suppose they need to let off some steam.'

Just then there was a crash as a rounders bat flew into the air and landed on the patio, breaking a plant pot.

'Come on, kids,' I heard Mike saying, in his usual calm voice. 'Let's put these things away and go to the park.'

'Yeah!' the three older ones cheered, as they threw all the toys into the shed.

'He's very good with them, isn't he?' smiled Carol.

'Yes, I couldn't do any of this without him.'

'Where were we?'

'Their mum's boyfriends,' I said. 'Do you know if there's any history of abuse?'

'No, we don't have any background information at all yet. Do you mean sexual abuse?'

'Yes. I suspected it from the first day, when they were in the playroom and Mike came in. Anita and Caroline both seemed to switch their behaviours.'

'How do you mean?'

'All I can describe it as is sexualised behaviour.'

'Surely not. They were probably just vying for his attention.'

'Yes, that's what I thought. It did seem very obvious, but they are so young. Perhaps I was imagining it. But Hamish said something last night.' I paused. 'He said that Wayne, the guy who broke Caroline's arm . . . he said that Wayne sexed Anita.'

'Sexed her? Are you sure that's what he said?'

'Yes, absolutely sure. But I didn't ask him what he meant or how he knew. Maybe he'll say more about it one day, when he's ready.'

'Perhaps you misunderstood him, Trisha,' said Carol, making a note on her pad.

'I hope so,' I nodded, knowing I hadn't.

Just then, the children tumbled back into the house, all rushing into the kitchen, followed by Mike, looking sheepish.

'Sorry, I couldn't keep them out there any longer. They're a barrel of monkeys today.'

'OK, kids . . .' I got up and stood in front of our tall fridge to prevent a food-fight in front of our visitor. 'You've worn Mike out, so you can come and sit back at the table and play quietly while Carol and I finish our chat. And you can have some of these.' I put out a plate of rock-cakes for them, which they all grabbed straight away and shovelled into their mouths before I had even got back to my seat.

'Have you thought yet about schools for Hamish and Anita?' asked Carol.

'Well, no. It's all been such a whirlwind, and it was just an emergency order to start with.'

'That's right, but now they'll be here for longer, with the full care order, I think it will help you to get the two older ones settled in somewhere soon.'

'So how did you get on with Carol?' asked Mike later that evening.

'All right, I think. She said she'd get a support worker to come for a few hours each week to give me a break.'

'So you can go out and lunch with your friends?' He grinned.

'Some hope! As if I'd have time for that when I've got all the shopping and washing and ironing and cleaning to do for everyone.'

'Do you think the kids have been any better today?'

'Not that I noticed,' I said. 'I wonder what tomorrow will bring.'

6

Fish and Chips

'All four children have suffered significant physical and emotional damage and deprivation.'

Independent social work report

I had been trying to get Hamish and Anita into schools – I rang every school I could think of, but it was always the same conversation.

'Their names and dates of birth please, Mrs Merry.'

That part was straightforward.

'Are you wanting them to start straight away?'

'Well, I'd like to settle them in here for another two or three weeks first. So maybe they could start after the Easter holiday?'

'You do realise that these children should legally be in school now?'

'Yes, I do realise that, but they've had a horrendous time before they came here, and they need . . .'

'What school did they go to before you moved to this area?'

'I don't know.' I didn't feel like explaining all the background before I even knew if the school had any places for them.

'I'm sorry?' Not so much an apology as a question.

'I don't know,' I repeated. 'As their foster mother, I wasn't told what school they went to.' There was a silence at the other end. I could almost picture the expression on her face.

'So . . . these are foster children?'

'Yes, that's right. They've been badly neglected I'm afraid, and they've had a hard time, so they do have a few problems . . .'

'Oh.' A very curt sound.

'So, can you take them from the beginning of next term?'

'No, we're completely full in those year groups,' she said in a snooty voice. 'I'm sorry.'

Well, I knew she wasn't sorry.

After the last school in the city turned them down, I wasn't sure what to do next. So I rang the education department at County Hall and told them the story of trying to find places and all the schools being full.

'They can't be,' said this clipped voice on the other end of the phone. 'We do have places in years one and two in some of our schools, so I don't understand why they turned you away.'

'Oh, but I do understand,' I said. 'None of the schools turned me down until I explained the children's backgrounds.'

'What do you mean, Mrs Merry?'

'Their being foster children, taken away from years of severe neglect and brought to us, damaged and starved. As soon as I mentioned foster children and problems, suddenly every school place was full.'

'I find that hard to believe.'

'Well, you don't have to believe. It's true. I could hardly send them to a school without any explanation, as they are both likely to carry their problems into the classroom with them, and they will need sympathetic, caring teachers.'

'All the teachers in our schools are sympathetic and caring, Mrs Merry.'

I know when I'm being patronised and I don't take it well. 'So what do you want me to do?' I challenged her.

'Well, you'll just have to keep trying.'

That was my red rag moment.

'No,' I raised my voice. 'That's it. I've tried every school in the city and they've all said no. So if you don't find my foster children places, I won't be sending them to school.'

'But you must. If you don't send them to school, you'll be breaking the law.'

'OK. Take me to court!'

On the second Friday after the kids came to stay, we took them out to the zoo. Everyone enjoyed looking at the animals, except for me, trying to keep them all together and calm them down – an impossible task. As we left, I looked at my watch. It was much later than I thought and I remember worrying that they would all be starving and I wouldn't have time to cook anything. Oh God, I thought, it will be manic when we get home and they find out there's nothing cooking. You see, I always used to make sure, if they'd been out with Mike, that when they came back the kitchen window would be open and they could smell the food as they got out of the car. But not today.

'Are you going to be able to cope with the kids while I start cooking their tea?' I asked Mike as we drove home. 'They're going to be starving.'

'Well, why don't we have fish and chips?' He grinned.

'But we don't want to give them junk food.'

'Fresh fish isn't junk food.'

'Well . . . Go on then. Let's have fish and chips.'

'Do you want fish and chips, kids?' he boomed into the back of the car, where they were all squabbling as usual. It brought them to a halt all right. Nobody answered, so I assumed that perhaps they'd never had fish and chips before. I turned round to face them.

'You'll like it,' I said. 'All golden and crispy.'

'Yes please,' said Hamish, and they all joined in, so that was that.

I turned back to look at Mike. 'So that's five fish and chips please, and just chips for me.' I'm vegetarian so I would find some cheese to have later at home.

We pulled up outside the chippy and Mike got out, then stuck his head back in through the window.

'Come on, Hame, I'll need some help to carry it all.'

So Hamish climbed out of the car.

'I want to go too,' wailed Anita.

'And me,' added Caroline, trying to clamber over her, until Anita shoved her back.

'The chippy's always full on a Friday night,' said Mike. 'So I can only take one of you in, and Hamish is the biggest to help me.'

So I sat in the people-carrier that we had to buy to fit us

all in safely, and the three younger ones sat in the back, Simon silently strapped into his car-seat and the girls starting off again with their squabbling. I just sat and looked at the door of the chippy, willing the boys to come out soon. It was before we had smartphones of course, but I did wish I'd had a video camera with me when Hamish emerged through that doorway.

He came through first, carrying a big pile of wrapped packages of fish and chips. You could almost see the air waving as the steam and aroma came out through the white paper. He had this amazing expression on his face – as if he was in paradise, his lips in a beaming smile and his nostrils quivering with pleasure as he sniffed the delicious smell. He sniffed right in, then let out a long, satisfied breath, as he held the precious packages in his arms out in front of him, as if it was gold. Even the queen's crown could not have been more precious to him than those fish and chips.

'Do you want me to hold it, Hame?' I asked him.

'No, no,' he replied quickly, putting his arm over to protect his treasure. 'I can look after it.'

When we got back to Church Road, we all went and sat down on our two church pews, one each side of the long kitchen table, as Hamish carried the white packages over. The smell of the fish wafted out, filling the kitchen before we even opened the paper. All their little noses were twitching. Of course, Hamish had seen the fish and chips being wrapped up, but the girls and Simon didn't know what it would look like.

I went to get the salt and vinegar and Hamish carefully lowered the pile down in the middle, then sat down himself.

I could see the children were all desperate to look inside and tuck in.

'Let's not bother with plates,' I said.

They all stopped and looked at me.

'But what about knives and forks?' said Hamish with a shocked expression.

I smiled at the irony of it. Of course, I'd been drumming into the four of them since the day they arrived that they mustn't eat everything with their hands, and they had just got into the habit of using cutlery . . .

'It's OK with fish and chips,' I explained. 'You can eat those with your fingers, you know.'

They all looked stunned for a second, as if this was some kind of trick I was playing on them. But then the unwrapping ceremony began. I watched them with amazement. It was as if they were all trying to keep up the suspense, slowly unravelling their paper, one corner at a time, sniff-sniff-sniffing as they did so.

'Ooohh,' gasped Anita dramatically, as if it was nectar.

'Go on,' I coaxed them all as I unwrapped Simon's package for him, sprinkled on some salt and vinegar and handed him a chip. 'Tuck in.'

As everyone savoured their first mouthful, Hamish puffed out his little chest with pride. It was so lovely to see him like that, his face beaming, with no worries about anything, perhaps for the first time ever.

All the portions of fish were huge and the chips were

piled up high as well. As we all sat there, eating and enjoying it all, nobody spoke a word. When it was finally gone and the papers were all empty I could hear each of them take in a big breath and let it out slowly, one after the other. Four big fat bellies and four very satisfied children.

Well, that was the start of a family tradition. The following Friday morning, I can remember Hamish coming down early and into the kitchen.

'It's our fish and chips night tonight, isn't it?' he said in an excited half-whisper.

'But I was going to . . .' I began.

His face fell.

'I know we had fish and chips last Friday,' I said. 'But it's not every Friday.'

There were only a few times that I ever saw Hamish close to tears. He hardly ever cried, but the lip was going . . . At that moment I'd have bought him a whole fish and chip shop.

Just then, Mike walked in.

'We'll have fish and chips tonight,' I said.

'Oh really?' he said with a quizzical smile.

So that was it, our ritual. Every Friday from then on was fish and chips night. I'd have scrubbed floors if I had to, just to make sure Hamish could have his fish and chips on Fridays.

Even when we took them on holiday we would take them all down to the quay and have a bag of chips and a Mr Whippy.

* * *

From the very first evening they were with us, all of the three older children behaved badly towards each other and swore like troopers. Simon didn't speak at all then, but even Caroline, with her speech defect, used all the swear words. With Anita, it was almost every word if she was angry. I do find children fascinating. As I watched and listened to them speak with each other, I soon noticed that both the girls only used the word 'cunt' to each other, but never to their brothers. And it was 'fucking hell' every time, in every situation. Especially Anita.

They used every single swear word you can imagine. And the sad thing was that with the older two it was usually in context, though Caroline sometimes got it spectacularly wrong.

It was strange for us, and upsetting or shocking for other people, but we had to remember not to show how we felt about the swearing at first. Of course, we're all used to hearing swear words in the shops, in the park, on the television . . . but this was different. We couldn't assume they knew these words were anything wrong.

'These children have been in a worse mess than we realised,' I murmured to Mike one morning, when the air was particularly blue.

I mentioned the swearing to Carol, the social worker, the next time she came round.

'Well, of course, your expectations might be a bit high,' she said.

I didn't say anything back, but I did think: Oh yeah? All five- and six-year-olds can wipe their bottoms, and know what toilet paper is, don't they?

One day, I took Anita to one side when we were in a shop and she swore loudly at Caroline.

'You know, Anita, "cunt" is not an acceptable word when you're with other people, especially with other children, because it's what we call a swear word, and a lot of people don't like swear words, so they prefer not to hear them.'

She looked a bit surprised, shrugged and that was that. I'm not even sure she understood what I was saying. But I always had to be careful, because all these words were presumably the normal conversation they had grown up with, till now, and if I'd been too disapproving of them, it would have been a slur on their parents, and I couldn't do that.

I had to just say: 'We don't say that when other people are around.' Or: 'Please don't use that language when we're in the supermarket, because it's not acceptable there.' 'If you want to use those words,' I used to tell the children, 'if you're angry about something, go upstairs and use them in your bedroom.'

They used their wide vocabulary of swear words all the time, whether they were angry with each other, or pleased with something they'd done. If Anita had completed a puzzle, it was: 'Fucking Hell. I've done it!'

I talked to Hamish one time when he shouted out a string of swear words at his sisters. 'That isn't a very nice way to speak,' I said.

I remember the way he looked at me. He was such a beautiful boy and he looked at me with his great big, brown eyes.

'Sorry. What did I say wrong?'

One day I sat them all down and told them that we were going to have a new chart.

'Right. These are all your names and this is our stop-swearing chart,' I explained. 'And this is the tricky bit. You know about wiping bums and washing hands – the things that you should be doing?'

'Yes,' chorused the eldest three, nodding.

'Well, this is about something you should *not* do – swearing. All the words you must try not to say. We don't want to hear them any more.'

'How do we know what words we can't say?' asked Hamish.

'Good question,' I nodded. 'Let's make a list of them around the chart so that you can try and remember *not* to say them. What word do you think I should write first?'

'Cunt!' yelled out Anita.

I turned away to hide my smile and listed all the swear words they told me, plus some others I had also heard them use. Then I got out four big jam jars, labelled them with their names and I put a few 1ps and 2ps in the bottom of each jar.

'What are they for?' asked Hamish.

'These are for your rewards.'

'Rewards?' Caroline tried to repeat the word as a question.

'Yes, for when you manage not to swear.' They all smiled and listened, so I carried on. 'Right, we're going to start with an hour at a time,' I explained. 'If any of you can manage a whole hour without saying any of these words, I will put a big tick under your name and 2p in your jar.'

I think I was expecting them to protest a bit, but they all seemed keen on the idea, so off we went. It certainly seemed to work to begin with, though of course they slipped up quite often in between. In fact, it worked so well that soon we made it 3p for two hours, then upped it to 5p for half a day.

Shopping and eating continued to be their number one obsessions, dominating our lives. But Caroline's continuous diarrhoea was my greatest concern. She had it when she came to us and it hadn't got any better. It was getting worse. No matter how often I changed her nappies, every one was badly soiled and the smell was repulsive.

One day, when it was particularly bad, I took her down to the hospital, with all the others in tow as well. It was a nightmare wait, trying to keep the older two from terrorising the other patients with their shouting and rushing around. It was like trying to make fish stop swimming, but worse. I think this may have worked in our favour, because it wasn't long before we were called through to be seen. I told the young man in a blue top why we had come.

'What do you think it could be?' I asked him, though he looked so young that I wondered whether he might not have done that part of the course yet.

'Well, I'm sure it's nothing to be concerned about,' he said with a cheery grin at Caroline, while Simon sat on the end of the bed, fingering the air holes in the hospital blanket, completely oblivious to the mayhem across the room, where Hamish and Anita had opened a cupboard and were busily taking out trays of instruments.

'Put those back in the cupboard and come over here,' I said. 'I've got some biscuits in my bag.' That did the trick.

'But surely there must be something wrong with her? Something causing this constant diarrhoea? Have you looked at her notes?'

'Who is her GP? Do you think she would be on our system?'

I told him and asked him to check her notes, which I think he did, but nothing came of it.

'What do they say?' I asked in exasperation.

'She's with you on a care order, isn't she?'

'Yes, that's right. They all are.'

'Well, I'm sorry, Mrs Merry, but that means I can't tell you what is in her notes without permission from the court.'

After all my years of fostering, I knew he was right, but it was so frustrating not being allowed to know what might be wrong with a needy child in my care.

'It will gradually get better,' he said. But it didn't.

'I'm going to take Caroline to see Dr Ogden,' I said to Mike a couple of weeks later. She'd been our GP for years and she had always been so good with our previous foster children, and not averse to bending the rules if it was in the child's interests.

'Good idea. Book her an appointment and I'll look after the others while you take her.'

So the following day I took Caroline down to the surgery.

'This child has permanent diarrhoea. Permanent,' I said before we'd even sat down.

'How often does she go to the toilet?'

'All the time. As you can see, she's still in nappies, and I've never changed a clean nappy on Caroline, no matter how often I change her.'

'Really? Have you given us her details?'

'Yes. Her name is Caroline Mackay.'

'Ah yes,' she said, picking up her records and starting to sift through. 'Mmm,' she said as she stopped to look at something, then leafed on. 'There's a lot in here for such a young child.'

'Yes, she's had quite a few injuries I believe, and she has a speech problem, and this diarrhoea must have been going on for a while before she came to us. Does it say anything in her notes about it?'

I waited while the doctor continued to skim through everything, until she came to one piece of white paper, which she unfolded. It looked like a printed letter.

'Here we are,' she said, turning to give Caroline a reassuring smile. 'Now, let me see . . .' She read through the details in the letter, then turned to face me. 'Well, Mrs Merry, this is dated eighteen months ago. It's written by a consultant at the family's local hospital and it says that Caroline was diagnosed with an impacted bowel.' She paused. 'That is just what I thought when you described how continuous it is.'

'I don't think so,' I said when I heard the word 'bowel'. 'She's not constipated. She's got diarrhoea.'

'Yes, that's right. You see, what can happen if the bowel is impacted is that the acids can make a hole in the middle, so that means constant diarrhoea, like Caroline has.'

'Oh, I see. Is there anything she can take to make it better, or does she need an operation?'

'No, I hope it won't come to that. I'm going to give you a prescription for her and if you follow the instructions on the label, you should see a great improvement within a few days.'

'Thank goodness,' I sighed. 'Thank you.'

We went to a chemist on the way home and started her on the medicine straight away. That was a Thursday evening and we gave her three spoonfuls a day. I didn't expect it to work immediately, but it did seem to be improving within hours, so I was really pleased. All through Friday the diarrhoea lessened, until it was barely an occasional trickle.

'It's amazing the difference that medicine is making to Caroline,' I said to Mike when we got up on the Saturday morning. But for the first time, she didn't eat all her breakfast. And she seemed quite listless and droopy. It wasn't a very warm day, so I wrapped her in a blanket and laid her down on the settee in the study while I went to make her a drink. When I was in the kitchen I suddenly heard a great commotion, and somebody was shouting for me. I ran to the other side of the house, where they were all gathered round her, with brown froth coming out of her mouth. She was covered in it and the froth was everywhere.

'Go and get the biggest towels you can find in the airing

cupboard,' I said to Mike. 'Put her in that and I'll pop round to the surgery.'

'Take her straight down to A & E,' said Dr Ogden.

Half an hour later, I was in a cubicle, next to Caroline's bed, holding her hand and soothing her as best I could. She'd had such a fright. We all had.

'When did she come into care?' asked a woman registrar. 'Do you know anything about her background?'

'Not a lot. But she was badly neglected and had a lot of minor injuries when she came, as well as a badly broken arm, which her brother told me was caused by a male visitor.'

I saw the look she gave the nurse. Then they both left the room.

I could hear their voices talking nearby, and a male voice too, but I only managed to pick out a few words. 'Foster mum . . . can't tell her . . . classic case . . . penetration . . . impacted bowel . . .' It was enough for me to work out what they were thinking.

Only a couple of days later, when I was talking to another woman I knew who had fostered children, I mentioned all this.

'Yes, we've had children with that problem too. I found out later that the most likely reason for a young child to have an impacted bowel is sexual abuse.'

I told Mike what she had said. 'Do you think that could be the reason for Caroline's impacted bowel?'

'Possibly,' he hesitated. 'But I expect there could be other causes too.'

'Yes. But I wouldn't be surprised if that was it. I just wish they'd tell me. It's so frustrating when everyone knows and they won't say anything to us.'

'Never mind, love. As long as we help her cope with it. That's the main thing.'

'Yes, you're right. Well, at least A & E took her seriously this time and gave her a thorough examination. If they'd done that the first time I took her, maybe it wouldn't have made her so ill.'

'Yes,' Mike sighed as he opened out his newspaper.

'But there's always something to worry about with these four. I wonder what it will be next.'

Knickerbocker Glory

'Simon's face is not responding. He needs time.'
My diary entry, 13 March 1997

Alongside the swearing chart, we had a behaviour chart, with stickers for good behaviour. The children all loved to see the columns and the jars filling up.

'What happens when the jar is full and we can't get any more money into it?' asked Hamish.

'I'll give you another jar.'

He beamed with pride as he went to bed that evening. But the next morning he was a different boy. The others were all sitting at the breakfast table in the kitchen, when Hamish stormed in. I don't know what had happened to change him, but he just went ballistic, shouting obscenities, punching Anita's arm, pinching Caroline, then throwing his breakfast bowl, full of cereal, onto the tiled floor, so it smashed into smithereens and splattered milk everywhere.

'What's the matter, love?' I tried to give him a cuddle, but he wriggled free and kicked my leg. 'Ouch! That hurt.'

'Good!' he shouted. 'I fucking hate you. I hate this fucking place—'

'Right,' I interrupted him. 'You've thrown away your breakfast and you've hurt and upset everybody, so I think we'll have to empty your jar and you can go up to your room. You can shout and swear as much as you like up there. Kick the furniture if you want. It's your furniture, so if you damage it, you're only harming yourself. Make as much noise as you want. Nobody will hear you, so that's fine. But don't come down until you are ready to start the day again.'

He looked as if he was going to refuse, and for a moment I wondered how I would deal with that. But the fire fizzled out. He turned around and stomped off, up the stairs. I heard the door slam, but nothing more for a couple of hours. I emptied his jar in front of the other three, leaving just 4p at the bottom, and they looked as subdued as I felt. This was a big setback for seven-year-old Hamish and I worried what would happen next.

The house was unusually calm after that outburst. The two girls played quietly together for once in the playroom. Simon sat by a box of cars, taking them out one at a time and opening their doors, opening and shutting the boot, or whatever else a particular car had on it. At least he was doing something. I was baking in the kitchen when I heard a sound behind me.

I turned round to see Hamish standing in the doorway, shifting from one foot to the other, his face a mixture of embarrassment and pleading, like a puppy who's just made a big puddle on the best carpet. He looked so uncomfortable and unsure of himself.

'Hello, Hame. Are you feeling better now?'

'Yes,' he said, barely audible.

'Good. Then you can come over here and give me a hug.' I held my arms wide and hoped that would break the ice for him.

He hesitated for only a couple of seconds, shrinking back like a wounded animal, then ran over and gave me that hug. I cuddled him, the flour from my hands all over his T-shirt, as I felt his tense little body relax.

'Look what a mess I've made on you,' I laughed.

'Sorry,' he whispered. Then louder, 'I'm sorry I was so horrible.'

'You're not horrible, Hame.' I ruffled his hair, growing through at last. 'It's not you. It's all that happened to you. All the responsibilities you had to take on. It must have been a very hard life for you. It's not your fault if remembering all that makes you angry sometimes. We must help you learn to cope with that anger. The only thing you did wrong was to take your temper out on your sisters and me.'

'Sorry,' he repeated, looking up at me with his sad brown eyes.

'It's all gone and forgotten,' I reassured him. 'Now sit down and I'll make you some breakfast. And after that we'll go shopping.'

That made him smile. Then his face clouded over again.

'What are you thinking about now?'

'I like going shopping every day,' he said. 'And making sure we have enough food. But . . .'

'But what, Hame?'

'Well, do you think we could buy some food for my mum too?'

I put some bacon on and filled a big bowl with cereals and milk for him. 'How could we get it to her?'

'Well, we could buy her some sandwiches when we go to the supermarket.'

'Yes, we could if you want, but we can't send sandwiches through the post.'

He looked serious, thinking about that as he scooped up spoonfuls of cornflakes into his mouth. 'Could you go to my mum and give her the sandwiches?'

'It's a long way to go, Hame. Do you remember, when you came here? It was a long drive, wasn't it? About a hundred miles I should think.'

'Yes, I suppose so . . . but she might be hungry.'

'Does she not go shopping herself?'

'No, I don't think so. She only had food sometimes when Dad was living there, or when the social workers brought it for her.'

'I see.'

'Dad's gone to Scotland and I think the social workers only came because we were there.' He paused. 'So who's going to make sure she has some milk?'

'Isn't she expecting another baby?' I asked him. I think it was Carol who had told me that. 'I expect the social workers will still be visiting her if she's going to have a baby.'

For the first time that morning he sort of smiled . . . with relief, I think.

I never did find out what had sparked Hamish off so

badly but there was a lot of anger seething below the surface in that little boy. It astonished me that he was so caring of his mum and whether she would have enough to eat, but he knew more than I did.

Hamish was a very serious child sometimes, but also a determined little boy. It didn't take long for him to build up some more coins in his jar and he tried doubly hard not to mess up again . . . for a while at least.

Most of the time, Simon was the least troublesome child of the four, if that's the right word, so it was easy to pay less attention to him when the others were demanding it in spades. But I was aware that he probably needed more attention than any of them, to get him to where he should be at his age. I began to feel guilty that I hadn't given him more of my time.

He was still silent and inactive, expecting me to carry him around. So I decided to stop that, unless it was necessary. He needed to move of his own accord. I've had children like Simon before, though nobody quite as rigid and detached. But the dislike of touch, skin to skin, I have come across a few times, so I knew what to try. It had worked with them, so perhaps it would work with him too.

I bought a set of face paints, with a sponge. That's the best thing. In fact, I've made my own face paints in the past. I started to bodge and splodge with the sponge, on his legs first, to get him used to the feel of it on his skin, which he didn't seem to mind. He watched as I sponged messy marks and patterns on his skin. Then I rollered his feet with paint and held him over a large sheet of paper.

'Put your feet down on the paper, Simon,' I said. 'So that you can see your own footprints.'

He seemed reticent, with a slight move, but not yet touching the paper.

'Go on,' I coaxed him. 'Look, I've made one foot blue and the other one red. Which one looks best?'

This time he lunged out with both feet and picked them up again to inspect the results. His face lit up for the first time.

'What do you think, Simon?' I asked, trying to persuade him to speak.

'Mmm,' was all he said at first. Then, 'Footprints.' We were getting somewhere now.

I wiped his feet clean with a large towel, then sat him down on the carpet, on top of some newspaper. He didn't seem too keen on that at first.

'I know it's a bit crinkly,' I explained. 'But I want us to have some fun, without getting paint on the carpet.'

He made no response, so I dipped the sponge in the paint again and this time began to dab it very gently on the tip of his nose, on his chin and the middle of his cheeks. Most children will look at your eyes when you're painting their face, but not Simon. He did look at parts of my face, but his eyes never strayed to mine – no eye contact.

'*Dgoo, dgoo, dgoo,*' I sang as I dabbed his face repeatedly round the edge with my painted sponge. Then I started to go a bit closer to the middle, all the time singing noises or talking to him in a funny voice. Finally, I handed him a mirror.

'Go on, Simon. Look what I've done to your face.' I helped him to hold up the mirror to look and he made eye contact with himself. I got him to hold it still and then, with my fingertips thick with paint, I daubed a bright orange stripe, right down the centre of his nose, then a big red blob like a clown on the end. That was the moment when he broke into a smile. What a breakthrough that was.

We had a bit more fun as I encouraged him to put his fingers in the paint and dab his arms and face as well. He was quite amused by his efforts.

'Face paints,' he said after lunch the next day. So this time we sat in the kitchen so it didn't matter if paint got on the floor and we both had fun, first painting his face together, and then mine! By the end of this session he was happily accepting the touch of my fingers on his face, my skin on his, and it was lovely to see his wide smile when he saw the results.

One rainy afternoon, the children and I were all sitting round the kitchen table playing games, colouring and doing puzzles. Somehow, as often happened when they felt safe and cosy like that, thoughts of their former lives came tumbling out. I listened and took it all in. It was important for them to know that I believed them, so I nodded or empathised when it seemed appropriate, but I tried not to comment, other than to soothe and reassure.

As usual, Hamish and Anita had the strongest memories. Caroline consciously remembered only snatches, with many of the worst things buried in her subconscious I suppose. But her older siblings occasionally said things that brought to life one episode or another. As usual, Simon sat silently, as he rolled some playdough into fat, stubby snakes.

'Mum chucked me out of the house once,' said Anita in a matter-of-fact voice.

'Yes, I remember that. It was when she had some of her boyfriends there and you were crying because you didn't like them.'

'I was frightened of some of those men. But when Mum chucked me out, I was very scared. I thought she wouldn't let me in again and I didn't know what to do. I was frightened that the big man over the road would come and get me.'

'Yes, we were all scared of him,' nodded Hamish.

'So what did you do?' I asked, trying not to betray my horror.

'I stood on tiptoes and shouted through the letterbox and somebody must have let me back in.'

'I got locked out one night,' said Hamish, with a despondent expression. 'I went out to get us some food, and Mum wouldn't let me back in. It was very dark and I kept shouting and banging on the door, but she just ignored me.'

'Maybe she was upstairs with one of her boyfriends,' said Anita.

'I don't know, but I did hear her shout at me after a bit.'

'What did she say?' I asked.

'"Fuck off."'

'Was that all?'

He shook his head and said nothing for a moment,

then, 'She said she wished I would die and she wouldn't care if I did.'

'Oh, Hame . . .' I leaned over and gave him a cuddle. 'I'm sure she didn't mean it.'

'She did,' he whispered, his body trembling.

'How did you get back in?' asked Anita.

'Well, I was getting frightened, so I kept on banging on the door, and one of the neighbours must have heard me because somebody called the police.'

'Oh good,' I said. 'So did they come and sort it all out?'

'No. They didn't come at all. I only found out about the complaint when the social worker mentioned it. But it was all right in the end. One of Mum's mates opened the door.'

Caroline had been listening to all this as she threaded some coloured beads. 'I don't remember any of that,' she said. 'But Mum used to tie me to the bed, didn't she, Hamish?'

'Yes,' he nodded. 'She used to tie you to one of the bed legs. I don't know why, but sometimes I managed to untie you.'

'You looked after me,' she said, smiling at him.

'Well somebody had to.'

The swearing chart was working well, with occasional lapses, of course, but the pennies were piling up again so we decided it was time to up the ante. First we extended it to a whole day without swearing – that would earn them 10p. I had to get change from the bank to make the daily payments. So finally we sat them round the kitchen table and made them a promise.

'If you can go a whole week without using any of these swear words . . . you can't use them in the garden or the house, you can't use them in the park, or on the bus or in the supermarket, or any shops. You can't use them anywhere at all. If you can all do that, every morning, every afternoon and every evening for six whole days, we will take you out on the Sunday to a proper restaurant for lunch, and you can all have a Knickerbocker Glory for pudding.' I stopped, expecting great excitement, but it was just blank faces and dead silence.

'What's a knicker-thingy?' asked Anita.

'Haven't you heard of it before?'

'No,' replied Hamish. 'Is it something nice?'

'Something nice?' I repeated. 'It's better than that. It's the biggest, boldest, best-tasting dessert you have ever eaten in your whole life.'

Now their faces lit up.

'Do you like ice cream, kids?' asked Mike, knowing what the answer would be. 'Well this is mega-brilliant ice cream, with all the trimmings.' He licked his lips.

'I'll tell you what,' I said to Mike. 'Maybe you should go down to the restaurant and ask them if we can borrow one of their menus to show the children.'

'OK, kids. Who's going to come with me?'

Well, of course, everyone wanted to go, so we all climbed into the people-carrier and Mike drove us there. He parked right outside the restaurant.

'I want to come in with you,' wailed Anita as he got out of the car.

'No, me!' shouted Caroline.

'I'll come and help you,' suggested Hamish.

And Simon said nothing.

Mike looked at me. I shook my head. 'Nobody is going in this time. We'll save that for the day we come to have that special lunch, and Knickerbocker Glory for afters.' Their faces fell. They were obviously disappointed, but I was relieved that nobody protested further. So we sat outside in the car and the children tried to peer through the windows. It had once been a pub, but now it was a restaurant.

'It's lovely inside,' I told them. 'All very clean and modern. I'm sure you'll like it.'

'Does it have tables?' asked Caroline.

'Of course it does you . . . silly girl,' said Anita, changing her choice of words just in time.

'Yes, tables and chairs, knives, forks and spoons, table-mats, proper napkins and waiters to serve us,' I said.

'Do they have Coke?' asked Hamish.

'Yes, and almost any drink you can think of.'

Just then, Mike reappeared with the ice-cream menu and there on the front was a big, colourful picture of the most delicious-looking Knickerbocker Glory you have ever seen.

'Wow!' breathed Hamish, full of awe and wonder. He was like that with most food, but especially this time.

'It looks amazing,' added Anita.

'How big is it?' asked Caroline.

'This big,' said Mike, exaggerating its size with one hand

waist high and the other at the top of his forehead, till he saw my exasperated expression, and moved his hands a little closer together. 'Well, nearly.'

'Ice cream!' shrieked Simon, unexpectedly, when he saw the picture.

'Let's take the menu home and stick the picture up on the whiteboard, next to the chart.' So that's what we did. 'Now remember,' I challenged them. 'Nobody must use those swear words all week.'

'What if somebody swears and we can't go?' asked Hamish, giving Anita a look. 'That wouldn't be fair.'

'Well, I'm really sorry, but that person would have to stay behind.'

'But we can't!' wailed Caroline.

'Yes, who would look after us if you left us behind?'

'Well, I'd ask someone to come and look after you.'

'What if you swear?' asked Anita, grinning at me.

'Then I would have to stay behind,' I laughed. 'Mike would have to take you without me.'

'Can I have your knicker glory then?' she asked.

'It depends how good you've been,' teased Mike.

It was quite a stressful week, as they tried and tried not to swear. They worked so hard to keep their mouths shut in case the wrong words came out, that hardly anybody spoke! The excitement grew and grew as the week went on and their columns of ticks rose, along with the pile of 10p pieces in their jars.

'Oh YES!' exclaimed Anita as Saturday evening came around and the ticks reached the tops of all their columns.

On Sunday morning, they were all up bright and early as usual, with a great sense of anticipation.

'Now, we've got to wear really pretty clothes,' I said to the girls. 'And proper shirts for you boys.' My daughter Jane and my grandchildren, Brett and Laura, came to help us get ready that morning. Our four all changed into their best clothes and had their hair done by me or Jane. Brett was just into a bit of gel, so he put some on Hamish who, having been shaved bald when he arrived, was now really proud of his thick, shiny brown hair, shaped by Brett.

'How do I look?' asked Laura, doing a twirl in the dress she had on. Anita and Caroline copied her in their new outfits.

'You look like beautiful princesses,' grinned Mike, as they made themselves so dizzy they fell into a heap together.

Jane, Laura and Brett waved us off and we soon arrived at the restaurant, parked outside and walked in. By now the children were at such a high pitch of excitement, you could almost touch it.

'We've booked for lunch,' said Mike. 'The name is Merry.'

'Table for six,' I added.

'Yes,' said the waiter and led us to our table, right in the middle of the packed restaurant, surrounded by other diners. As I looked round, they were mostly middle-aged or elderly, so ours were the only children. Please God they behave themselves, I thought. A few people smiled as we passed and I smiled back.

'Oh look at this,' I said as we sat down. 'We've got the best table.'

The waiter came back with menus, including one specially for children. So we ordered some drinks, including Hamish's Coke of course. He was very pleased with himself when it arrived in a tall glass with ice-cubes and a straw. I can't remember now what any of us ate for our main course, but I do recall that they chose everything they could.

'Can we really have this?' asked Anita.

'Yes.'

'And that too?' asked Hamish.

'Yes.'

'When do we get our Knickerbocker Glory?'

'When you've finished the main part of the meal. Then the man will come and take the plates away and you can tell him what you want for pudding.'

We all enjoyed our main course, and the children scraped their plates clean. The anticipation was rising and I had a sudden, frightening thought. What would we do if they didn't have any Knickerbocker Glories that day? World War Three might be about to break out.

One of the waiters came and cleared our table. Now was the 'what if' moment I dreaded. The menus were brought and passed round.

'Do you have an ice-cream menu for the children?' I asked.

'Yes, of course, madam.'

Simon was sitting up in his high chair, watching

everything that went on. Even he looked excited. They were all sitting up straight, hardly able to contain their excitement by now.

The waiter brought back the menu . . . and there it was. The picture we had on our whiteboard.

'Knickerbocker Glory!' exclaimed Hamish.

'So what do you want for pudding, kids?' asked Mike, and they all shouted it out.

'Knickerbocker Glory!'

'That will be six Knickerbocker Glories please,' I told the waiter and off he went.

Anita fidgeted in her chair for about half a minute before she got down and stood where she could see round the corner, in the direction of the kitchen. She knew he would come that way and wanted to be the first to see him. She couldn't take her eyes off that doorway and it seemed like an age for us all. Finally, out he came, holding a tray of wondrous desserts, heading straight for our table.

'Sit down, Anita,' I said.

She immediately sat on her chair, which meant she was higher up and as the waiter came nearer she had a better view of the six tall glasses and their delicious-looking contents.

As he lowered the tray, she opened her mouth, took in a deep breath and out it came, at the top of her voice.

'Fucking hell!'

We all looked in disbelief. Everyone in the restaurant stopped and turned round to look, their mouths wide open. Then the tut-tutting began, and the comments.

'Oh my goodness. Did you hear that?'

'Deary dear.'

'How dreadful.'

'Children shouldn't be allowed if they don't know how to behave.'

'It's the parents' fault, not teaching their children any manners.'

Anita went red. I'd never seen her blush before. She gave me an anxious look.

'Don't worry, Anita. Don't worry. Just ignore them.'

She relaxed a little. I don't think she cared about what people were saying. It had never bothered her before. But I'm sure she thought she had ruined her chances of having her Knickerbocker Glory, so we made it clear that she would still have her prize. Then I looked at Mike and he looked at me. We didn't dare laugh there, in the restaurant, with all those disapproving biddies around us, but it was almost impossible to keep a straight face. The only way was to tuck in, so we did.

We all ate our Knickerbocker Glories and, oh, the looks on those children's faces, as if they were in heaven, eating the nectar of the gods.

We finished, we paid and we left.

Once we had all climbed back into the car, we could hold in our laughter no longer. I don't think I've ever laughed like it. Mike was the same, and even the kids saw the funny side of it. We were laughing so much that we couldn't drive away until we finally calmed down.

'Well done, kids,' I said, wiping the tears from my eyes. 'You did brilliantly.'

'All of us?' asked Anita tentatively.

'Yes, all of you.'

'Wasn't it funny?' said Hamish, as I was getting them ready for bed that evening.

'The funniest day out I've ever had,' I agreed.

Everyone looked happy except Anita.

'What's the matter, love?'

'I don't like the dark.'

'But it won't be dark with the landing light on.'

'It used to frighten me when the lights went off.'

'She means when the electricity went off,' explained Hamish. 'The meter always ran out of money and we had to go to bed in the dark.'

'Well, you'll always be all right here, because we don't have that kind of meter. Our meter keeps the lights on whenever we want them, so you don't need to be afraid.'

'But I can't help it. What if a bad man comes to get me?'

'We don't have any bad people here, Anita. Only Mike, when I gave him two naughty stickers for saying I looked fat in this top!'

That made her laugh, and we all laughed when Mike himself popped his head in.

'What's the joke?' he asked.

'You are,' said Anita, and we laughed all the more. Mike joined in too. It had been the best day we'd had since the children arrived and that night we all went to bed happy.

8

Mary Poppins

'Anita says Mom doesn't mind her being dirty with dolls or Hamish or anyone.'

My diary entry, 21 March 1997

Ever since the children arrived on our doorstep, our lives had been a whirlwind. Nothing was 'normal' in our house and I never seemed to have time to conquer the mountains of washing and ironing, daily supermarket sweeps, nappies, changing beds, and all the rest, let alone have time to have a cup of tea and put my feet up for a few minutes – an unattainable treat. I couldn't even sit on the loo without everybody shouting and ranting at me.

So I was excited when I woke on the day our promised support worker would come for her first visit.

'Kay will be your super-nanny,' Carol said on her last visit, but I didn't realise just how apt that description would be.

First impressions were very encouraging. When I opened the door to this smiley woman with twinkly eyes and bright-red spiky hair, she was not at all what I expected.

'Hi, Trisha. I'm your support worker and I've come to give you a break; lots of breaks.'

'Great. I'll put the kettle on.'

Kay was someone quite different from any social worker I had ever met. She was what every foster mother in England, or even the world, should have. She was a real-life Mary Poppins.

'If you want to go out for an hour or two, I'll have the children here. Or I'll take the children out for you if you like. Whatever suits you best.'

'What, all of them?'

'Yes, all of them.'

'All at once?'

'Yes. All at once, or even in twos or one at a time if you prefer. You can just tell me what you want me to do. The whole point is to give you time for yourself, either at home or to go out without having to take them all with you.'

'I'm sure I must be dreaming!'

'Sometimes you might need to have individual time with one of the children, or I could take the two bigger ones out one day and the younger ones the next time. It's your choice.'

'My God! You're giving me a lifeline.'

'Well, that's my job.'

'I can hardly believe you're real!'

'Well, I am, and I'm going to start by taking all four children to the park for the rest of the afternoon. I know lots of games we can play and we'll all have fun. I'll bring them back for five. Will that be all right?'

'Are you joking? It will be bliss.' And it was.

The next few times she came, she changed things around.

'I'll take Anita into town if you like,' she suggested one morning. 'Does she need any new clothes?' Anita was in heaven, having someone entirely to herself, looking at girly clothes.

'What about if I take Hamish to the leisure centre and start teaching him to swim?' she asked another time. Hamish loved that.

One day she took both Hamish and Anita to an adventure playground on the other side of town, so I could have a bit of individual time with Caroline and Simon in turn. That was invaluable for both of them. But they didn't miss out on the fun, as on another day she took them to a petting farm, where they could stroke the animals. That was a great experience for both of them in different ways.

Kay was brilliant. She really understood children – their very breathing she knew. She was superb and they all loved her. So did I.

One day, when it was pouring with rain and the children were playing happily for once in the playroom, we sat and had a good chat over a cup of coffee.

Caroline's bathtime fiasco was still a daily trial. I explained it all to her.

'There's definitely something wrong about this,' I said. 'To be so afraid of even going into the bathroom.'

'Well, you're right,' she agreed. 'It's not a normal reaction.'

'I've tried putting the ducks in, using blue bubbles, letting her turn the taps on and off herself, but it makes no difference. She just screams and screams with terror.'

'It all sounds very stressful.'

'Yes. It is. I sometimes feel like I'm being so cruel to her, forcing her into the bath each time.'

'Do you have a separate toilet in the house?'

'Yes, just off the hall.'

'And is she afraid of going in there?'

'I don't think so,' I said. 'She doesn't use the toilet yet, because she's still in nappies. But we use that basin for the children to wash their hands before meals and she's got the hang of that all right now, without any tears or fuss.'

'Well, I know it would be lovely for her to be able to enjoy having a bath, like the others do, but what about trying a different tack?'

'What do you mean?'

'What if you get Mike to watch the other three, and you take Caroline to have a thorough wash in the basin downstairs instead, so that she can get used to the idea of washing in peace and safety. Then maybe you could gradually coax her to join the others just for a minute or two at the end, or maybe leave it till you think she's ready?'

'That's a good idea. I'll talk to Mike about it.'

'Are you keeping notes of all these early problems?' asked Kay. 'And the fun things too?'

'Yes, I keep my fostering diary to jot down problems, and I've started a memory box for each of them.'

'That's great.' She smiled. 'I always think a memory box is much better than an album or a scrapbook, because memories don't always come in date order, do they? At least, they don't with children. And that way, you can put objects in too, like a flower, or a piece of fabric, or even a special toy, to remember things by.'

'Yes, we have one special box for each of the children to keep in their bedrooms and go through any time they want. They all love their memory boxes already. I've done it with all our foster children. It's great when they're feeling a bit down and I can say "Why don't we go through your memory box together?" Good memories make everyone smile, don't they?'

While we were talking we went down to the playroom to check on the children, who had caused the usual mayhem, pulling everything off the shelves and out of the toy-boxes. They were as hyper as monkeys and very fractious with each other. But when I turned to look at Simon, he had curled up on the sofa and fallen asleep.

'I know he's still quite young,' said Kay. 'But does he often fall asleep like this?'

'Yes, he does it quite a lot. Hamish says he used to have nothing to play with. His mother either carried him around or put him in his cot in their main room, where I suppose there was nothing else to do but sleep.'

'Let's wake him up gently and try to get him into playing with the toys.'

Ever since that first weekend, when I'd noticed what seemed like sexualised behaviour in both the girls, but especially Anita, I'd seen it more and more. One day when I walked into Anita's bedroom, she was sitting on the floor with two naked Barbie dolls and putting them into sexual positions. She was so engrossed that she didn't notice me standing in the doorway. She had them on top of each other at first, with one going up and down. Then she changed them round and had one standing and the other kneeling in front. Variations of these positions went on for quite some time, with her quietly using a lot of swear words in her 'talk' between the two dolls. Finally she suddenly flared up angrily and threw the short-haired doll right across the room. At that moment she caught sight of me, so I put the ironing away in her drawers.

'Did you get cross with your dolls, Anita?' I asked, as I paired up her socks.

'This one's Mum,' she said. 'And that one is Larry. Mum made us watch them sexing together. I hate it when Mum's friends do that to me.'

'Do what?'

'Put their thing in me.' She paused. 'They do it to Caroline too.'

'Well, that's not going to happen here.'

Anita and Caroline seemed to pose for any man that came along, including Mike. I don't think they were even aware of how inappropriate their sexualised movements and mannerisms were.

'She's just looking for a bit of attention, Mrs Merry,' they said at Social Services when I rang up to try to find out more about what had happened to Anita in particular.

'No, no, no. Nothing happened,' they always insisted.

'Nothing in the notes,' they claimed. And I'm thinking *You haven't even looked.*

It was very clear to me now that they had both been sexually abused.

At about this time, Anita developed a fetish about her hair. Much as she craved attention from anyone, a part of her seemed to want to hide who she was and to look like a different person.

'I don't want to have brown hair any more,' she said to me one day. 'Don't look at me. You mustn't look at me, not till I've grown my hair and it goes blonde. I'm going to have long, blonde hair, and then nobody will recognise me. But you mustn't look at me now.'

'No,' I humoured her. 'We're going to let it grow and make it all clean so that it's lighter.'

Wednesdays and Sundays were nit-nights, with the metal nit-comb.

'Once we've got all the head lice and nits out, your hair will grow quicker.'

She smiled. 'And I want to grow the fringe right over my face, so that people can't see me.'

'Let's wait and see about that, An.' I never knew if I was saying the right things. I felt that all the children needed someone with a lot more expertise than I had. They really needed a therapist or counsellor to help them through all these problems, but the Council refused to pay for one, so I tried to persuade the agency to pay for it, but I'd have to keep working on that, especially as we didn't know how long they would be with us.

I began to wonder again whether I was getting too old for all this!

Social Services rang up one day to arrange a visit between the children and their mother. The court had granted her fortnightly visits, as long as they met in a family centre in a nearby town. We agreed a date towards the end of the week, so that I could prepare the children for it. First I would have to tell them, but I really didn't know how they would react.

'I had a phone call this morning to say that your mum is coming up to visit you on Thursday—'

'She's not going to come here, is she?' interrupted Hamish.

'No, not to the house.'

'She mustn't come to the house,' he insisted. 'I don't want her to see where we live.'

'Well, it's all right, she won't be coming here. You're going to meet her in a family centre a few miles away, where they have a really nice room with cosy chairs and toys and things.' I couldn't be sure about the details, but I wanted to reassure them and that's what family centres were usually like.

'Do we have to see her?' asked Anita, which caught me by surprise.

'Well, I don't know whether anyone can force you to see her, but she's coming up specially and I think you should at least be there to meet her and let her see how pretty you look in your new clothes.'

'OK,' nodded Anita. She was always a sucker for showing off her favourite clothes. 'She probably won't recognise me anyway, now that I'm growing my hair.'

'Will she be on her own?' asked Hamish. 'She won't bring any of her mates, will she?'

'Like who?' I asked.

'Kevin,' he said. 'Or Larry, or Wayne.'

'No, I'm not going if she brings Wayne,' shrieked Anita in a sudden panic.

'Don't worry about that,' I tried to reassure her. 'I'm sure nobody like that would be allowed to come in with her. It will be relatives only.'

'Will you come in with us?' asked Caroline.

'I will take you there and wait for you, but I don't think I'm supposed to go in with you.'

'What if we refuse to go in unless you come in too?' asked Hamish.

'I don't know,' I replied, honestly. 'Why, do you really want me to come in that much?'

'Yes,' they all chorused in unison.

'All right, I'll ask if I can, as it's the first visit, but I can't promise they'll let me.'

We spoke quite a lot about the impending visit and the older three all seemed apprehensive about seeing their mum, and the tension rose to a crescendo when we pulled up in the car outside the modern family centre building.

'Do I have to go in?' asked Hamish.

'I think you should,' I said. 'Your mum has travelled all that way. She'll be upset if you don't come and say hello to her.'

They all piled out of the back seats and we climbed the

shallow steps to the front entrance. Inside, a smiling woman welcomed us and took us to the room where the meeting would take place. As I predicted, there was a lovely play corner, full of books, toys and puzzles, so they all made a beeline for that. Even Simon, who by now was walking a bit more confidently, pattered off after them.

'She's not arrived yet,' said the woman. 'I'll bring her straight through when she gets here.'

I passed by the comfortable-looking easy chairs, grouped around a square coffee table, and went over to join the kids in the play area. They had so many lovely picture books there that I chose one and started to read it to Simon and Caroline, while Anita had a go at a jigsaw puzzle and Hamish emptied out a box of Lego to build with.

I didn't notice how much time had passed until the woman came back in, alone.

'No sign of her then?' I asked.

'No. She's already half an hour late. Shall I call Social Services to see if they know anything?'

'Yes, that's a good idea. Thank you.'

Another five minutes and back she came again. 'I phoned them and spoke to somebody called Steve,' she said. 'He told me that they'd given her a train pass and ordered a taxi to take her to the station. But when the taxi got there, she said she had some friends round, so she would have to come another day instead.' This pleasant woman looked as dismayed as I felt. Having spent the past couple of days building the children up to be ready for this meeting, how was I going to let them down gently? I had to tell them their mum wasn't coming, but I couldn't tell them why – that she preferred to spend the afternoon with her friends than with her own children who she hadn't seen for several weeks.

I felt sure there would be repercussions over the next few days, but when I told them, they seemed to take it in their stride, as if they half expected it.

'She never goes to appointments,' explained Hamish. 'So I thought she might not come, unless somebody drove her all the way here.'

'Oh, I don't suppose they could do that,' I said.

We all went back home and they just carried on as usual, as if nothing had happened.

'I'm just waiting for the aftershocks,' I told Mike that evening when they'd all gone to bed.

'Don't worry, love,' he said. 'You'll cope with it. You always do.'

9

Dicing with Death

'The centre reports that the care of these children isn't good enough. They are neglected, unkempt and infested with lice. The children constantly ask for food and have eaten ravenously when food is offered to them.'

Social Services report

I knew it couldn't last. The morning after the missed visit from his mum, Hamish's fury erupted. He stormed down the stairs and into the kitchen, banged his bowl and spoon about on the table and spat at Anita sitting next to him.

'You wanker!' she shouted at him.

'You're the wanker!' he yelled back at her.

'Get away from me.'

He got up, threw his spoon across the floor, opened a cupboard and slammed it shut again.

'Steady on, Hame,' said Mike in his calm voice.

'I fucking hate you,' Hamish replied. 'I hate you all. I hate this fucking place.' He stamped around the outside of the room, muttering obscenities, seething to himself. He stopped, red in the face when he got to me.

'I'm just going to do a cooked breakfast for Mike,' I said, trying to calm him down. 'Would you like some?'

'Keep your bloody bacon!' he yelled, as close as he could to my face, and spat at me. I could feel a gloop of saliva landing on my cheek and running down onto my chin, before I wiped it away with some kitchen towel.

'Right, young man. It's back to your bedroom for you. I'm not having that kind of behaviour down here. If you want to shout and swear and spit, go and do it in your own room. And don't come down until you are ready to be civilised to everyone. I understand why you are angry, but that is no reason to upset your brother and sisters, Mike and me.'

He stood his ground. How could I resolve this?

But Mike came up with the answer. 'No fish and chips for you tonight, Hamish, unless you go up to your room. And don't come down until you are ready to apologise.'

He thought about this for only two seconds, turned smartly and marched off upstairs. I heard the door slamming, but all was peace and quiet after that.

'I'm really sorry,' said his sad voice from the doorway, an hour or so later. 'I was just so cross with Mum.'

'I know, love.' I went over and gave him a hug. 'It's hard coping with everything that's happened to you, isn't it?'

He nodded.

'Come on, let's get you something to eat.'

As he ate his late breakfast, I sat down at the table with him and sewed a button onto one of Mike's shirts. 'I don't know what Mike does with his buttons. They're always going missing.'

'Mum wouldn't do anything like that. She's very lazy,' he said.

'Well, lots of people don't bother with sewing unless they have to.'

'But she doesn't do anything. No cooking, no cleaning. The house was always filthy. I hated that. I hated having to wear dirty clothes too. Mum hardly ever did the washing, so I sometimes did it when we went to bed, but I couldn't get the clothes dry in time for morning, so we had to wear wet clothes to school. My teacher told me that she had made a complaint about my wet clothes, but they never did anything about it.' He paused. 'It was the same with the food.'

'What do you mean?'

'Well, I was always hungry. We never had breakfast, so I used to ask for food at nursery when I was younger, and then at school. Some of the teachers used to give me a biscuit, but I was still hungry. I used to look through the school bins at playtimes, looking for something to eat.'

'Didn't anyone see you?'

'Yes. My teacher asked me why I was so hungry and I didn't know what to say.'

'Did she contact Social Services about that too?'

'I think she did. I don't know. Nothing ever happened about it.'

'That must have been very difficult for you, being so hungry all the time.'

'It wasn't just me,' he said. 'The others were hungry too. I had to find food for them as well.'

He finished his cereal, so I made him some Marmite toast.

'I don't know why I was so cross this morning,' he said between mouthfuls. 'I knew she wouldn't come. She just sleeps late and lays about the house with her friends.'

'Who were the friends?'

'I don't know. Just men. We used to get left with them sometimes. But we were left on our own a lot too.'

'Did that worry you?'

'No,' he shrugged.

'I know Anita was at school with you before you came here. But what about Caroline and Simon?'

'Caroline was supposed to be going to nursery, but Mum hardly ever took her. Sometimes one of her mates did.'

'One of the men?'

'Yes.'

'Didn't they buy food when they were at the house so often?'

'I don't know. I don't think so. When I was at school, I used to worry about Caroline and especially Simon, because he was always at home. He was Mum's favourite, but I used to worry that she wouldn't change his nappies or feed him.'

'He must have been very smelly by the time you got home.'

'Yes, but sometimes Simon and Caroline pulled their nappies off, so there was a lot of mess when that happened.'

'Oh dear.'

'I don't think Mum liked Caroline, so she used to tie her to her bed when I wasn't there.'

'Yes, Caroline told me that. She said you untied her. Do you think the social workers knew about that?'

'I don't know. Mum didn't like the social workers. She argued with them. I remember Mum was right in front of me when she punched one woman in the face.'

'Oh dear. Was the woman all right?'

'I don't know. We never saw her again.'

'You told me that Simon had nothing to play with in his cot.'

'None of us had any toys. Two social workers brought us toys for Christmas presents one year, but I think Mum sold them.'

'So what did you play with?'

'There was an old wrecked car on our drive.'

'Whose car was it?'

'I don't know. But it didn't have any tyres and the doors were falling off. It was good fun to play with. We played games in it. I used to like pretending I was driving the car on a long journey. Sometimes we pretended it was a pirate ship. That was good.' He smiled. 'Sometimes me and Anita went down to the river with sticks and we tried to pierce the fish, but they were usually too quick for us. I did catch a fish once and I took it home to show my dad. He gave me a pound coin and told me to go and throw it back into the river.'

'Do you remember your dad quite well?'

'Yes, a bit. He left when I was three or four I think. I

remember the police kept coming round to arrest him and take him away.'

'Come on, sunshine,' I said, standing up. 'I think we'd better go and see how the others are getting on.'

'Can we take some food down with us?'

'Yes, but let's make it healthy food. It's not long till lunchtime.'

We took four apples down to the playroom, where they were all busy demolishing a toy farm, with Anita about to jump on it.

'An! Don't do that,' I said. 'Simon likes to play with the farm. I'll put it over there for him.' I don't think he'd ever played with it, but I thought he might like it, so I lifted it up and placed it in front of where he was sitting. Hamish, bless him, brought over some of the farm animals that went with it and set them all out on the floor. Simon picked up a cow and took a close look at it. Then he gathered some of the other animals and started to reposition them.

It was nice and quiet while they crunched their Granny Smiths. I had cut up one of them to make it easier for Simon to eat and he carefully picked up one quarter and started to nibble on it.

'Thank you,' he said.

'That's all right,' I replied, in shock. 'Good boy.'

Hamish picked up a picture book and started to read it out loud, word by word. That made me feel guilty.

'Well done, Hame. Do you miss being at school?'

'A bit,' he nodded. 'But I'm glad I haven't got to walk to school any more.'

'Why is that?'

'I used to walk Anita to nursery to start with, before I went to school. I was only five and I used to get her up and help her get dressed. Then we had to walk down the path by the canal.'

'Hamish saved my life,' Anita chipped in.

'Really?' I couldn't help being shocked. 'What happened?'

'Yes, she fell into the canal and I had to pull her out,' he said matter-of-factly.

'I don't remember falling in, but I remember panicking. I was struggling.' She acted it out dramatically. 'I tried to climb up the wall, but I couldn't. I was scared because I thought the fishes would eat my toes.'

'I got a stick,' Hamish continued, 'and reached it out to her to grab hold of, so that I could pull her in to the side.'

'I nearly drowned,' added Anita. 'I lay on the ground and I couldn't get my breath back.'

'Then we walked further down the path and this man with a beard came out of the bushes. He was watching us, but he didn't come to help.'

'I was frightened of him,' said Anita.

'I think his name was David. He used to babysit us. He was dangerous. He beckoned us to go to him, but we ran away.'

'So where was the nursery?'

'Not far from the canal. I used to take her there and then walk the rest of the way to school. But this year she has been coming with me to school. It was OK until we got to the dual carriageway. I never really knew how to cross it, so at first I just closed my eyes and ran across. Later I tried to look for a gap.'

I was horrified. 'Didn't anybody see you trying to cross?'

'Some of the parents saw us from outside the school. One of my friends said his mum told the head teacher. I had to go to her office and she asked me some questions.'

'Did anyone do anything about it?'

'I don't think so.'

'It sounds like you were dicing with death!'

'Hamish always looked after me,' said Anita, with uncharacteristic admiration.

'And me . . . and Simon,' added Caroline.

After I had tucked the three younger children into their beds that evening, I came into Hamish's room. He was standing in his pyjamas, looking at his face in the mirror, with a solemn expression, which slightly unnerved me. He was still very small for his age, but he had the look of an old man, careworn and anxious.

I walked up behind him, so that he could see me in the mirror.

'What's up, Hame?'

He said nothing.

'You look worried.'

He hesitated. Then out it came: 'I don't know who I am.'

I was shocked, uncertain what to say, so I put my arms gently around his shoulders, then turned him around to face me. He didn't resist. His big brown eyes, deep and doleful, stared into mine as he let out a long sigh.

'What's the matter?' I asked him as we went and sat together on the edge of his bed, my arm still around his bony shoulders.

'I don't know who I am,' he repeated with a small voice.

'Really?' I tried to understand what he might be thinking. 'What do you mean?'

'I don't know what I'm supposed to do any more.'

'You mean, because you don't have to go and find food any more, or keep the others safe, or nag at Mum to change Simon's nappy, or—'

'Yes.'

'I've taken it all away from you, haven't I?'

He nodded, his bottom lip quivering.

'But you do remind me whenever you think I've forgotten. That's very helpful. I have so much to do in the house that I like it when you remind me about mealtimes or snacks or nappies, and you always know what we need when we go to the supermarket, so I know I can rely on you. I reckon you've got a much better memory than I have. Mike said that just a couple of days ago.'

'Did he? Really?' His face brightened up.

'Yes, really. And the younger ones always turn to you for help when something goes wrong, or they're not sure what to do. So you see, you will always be their big brother-hero, not just for saving Anita's life, but in lots of ways, every day.'

He lifted his hunched shoulders and looked me straight

in the eyes. 'Thank you,' he said, a slow smile lighting up his face.

'He really is old beyond his years,' I said to Mike later that evening, as I told him about what Hamish had said. 'A part of him just wants to be a little boy, but he can't let himself . . . yet. I suppose it feels like we've pulled the rug away from under his feet.'

'Yes, he's a good lad, and he must know he's come to the right place. If anyone can help him adjust, you can.'

'I hope so, but you'll have to do your bit too.'

'Haven't I always?'

'Yes, love. You've always been my rock, and you never complained . . .' I paused. 'Do you remember those days when we used to have lots of emergency placements and you never knew who would be here when you came home from work?'

He laughed. 'Yes, there'd be three round the breakfast table when I left in the morning, and six eating their tea when I got back home again. That took some adjusting to.'

'For both of us! But you always took it in your stride.'

'Hamish will be all right . . . even if we're reduced to a frazzle!' He grinned.

After more than thirty years of fostering, I was shocked to be invited to attend a case review meeting. In the past, I didn't even know when they were, and only discovered afterwards what had been discussed and decided. But now that we were with John's agency, he made sure we could be included.

'Nobody knows these children better than you,' he explained. 'We need to know what you think about their progress and how best to meet their needs.'

So they were not only telling me the date, they were asking me to go along and *give my views*! I certainly had a lot of questions to ask and things to say.

My biggest concern at that moment was Caroline and her abnormal fear of the bathroom, so I really wanted to talk about that, and what it might mean.

I walked into that big room, full of social workers sat around a long table, all looking at me as I sat down on the last chair.

If I could have read their thoughts, I think they would have been 'troublemaker'.

'I really just need more information,' I said when it was my turn to speak. 'Because I think these children have been abused.'

'Oh, no, no, no, no. These children haven't been abused.' It was like a brick wall.

'The children have told me about all the men in and out of the house and some of the things they did to them. I'm wondering if they were paedophiles.'

'No, no, no. We wouldn't let that happen.'

'Well, I'm sorry, but . . .'

They weren't listening – maybe they didn't want to listen. Of course, what happens in that sort of situation is you start thinking, well, perhaps it's me, imagining things. Perhaps I'm not reading it right. That's how I felt. But then as I watched them continuing their self-righteous discussion, I thought no, I know what I've seen, and what the children have said. How could they make up some of those things, if they hadn't happened?

'How have they settled in, Mrs Merry?'

I glanced across to Carol from John's agency, the only friendly face in the room, and she tilted her head slightly, as if to encourage me to say some of the things we had often discussed.

'They were all in a terrible state when they arrived,' I began. 'Straight out of the workhouse. That's what they looked like. But they've settled as well as we could have expected, considering all their problems. And this little family had more problems than I've ever known, in all the nearly seven hundred children we've looked after, from starvation to fear, and everything in between.'

'Is there anything major that still worries you?'

'Yes, a lot of things, in all four children. For example, Caroline has a screaming fear of the bathroom, and we can't work out why. We've tried everything, and we hate having to carry her in kicking and screaming. So I've taken to giving her a thorough wash at the basin in the downstairs loo. But we can't go on with that indefinitely.'

'No, that does sound unusual,' said a young man sitting next to Carol.

A rather pinched-faced woman glared at him.

'Something must have happened to her in a bathroom,' I suggested.

'No, it sounds more like attention-seeking to me,' she insisted.

Oh, here we go again, I thought, so I changed the subject. 'Well, these children have all been badly neglected. And the only way I can do my job well is if you give me all the information. I don't care how bad it is. Just tell me.' Stunned silence. They were invisibly closing ranks.

'What about their mother?' I asked. 'I'm wondering, does she have learning difficulties?'

'No learning difficulties,' replied the pinched-faced lady, so adamantly it gave her away.

'What about mental health problems?'

'No mental health problems, nothing like that,' said another woman, her fingers fidgeting.

'They all have a bit of a speech problem, especially Caroline. It's often difficult to understand what she says. Do you know if there's a history of speech or hearing problems in the family?'

'No.'

'Why have they never been to the dentist?' I asked. 'Couldn't a social worker have taken them? And not knowing their medical history made it difficult when Caroline was ill and we had to take her to the hospital.'

'You're a gobby carer!' scowled pinch-face.

They were all looking very uneasy now, even Carol.

I thought I had been invited to that meeting to discuss the children's needs, but I left more frustrated than ever.

Mike was pleased to see me back and I told him about the meeting over a nice mug of tea.

'They wouldn't even tell me about the speech problems,'

I said. 'Whether anyone in the family had speech or hearing difficulties.'

'Well, perhaps it's simpler than that. If nobody talks to you, how are you going to learn to speak properly?'

'That's true,' I agreed. 'How did your morning go with the children?'

'Well, you know what they're like. Hamish was edgy and couldn't settle to anything. Anita was her usual hyper self – off the wall, swearing like a trooper. Caroline was constantly tugging at me, in between pinching Anita and shoving Simon away, anything for attention. All being spiteful to each other and spoiling each other's games.' He shrugged. 'I think sharing passed them by!'

'A normal morning then?'

'Yes.' He made a face. 'So I just took them all over to the park for a good runaround. They were better after that.'

The phone call came from Social Services. 'We've arranged for both of the children's parents to come up and visit them.'

'Together?' I had visions of the nightmare that might be . . . if they both turned up.

'No, the same day, but different times.'

'When?'

'Tomorrow.'

'Not much notice then.'

'Sorry about that, Mrs Merry. Gary will come at noon and Jill at two.'

'Is somebody driving them here?'

'No, Jill asked me to bring her, but I'm not driving her anywhere in my car!'

'Why is that?'

'Personal hygiene. And she's with Kevin, the paedophile, and I'm not having him in my car. So we've given them both train passes.'

I shuddered, remembering the smell of the children when they arrived, and having to pick off the lice crawling on their bodies. Eugh!

Later it occurred to me that this mention of Kevin's status had been an unintentional slip. So they did know that Jill had paedophiles in the house. But they'd always sworn blind to me that this was nonsense.

The next morning, I put together some food and we all piled into the people-carrier.

'It will be Dad first,' I explained. 'Then Mum after lunch.'

'How will Mum get here?' asked Hamish, his face creased with anxiety.

'On the train. They've given her a ticket.'

'But she won't know how to do that.'

Children like Hamish, with all the cares of the world, can be very perceptive sometimes.

'Maybe she will bring a friend with her.'

'I don't want to see Mum's friends,' wailed Anita.

'Don't worry, it will be all right. I'll tell the lady at the centre not to let anyone else in.'

'What about food?' panicked Hamish. 'Where are we

going to eat?' Food was still his number one priority. Some things never change.

'I've made us all lots of sandwiches and cakes and I've packed drinks and yoghurts and fruit as well.'

'And chocolate biscuits?' asked Caroline.

'Yes. It's for Dad and Mum too. We'll spread the cloth on the floor and put all the food out. Then you can just help yourselves.'

Hamish nodded his approval, so I knew I'd passed the test.

First it was Dad. He came down on the early morning train from Scotland to visit them. Hamish and Anita were quite excited, because it had been a long time since they had seen him. Caroline and Simon didn't remember him. They were all sitting in the play area when he came in through the door, so he sat down on the nearest chair and lit up a cigarette.

'Hello, kids,' he said as he delved into a carrier bag and pulled out a can of lager, which he opened and started to drink.

'Do you like my dress?' asked Anita, doing a twirl. But her father wasn't looking. 'Look at me, Dad,' she insisted crossly.

'Very pretty,' he said with a quick glance and a preoccupied expression.

He turned to Hamish. 'What about you, son? What have you been up to?'

'I help Mike collect the fish and chips on Fridays,' said Hamish proudly. Then his face clouded over. 'Why didn't you take me to Scotland?'

'I couldn't,' was his only reply.

Caroline tried to climb onto his knee, but he brushed her off gently and she sat scowling on the floor by his feet.

'Farm,' said Simon to me, pointing at the toy farm in the corner, so I took him over to help him play with it.

'Do you want a sandwich, Dad?' asked Hamish, bringing a plate over to him.

'No, I'm all right, son.'

Their dad stayed for a while, but didn't really interact with the children. He just sat there and drank and chain-smoked, then finally he gave them all a wave. 'Bye, kids,' he said as he left.

The children demolished the sandwiches enthusiastically.

'That went OK, didn't it, Hame?' I said to the eldest.

'Yeah, I suppose. But he could have talked with us.'

The time for their mum's visit came . . . and went. Then, finally, as we were beginning to pack up, she ambled in. Caroline made a beeline for her and got there first.

My heart lurched as her mum just pushed her away, sending her sprawling on the floor. Caroline cried and cried, but her mum ignored her. So I put my arm round her narrow shoulders and took her into the play area, where I read her a book called *The Tiger Who Came to Tea*.

'That's my Anita,' said Caroline.

'Yes, she does look a bit like her.'

I called Anita over and we read it through again.

Meanwhile, Jill had picked up Simon and was carrying him around the room.

Hamish kept getting in front of her, trying to tell her

things, about the fish and chips, the park opposite our house, the playroom in our cellar . . . But she made no response, just ambled about with a bored expression, looking intently out of the window every now and then. I don't think the children noticed that, but I knew why. Kevin was lurking somewhere.

Looking at Jill, I wondered again about learning difficulties. When Anita took the tiger book to her birth mother, she wouldn't even look at it, just turned away. Perhaps she couldn't read. She didn't make any effort to please her children, or seem to understand the effect she had on them.

'I don't know why they took my kids away,' she said to me at one point. 'I did everything I could for them. Why did they interfere? I didn't need their interfering, just more money.' She paused. 'They never helped me. I can't do it all on my own.'

From what the children had told me, it didn't sound as if she had been alone, much, but I just nodded sympathetically and said nothing, which is quite unusual for me!

The only child she showed any attachment to was Simon, and that was more passive, just carrying him around, rather than any active show of affection. Even he plodded off with his strange walk as soon as she put him down to light a cigarette.

Caroline let out a sob every now and then, clinging to me most of the hour that her mother was in the room. Finally Jill left to meet Kevin for the train home. The children seemed unconcerned.

Caroline sobbed and sniffed by turns, all the way home

and for most of the evening. I gave her lots of cuddles and even the other children were unusually kind to her that bedtime, letting her sit on my knee for the whole story.

I was surprised that the other three showed no reaction following their parents' visits, but over the next few days Caroline started stealing food from the kitchen cupboards and hiding it in her room.

10

Mum's Boyfriends

'Exposure to Schedule 1 offenders, very dangerous to children, often staying overnight in the house. Mrs Mackay was warned about this, but is unconcerned about the risk this poses to her children.'

Independent social work report

A few days after their parents' visits, Hamish went into overdrive again with his ballistic behaviour. He was spiteful towards his brother and sisters, rude and rebellious to me and Mike and at times quite wild, throwing things about, stamping, shouting and of course swearing. It wasn't the same every day, but most days were challenging anyway, and he pushed us, especially me, almost to the limit. After a particularly spiteful outburst, I gave Hamish a long, intense gaze that must have made him feel uncomfortable. He hung his head to prevent eye contact with me.

So I sat down next to him at the table. We stayed there like that, the two of us, in silence, while Mike was out in the garden with the other three.

'What's up?' I asked him eventually.

'I'm cross with Mum. I don't think she really cares about us.'

'Why do you think that?'

'She didn't ask me what I've been doing, and she was mean to Caroline, pushing her away like that. All she said was that she'd brought Kevin to see us but they wouldn't let him come to the family centre with her.'

'Did you want to see him?'

'No. I did not! I didn't want to see any of the men that used to come and stay in our house. I didn't like any of them. I didn't like the things they did.'

'What sort of things?' I don't suppose I should have asked that question, but it came out.

'Like Larry. He used to tape up our mouths to keep us quiet. And he used a stick to make us good. Then he sometimes gave us money or sweets if we were.'

'Was Larry at your house a lot?'

'Sometimes. But he used to get in trouble with the police for being dirty with kids.'

'Was he ever dirty with anyone in your house?'

'I couldn't see what he did with Anita or Caroline when he took them upstairs. But I didn't like him being in our house.'

'Was he ever dirty with you?' I persisted.

Hamish dropped his chin to his chest and said nothing.

That afternoon, as I was putting some of the laundry away in the children's drawers, I was in Anita's bedroom when she came in to change into dry socks.

'Here you are Anita.' I handed her some clean pink socks.

'I like socks,' she said. 'I never had any before I came here. And my shoes didn't fit.'

'I remember when you came.'

'I never had new clothes till I came here.'

I finished putting her things away and closed the drawer.

'And I didn't have a proper bedroom. It was always busy in our house.'

'How do you mean?'

'A lot of people, Mum's boyfriends. There was always something going on.'

'I expect your mum liked having lots of her friends around.'

'I don't remember much about Mum,' said Anita. 'She didn't talk to me. One day she was running around the house in the nude, with one of the men who sometimes picked on me. Then he took me outside and made me chase him down the street in just my knickers. And the twins were there too. They played around with my mum and one of them picked on me too. I didn't like them. They were scary and they hurt me. And Kevin always got cross with me.'

'Was this when your dad was still there?'

'No, he went before that.'

'Wayne always wanted me to go upstairs with him.'

'Was he there a lot?'

'Yes, and other men too. I remember one day. I don't know who this man was. He had green Y-fronts on and they were round his legs, under his knees. I just remember his tummy, and the green pants around his legs.'

I was horrified at how matter-of-fact Anita was about

all this, at only six years old, and that she even knew those pants were called Y-fronts. I didn't know what I could say.

'Mum always took her clothes off with men. I remember one time,' she continued, 'I don't know if it was Kevin, or a friend of Wayne's, but him and Mum made Hamish, Caroline and me watch them sexing together.' She looked down at the carpet.

I sat down next to her on the bed and took her hand in mine, but I said nothing.

'Wayne . . .' The tears came and her little body began to tremble. 'He always made me . . .' She sobbed, unable to speak any more.

'*Shh, shh* . . .' I put one arm round her shoulder, stroking her hair with my other hand, trying to soothe her. 'You don't need to say.'

She remained silent, her little chin quivering as her whole body shook. I gave her a big cuddle. 'It's OK, An, they're all a long way away now.'

She nodded as the tears streamed down her face.

'Come on. Let's go downstairs and see what the others are doing.'

She let me hold her hand across the landing. 'If we don't go back soon, Mike will be pulling his hair out. He won't have any left!'

I don't suppose she understood what I meant, but it raised a smile.

'Mike is funny,' she said.

* * *

As I was cooking tea, all the children were at the table.

'I don't want to go back to being hungry and cold,' said Hamish, out of the blue. 'I like having cooked food.'

'You a good cooker.' Caroline smiled.

'Thank you. It's nearly ready, so time to go and wash your hands while I clear the table.'

'I'm drawing rude men and ladies,' announced Anita, holding up her paper for me to see. 'This is what ladies do.'

'I'll look at it later, Anita,' I said gently. 'I'm glad you like drawing, but it's time to go and wash your hands for tea.'

As I gathered all their puzzles and colouring things into a box, I took a look at Anita's rudimentary but revealing pictures. I folded up the piece of paper to show Mike later, and Carol on her next visit.

It had been quite an upsetting day for both Hamish and Anita, and Caroline was still reacting to her mother's most recent rejection, so they were all on edge. I sat with them as they ate their tea. Usually it was a noisy, boisterous time, but today seemed more subdued.

'You sound a bit snuffly,' I said to Simon as I reached for a tissue to help him blow his nose. 'I hope it's only a cold.'

'You can take Night Nurse for a cold,' announced Anita.

'That's right, some people do,' I said, surprised that she knew about that. 'But I prefer natural medicines, like honey and lemon. That's much healthier.'

'Yes, Mum had a bottle of Night Nurse. I drank half of it, but it made me ill. And I didn't even have a cold.'

'Half a bottle? I think that's for grown-ups. It should be only a spoonful at a time.'

'I didn't know that. The top was off so I drank it.'

'What happened?'

'She went to sleep,' said Hamish. 'She wouldn't wake up and I thought she was going to die.'

'I only remember lying on the sofa, like I was in a cloud, with lots of people talking to me. I was asleep and they told me to wake up. I tried to open my eyes.'

'You were very floppy,' added Hamish. 'When the social worker came, she called an ambulance.'

'When I woke up I was in hospital. That was good.'

'Why?'

'Because a nurse gave me the best hug. And then I rode a trike round the ward.'

It was one of those bright, warm spring afternoons, with the smell of blossom, when we arrived at John's house. In all my previous thirty-five years of fostering, I had never before been invited to any get-together like this. John had asked all his carers to bring along their foster children one Sunday afternoon. He had a beautiful garden that led down to a shallow stream, with a climbing frame and swings in one corner and lots of balls and games out for the children to play with. Play they did, rather wildly as I remember, but that was nothing unusual – they were just having a good time.

'Hi, Trisha,' John called with a smile as he came across to me, standing with a group of other foster mums. 'Did you know?' He turned to them, offering a plate of jam tarts and mini-éclairs round the group. 'This woman was voted Mum in a Million?'

'No? . . . Really . . . Well done . . .' They were all very gracious about it. Too nice really.

'But the people who voted would have been shocked if they saw the state of my house after the kids have trashed it.' I grinned. 'Or heard me bellow when I have to shout above their noise! I'm not very motherly then!'

'No, I'd never win something like that,' said the young foster mum standing next to me. 'But you have to be tough, don't you? Even with one child. I can't imagine how you cope with four!' She looked pointedly at the havoc they were creating, pushing other children off the climbing frame and pinching their skipping ropes.

'I don't think I do,' I shrugged, making a mental note to talk to the kids about being kinder to others. 'I just try to keep my head above the troubled waters, one day at a time!'

'That's so right!' said another woman. We all laughed, pooling our experiences. It was such a lovely afternoon and it was all down to John and his partner Suzy, who plied the children with cakes and buns. My four loved her for that.

The children were beginning to get used to us and our ways, though it was always two steps forward and at least one back from day to day. Nothing was ever predictable.

One morning, the hoity-toity woman from the education department phoned me.

'I'm just ringing to check,' she said. 'Are your two older foster children attending school yet?'

Here we go again, I thought. 'No. As I told you before, I

tried all the schools and as soon as I said the words "foster children" and "problems", nobody would take them.'

'Well, try some more schools outside the city.'

'You try them,' I said, losing patience with this jobsworth woman. 'Look, four weeks ago I told you that if you couldn't find Hamish and Anita places at the same school, I would have to keep them at home.'

'But you can't do that.'

We'd been here before. 'Yes, I can. I refuse to send them to school until you find them places,' and I put the phone down. I probably shouldn't have done that, but it worked!

Everyone came out of the woodwork and within an hour the phone rang again.

'Have you tried any of the smaller village schools outside the city, like St Mary's?' asked a warmer female voice, quite different from the first woman. 'I wonder if Hamish and Anita might settle more easily into a small school. What do you think?'

'Well, I assumed they would have to go to their local school, and I thought a bigger school could more easily handle them. But now you put it that way, a village school with smaller classes might be better, more personal, more like a family. Do you think St Mary's would be willing to take them?'

'I've just called to see if they have spaces and they do. It's not too far to drive. You could give them a try. I said you might call.'

So that's what I did.

'Yes, Mrs Merry. We do have places in both Year 2 and Year 1.'

'Did the education department tell you they are foster children who have a lot of adjusting to do and may have problems settling in?'

'Yes, they did. And we'll discuss with you the best way to meet their needs.'

'Thank you, thank you!' I was so grateful to have found a small school with a good reputation to start them in at last. That woman was right. They might have felt lost in a big school, but small classes in a village school – that would be much better.

I began to get them into school routines: getting up at the right times, doing some reading and writing practice with me in the mornings, and counting out the money in my purse.

Simon and Caroline used to sit with us too during these morning sessions. Of course their needs were very different. Simon, at nearly three, was just beginning now to play with wooden bricks or his beloved farm animals, so he sat on the floor with them while Caroline, coming up to five, joined us at the table. I would set both Hamish and Anita a handwriting or adding task, while I tried to teach Caroline some numbers and colours, but with no success. She could repeat them after me, but she didn't retain them.

So Caroline didn't know her colours, couldn't count at all, had a speech problem, was still in nappies day and night and . . . who's going to take her? Well, I'd worry about that later, once the older two had started school.

One morning the health visitor arrived to do her weighing and measuring. All four children had been very small for their age, so this monthly ritual was an important factor in judging their progress since coming to us. Then she observed them playing, over a cup of coffee with me in the garden.

'How do you think they're doing?' I asked.

'Very well, I'd say. They're all putting on weight and climbing the charts to get closer to average now,' she explained. 'How are they mentally and emotionally?'

'That's the bit that is huge for them. I feel I've barely scratched the surface of the damage there. They really need therapy, all of them. They need a good, perceptive counsellor in the long term, who can help them sort it all out in their heads, but nobody will pay for it.'

'Who needs it most?'

'They all need it badly, but maybe Hamish, because he's suffered for longer, and he's been more a parent than a sibling to the other three.' I explained some of the things he had done. 'And he can't let go of all that responsibility. Even now, if Mike takes him out with him to get the paper or anything, my phone is sure to go and it's always Mike's mobile. "Hello, it's Hamish. Don't forget you have to feed Simon and change his nappy." He can't shrug off that mantle and let himself be a normal carefree boy. I wonder whether he ever will.'

'It sounds like he has been quite a hero.'

'Yes, that's what Anita said.'

We sat and watched the children running around and showing off.

'Anita looks quite athletic,' said the health visitor.

'Perhaps she might like to join a club, like gymnastics or trampoline, or something like that.'

Later I asked Anita. 'The health visitor said you look athletic. That means you move your body well and you could be good at sports. What do you think?'

'I like running and doing cartwheels,' she said. 'Are they sports?'

'Yes, I think that's what she noticed when she was watching you in the garden this morning. Do you think you'd like to join a sports club?'

She put her head on one side and thought about it. 'Is dancing a sport?'

'Yes, in a way. Would you like to have dancing lessons?'

'Yes. I'd like to be a dancer.' Ever the exhibitionist, Anita did a twirl and bowed to her imaginary audience.

'Do you remember Steve, your old social worker?' I asked at breakfast the next morning.

'Yes, I do,' nodded Hamish. 'He had glasses and brown hair.'

'I remember him too,' added Anita.

'Well, he's coming to see you all this afternoon.'

'It's a long way,' said Hamish.

'Yes, he said he couldn't stay long, so I want you all to talk to him and show him your bedrooms, so after breakfast you can go and tidy them up.'

'What do we have to talk to him about?' frowned Hamish.

'Oh, just anything you want to tell him.'

'Like what?'

'Well, are you worried about anything?'

'Yes. Is there any Weetabix left?'

Steve was supposed to come every six weeks, but it had been more than two months now. Whenever I had phoned him to ask for any information, which he wasn't allowed to give me, or to try to get him to agree a date for this visit, he had always blamed the delay on work. I had to badger him to come at all.

'What day are you coming next week, Steve?' I said. 'I'll put a lunch on for you.' I knew he'd go anywhere for the opening of a sandwich, and sure enough he arrived, just in time to eat.

'Hello, kids,' he said to them cheerily as he came in. 'Gosh, haven't you grown!'

'Have we?' asked Hamish anxiously.

'I'll soon be as big as you,' Anita taunted him.

'No, you won't. I'm growing faster than you.'

'No, me,' wailed Caroline, standing on tiptoes . . . and falling over.

'Let's not argue while Steve's here,' I said.

Over lunch all the children in turn told him about their lives with us. Hamish about the swearing chart and the fish and chips, Anita about the Knickerbocker Glory, her girly clothes and growing her hair, Caroline about eating her favourite pasta and having lots of toys and Simon . . . well, he just pointed at his favourites, the farm and the bricks in the corner of the kitchen.

After lunch, the children were still hungry, so I sent Hamish down to the playroom with a packet of cereal bars and the other three all rushed down the stairs after him. Steve and I followed.

We watched the children getting out the toys to show Steve.

'I'm sure Caroline has some sort of learning difficulties,' I said to him. 'And after watching Jill on her two visits, she appears to have learning difficulties too—'

'Oh, I don't think so,' he interrupted.

'I'm wondering whether Caroline has inherited her mother's learning problems.'

'She looks all right to me.'

I could see I wouldn't get anything out of him about that, so I changed the subject and told him about Caroline's impacted bowel and what I had overheard in the hospital. I hoped it would prompt him to tell me more, but he kept his lips sealed.

'It would have been really helpful if I had known that she had that condition before she came to us.'

'I expect it would.'

'Are there any other health problems that I should know about?'

'Not that I'm aware of.'

'Can you look it up and let me know?'

'I'll text you,' he said, shifting uncomfortably. I knew he never would.

'Why did it all go on so long, Steve, all the neglect and abuse they had to suffer?'

'I did everything I could,' he answered defensively. 'I put in a support worker every day.'

'Well, it doesn't sound as if any of those support workers did much good,' I said.

'No,' he shrugged. 'Jill hated them coming and refused to let them in, or shooed them away too soon. She even punched one of them in the face.'

'Yes, Hamish told me about that. Was she all right?'

'Yes, a bit bruised, but nothing broken. We took the Mackay children off her caseload.'

'Couldn't you have removed them sooner?'

'We didn't know how bad it was for a long time. Then I filled in all the paperwork three times to have them removed into care, but my boss threw it out every time. I was sorry I was away when they were finally removed.'

'I think it's time you told them why they are still here and that they are not going back. That should come from you. I shouldn't have to tell them that, or they might blame me. But they all need to understand.'

'Yes, I suppose so.' He looked a bit uncomfortable.

I have to say, he did a reasonable job of it, with me breathing down his neck. He sat them all down together and explained.

'The judge said that your mum could not look after you any longer.'

'Did she cry?' asked Anita.

'Yes, she did. But it was too late to make any difference. The judge told her that she had neglected you for too long and she wasn't able to look after you all properly. So he signed an order and made her sign it too, to say that you could live with Trisha and Mike instead.'

'Forever?' asked Hamish.

'Well, I don't know about that. But you are all going to stay here for a long time.'

'Goody,' said Caroline, clapping her hands together.

'Trisha and Mike are obviously looking after you all very well, so I'm sure the judge is right. What do you think, Hamish?'

'Yes,' he replied with a nod. 'The judge is right. But who is looking after Mum? She can't look after herself.'

'No, you're right. She has a partner living with her full-time now and he looks after her.'

'Is that Kevin?' asked Hamish warily.

'I hope it's not Wayne,' whispered Anita.

'I'm afraid I can't remember his name.'

'What about the next baby?' asked Hamish.

'Yes, your mum is expecting a baby and we are keeping an eye on her, with regular visits to check that she is eating properly.'

'But she'll be the same with the new baby when it's born,' sighed Hamish.

'No,' Steve said gently. 'We will take the baby straight into care so that it has a happy, safe and healthy childhood.'

That was a lot for the children to take in and I wasn't sure that anyone other than Hamish really understood it fully, but I knew it would sink in gradually and I could be there to sympathise and help them, which was my role. None of them reacted badly to this news at the time. In fact, they all seemed relieved to know they would be staying for a longer time.

'Thank you for doing that,' I said. 'How do you think they look now?'

'Loads better,' he smiled. 'They all have colour in their cheeks, healthy skin and their hair is growing well too. It's great to see them in good clothes. They always wore rubbish jumble-sale tat before.'

We finished our coffees and he stood up. 'I'm afraid I've got to go now.'

'Not till you've been upstairs to see all the children's rooms.'

'But . . .'

'They've tidied them up specially. Come on, kids, take Steve upstairs and give him a tour of the house.'

It was nearly an hour later before we finally let him leave!

'Don't be so long before you come next time,' I said. 'Hamish and Anita will be starting school soon, so make sure you come and hear all about it.'

A few days later there was another supervised visit from their mum. The children again insisted on my presence and this time the social worker stayed in with us. Jill must have come on the right train this time, with Kevin again I believe, but he had been told not to come anywhere near the family centre this time, so Jill seemed a bit less distracted.

The plan this time was to split the visit. I took the two younger children there for the first hour. This went quite well as Hamish and Anita didn't monopolise their mother's attention and she didn't overtly reject Caroline, although she still spent much more time with Simon. The social worker and I tried our best to get her talking with both children, but with little success. It was hard going.

Mike brought Hamish and Anita for the second hour and took Caroline and Simon home again. Without Simon to carry around, Jill seemed more aware of the older two, but still hardly paid them any attention. She seemed uninterested and I could see they were bored and restless; almost impatient with her. It was hard work trying to engage her in their play, and she remained detached. Yet again, this was a lost opportunity.

I could see now just how limited Jill's understanding was of what her role should be. I expect she did love the children in her own way, but she appeared only to be conscious of her own immediate needs. Hamish and Anita seemed relieved when her taxi came to take her back to the station and we could go home and get on with our own lives.

In my diary that night I wrote: '. . . *better for all the children, but not so good for me.*'

11

Starting School

'The children did not start school immediately. They spent the first few weeks with carers, focusing on their basic needs. This provided the stability they obviously craved.'

Review notes

It was a big outing the day we went to buy Hamish and Anita's school uniforms for St Mary's First School. Kay took out the two younger ones for the afternoon so that Hamish, Anita and I could concentrate on kitting them out with all the things they needed.

The school colour was red, so they needed smart red sweatshirts with the school logo on them and we ordered those from the school. The rest we bought in town.

'I love my new uniform,' said Anita with pride. She couldn't stop grinning. 'Can I wear it when I get home?'

'You can put it on to show the others,' I said. 'But we must keep it smart for your first day at school next week.'

'I'm going to show them mine too,' added Hamish with a smile. 'I never had any uniform at my old school, and I hated being different from everyone else. This time I'll be just like them. I can't wait to start school again, and make some new friends.'

'And this time you won't have to dice with death, crossing any dual carriageways, Hame, because I'm driving you all the way to the school gate.'

They were both in a good mood that evening, excited to be parading their new outfits for the family, but as usual their exuberance got the better of them. It was almost as if they were drunk they were so loud, and over the next few days they pushed the boundaries so far . . . The first day of school couldn't come soon enough.

I dropped them off that first morning and went back home to wait for the fireworks. I was not wrong. Hamish and Anita both stood out like beacons.

'They won't sit down, Mrs Merry,' was the first call in the middle of that first morning. I felt like saying: well, what do you want me to do about it?

The next call followed at lunchtime. 'Hamish won't write. He won't do anything I ask him to do,' said his class teacher. 'What can I do about it? And Anita's teacher says she shouts out all the time in her class.'

I don't come to you, I thought, with my fostering problems, so why are you asking me about teaching? It's your job.

By the time I drove over with the younger ones in the back to collect Hamish and Anita from St Mary's, I imagined they had probably started a full-scale riot, or worse. I dreaded finding out. But when I went to meet Anita from her classroom, her teacher smiled warmly.

'Anita has settled in quite quickly, Mrs Merry. She is happy and cheerful, and has already made a couple of friends.'

'But I heard she was too noisy this morning.'

'Yes, but she was much calmer and quieter after some lunch and a good runaround on the school field.'

Next we went to pick up Hamish. He saw us coming and ran over to meet us in the playground, waving his new red book-bag at us.

'I've got a book to read tonight—'

'So have I,' interrupted Anita, never one to be outdone.

'Hello, Mrs Merry,' said Hamish's teacher, who had followed him out.

'How has he been since you rang me?' I asked.

'Well, funnily enough, he settled down a bit better after that. He still didn't want to do what I asked a few times, but I think it's about adjusting to school rules and classroom routines. He does seem bright and eager to help, when he's not too busy protesting!'

'I think it's mainly because he had to assume the role of a parent to his siblings for the past few years,' I explained. 'So he finds it hard now to become a child again, and relinquish control.'

'I see. Yes, that would explain it.' She looked a little uncertain. 'He does seem very fidgety as well, as if he finds it difficult to stay within the classroom or to sit down and work on a group task.'

'Yes, I know what you mean. But he's always had to be so self-reliant, that I think he finds it hard to cooperate with others or let anyone take over.'

'Right, I'll try to bear that in mind.'

Off we went home, with Hamish and Anita chattering on about school all the way home. They had clearly enjoyed the first day, oblivious of the minor troubles they had caused.

'Right, go and get out of your school clothes while I butter you some toast,' I said, and they both scampered upstairs to their rooms.

A couple of minutes later, Hamish came back down. He had taken his school clothes off all right. In fact, he had taken me rather too literally. He was completely starkers!

'Oh, Hame,' I said, trying not to laugh, 'you could have kept your pants and socks on!'

For a moment he looked unsure, but then he saw the funny side of it and went back upstairs.

Most days after that, somebody from the school would phone to tell me of some misdemeanour or other. Quite often I had to drive back to St Mary's to help them sort it out, whether it was cajoling Hamish to come off the field and go back into his classroom after break, or persuading Anita to let other children have a turn on the climbing frame.

Once the older two had been in school a couple of weeks, I turned my attention to Caroline and Simon. Although at the age to start her formal education, no school would take Caroline in nappies, so the agency helped me to find her a place in a nearby nursery. She started there, very clingy that first morning. I chose my moment and left her to settle in. I don't know exactly what happened, but her temper was what prompted the call, later that morning.

'I'm sorry, Mrs Merry, but could you please come and collect Caroline?'

'What's the matter?'

'She's very aggressive, isn't she?'

'Yes. She's had a very difficult life.'

'I'm sorry to hear that. But we have to think of all the other children in our care.'

'I see,' I said and went to collect her. So now Caroline had something new to put on her CV. 'Excluded from nursery school on her first day for aggressive behaviour.'

Fortunately, they agreed to try having her again the next day, as long as I stayed with her this time, so I left Simon with Mike while I played all morning with Caroline and some of the other children. This seemed to help her settle more, but she still found it almost impossible to understand the concept of routines and rules. And there weren't enough adults to give her the individual attention she needed, so this placement didn't last long and I started looking again.

This time, although she hadn't been officially diagnosed with learning difficulties, I was sure that was a key factor, so I booked her into a special needs nursery. This one was a marginal improvement, but still understaffed. Caroline was physically better looked after here, and she seemed to be less obstructive, but I felt her learning needs were not adequately met.

This worried me quite a lot. Should I keep her at home and try to help her learn the basics with me, or was it more important for her to socialise ?

Simon was a different story. I got him into a different

nursery school, where they took very young children and seemed to accept his immaturity and detachment. Because he wasn't loud or aggressive, he never caused any trouble.

'He's like a little dumpling,' said one of the nursery nurses, fondly. He went to the nursery, he stayed there all day, but I don't think he made his mark there. He wasn't naughty, but he didn't take part at all, and he wasn't really learning anything.

It was bad enough being called out during the day, in the middle of mixing a cake or doing the never-ending laundry, to deal with a recalcitrant child, or a displeased adult, but the morning and evening run was always a nightmare, with St Mary's being five miles away to the north of the city, and Caroline and Simon's nurseries being in different directions across the city. I was fed up with battling so much rush-hour traffic from place to place every day, trying to get them all dropped off at their required times.

One particularly fraught day, when I'd already had to go and collect Caroline from her second nursery for spitting at other children, the phone went as soon as I came through the door.

'Hi, Trisha, it's John from the agency. We've decided to start our own nursery for our hard-to-place foster children and we'd like to offer you places for both Caroline and Simon.' He paused.

To be honest, I was so surprised . . . and distracted by what I was going to do with Caroline, that I was stunned speechless. This couldn't have come at a better time.

'From what Carol tells me, you might be interested in their joining our group. We've changed our headquarters around to free up some of the large ground-floor rooms for the nursery. We are taking on some very experienced and well-qualified staff, with a high adult-to-child ratio—'

'That's music to my ears, John,' I interrupted him. 'Can I book their places right now?'

Teatime that evening, I was on a cloud, thinking about how wonderful it would be to have Caroline and Simon at the same nursery, and of course that they would be so much more appropriately cared for and their needs met. Perhaps my good mood rubbed off on the children, because I noticed how well behaved they were all being that evening. Anita was using her cutlery to eat her beans and egg on toast. Hamish passed the ketchup to Caroline and helped her put some on her plate.

'Thank you.' She smiled at him.

Even Simon remembered to put his hand in front of his mouth when he coughed. Were these the same children who only a few months before had stuffed every kind of food into their mouths with their hands and gobbled it down like wolves?

It was a great step forward . . . but I knew it couldn't last.

I collected the children early from school and nursery for Jill's next visit and we all went to the usual family centre near Stonditch. We went in and the children zoned straight in on the snacks in my bag and the play area, in that order. We settled down to do some puzzles and play with the toys until Jill came . . . but she didn't turn up.

'Has there been any message?' I asked the lady in the reception office who usually came in to supervise Jill's visits.

'No, nothing. I'll give Social Services a ring and see if they know anything.'

I waited while she phoned them, listening to one side of the call while also keeping an eye on my exuberant clan through the window in the door.

'No, Mrs Merry,' she said as she put the receiver down. 'They gave her the ticket yesterday, and she was meant to be coming. What time was she due?'

'Three o'clock.'

'Well,' she said, looking up at the office clock. 'It's four now, so I'm afraid it looks like she's not coming. Will the children be very upset?'

'I never know,' I shrugged. 'I'll gather the hooligans and we'll go on home.'

'Oh, they're not that bad,' she laughed.

'You don't know them!' She probably didn't realise I was only half joking.

'I thought she wouldn't come,' scowled Hamish in the car on the way home, but glancing in my mirror I could see that the others looked completely unconcerned.

I did ask them all later: 'Are you fed up that Mum didn't come today?'

'No,' said Anita. 'It's boring when she's there, because she doesn't want to play with us. It was good today because we could get all the toys out and have fun.'

'Not really,' agreed Caroline. 'I liked playing with Anita.'

Simon said nothing at all, as usual; just a slight shake of the head.

Only Hamish had shown any reaction in the car, so I repeated my question to him.

'What about you, Hame? Were you upset?'

'I would have liked to see that she had been eating properly. Do you think Steve will make sure she eats proper food?'

'I should think so, Hamish, because she's expecting the baby.'

'That's all right then,' he said and gave a half smile. 'I didn't think she'd come anyway.'

'Well, never mind. I expect she'll come next time.'

'I don't really care,' said Anita. 'She's probably at home watching horror films with her mates. She used to make us watch horror films. The first one I remember was nightmare something.'

'*Nightmare on Elm Street*,' said Hamish.

'It was very scary and I didn't want to watch it when it was on, but I couldn't stop. I don't know why I liked being scared. But it did give me nightmares.'

'You always had nightmares,' commented Hamish.

'I still do. But not so many now.'

'I still remember being sat in front of *Chucky* and being made to watch it,' said Hamish. 'I never want to see that film again.'

'We had to watch rude films as well,' added Anita. 'I don't want to go back home.'

'Why not?' I asked.

'Because Mum will let people hurt me.'

'What people?'

'Her boyfriends,' said Hamish.

'Larry is nasty to us,' explained Anita.

'And Wayne tries to put his hands over our faces,' continued Hamish. 'So that we can't breathe. He tried to kill us when Mum and her other boyfriends were in bed.'

All the children's behaviour was up and down – good days and bad days, but a few more good days than there used to be.

They'd been with us for a year now and I decided it was time to start trying to potty-train Caroline. She wanted to go to a Saturday morning club with Hamish and Anita.

'You can only go to Saturday Club when you stop wearing nappies,' I told her and that really motivated her. So we gradually got her dry during the daytime.

'Well done, Caroline,' I congratulated her one day. 'You worked hard to get dry in the daytime. Now you deserve a reward.'

'What's that?'

'You can choose something you want to do.'

'Can I go to Saturday Club tomorrow?'

So off she went in Mike's car with the others the next morning, proud as Punch. It would be a long time before any of the younger three would be dry at night, but it was a big first step for Caroline. Simon would take a little longer.

Both the younger ones were much happier at the agency's nursery, with other children from difficult backgrounds, so there was a lot more tolerance and understanding amongst the staff and the children were not so fazed by the actions of others. Caroline continued to be slow and wary, but she was learning to dress herself at nursery, so we did the same at home and she soon got the hang of it. Simon too could now put on his own socks and shoes. Maybe we're winning, I thought as I sat with them one breakfast time, until they suddenly started fighting at the table, which ended up in a frenzy of hair-pulling and biting.

I had to call Mike to come and help me pull them apart.

In my diary that night I wrote '... *going through the terrible twos stage, a bit late — what fun!'*

12

Whistleblowers

'I was shocked at the kids' reaction. Caroline was rigid. They all looked frightened . . . nightmares, sleepwalking.'
Extract from my diary

A large, brown, handwritten envelope arrived one morning, sent in the post. No official stamp like the Social Services mail always had.

I opened it at one end and extricated the contents – some sheets of paper stapled together, sparsely typed with dates and notes. There was no letter or compliment slip. My hands started shaking as I realised what this was. Who could have sent it to me? And why now?

As I stared at the top sheet, the children's names jumped out at me, and the name of an older sibling too. I began reading the first page, going right down to the bottom. I stopped and put the sheaf of papers down on the table, pushing it away from me, and then sat back looking at it.

This is wrong, I thought. I can't read this. Oh my God, I could be in trouble. Somebody must have sent me these case notes in error. What happens if I read this and I shouldn't have done? But I wanted to learn more. It was difficult to take in, but I just had to continue reading.

'There's something very strange about these notes,' I said to Mike that evening, after the children were in bed.

'What do you mean?'

'Well, they look like case notes, and they do give a basic description and list events with the dates, but it feels like it's not the whole story.'

'So, do you think the notes were not very well written by the social worker, not detailed enough? Or are you saying you think they've been doctored?'

'I wish I knew!' I paused. 'It's like I'm having to read between the lines. It says a lot about surface goings on, but I feel cheated somehow. I can't really explain it. I feel as if the worst things have been deliberately left out.'

'Or maybe it's just an unobservant social worker who couldn't be bothered to write much.'

'Trust you to defend the social worker for not doing their job properly!'

I passed the notes to Mike. 'Here, have a look. See what you think.'

As I watched him skim through the first page, I began to feel guilty that I'd read it.

'Do you think I should ring Social Services and tell them I've been sent these notes?' I asked him.

Mike looked up. 'Who are you going to tell? You could get someone in trouble for revealing confidential information.'

'Oh, I hadn't thought of that. Do you think it could have been a whistleblower?'

'I think it must have been.'

'Surely we have a right to this information? But I can't do anything with it, because I'm not supposed to know about the older sister having severe learning difficulties, or the parents' previous marriages, or the grandmother's learning difficulties . . .'

'Well, at least you've learned a few revealing things you didn't know.'

'Yes, the social worker clearly knew the children went to school in wet clothes, without eating anything. And all the missed appointments, and the state of the house. The person who wrote the notes even mentioned the Schedule 1 offenders coming in and out. Offenders – surely that means they must have been convicted paedophiles? Why didn't anyone ask the obvious questions? Why did they continue to leave the children at such great risk?'

'It sounds like they've failed this family badly.'

'Yes, it mentions severe neglect as if it were ordinary, but it doesn't actually say anything about abuse at all.'

A few weeks later, I had a call from Social Services. I gulped, thinking they'd rumbled us and we'd need to own up to having the case notes. But no.

'I wonder if you could help us, Mrs Merry?'

'Well, I can try.' I couldn't help but smile at the irony of this situation.

Jill had the baby and it's a boy. We placed him with a family for adoption.'

'That was quick.'

'Yes, we had to be quick.'

Yet more irony, I thought, considering how long they had taken to remove our four.

'We've received a request from Michael Warren, the carer who hopes to adopt the baby, asking if he can have your phone number to find out about the baby's half brothers and sisters.'

'Right.' I had to think quickly here.

'Would you be happy for him to contact you?'

'I'd rather give you my email and postal addresses and we can do it that way?'

'Very well, Mrs Merry. I will pass those on to him.'

A couple of days later, we had a short, handwritten letter from Michael Warren:

Dear Mrs Merry,

My name is Warren. My wife and I are in the process of adopting Jill Mackay's baby, Lee, who we have been looking after since his birth. But we are encountering some difficulties. The main problem is that we can't get any information out of the Social Services.

The only thing they could tell us was that you are fostering four of Lee's half sisters and brothers. So we are hoping you can give us some background information. It all seems quite confusing. Can you tell us what's what in this family?

I would be very grateful if you could perhaps call me on the above number so that we can talk about all this. I think you may be the only ones who can help us.

Regards,

Michael Warren

I talked it through with Mike and we both felt these people must be as much in the dark as we had been, and still were in some ways, so we wanted to try to help them. I rang him that evening.

'I've got a great big wodge of paper about your children,' he said, as soon as we got the introductions over with.

'What do you mean?'

'Oh, since I wrote to you a couple of days ago, we've received this thick packet of what looks like detailed case notes about your children. More than a hundred pages I should think.'

'Really?' I was shocked. What was he doing with detailed notes about our children, sent officially by the Social Services, when all we'd had were a dozen or so pages of very sparse notes sent anonymously?

'Right,' I said. 'Why would you want notes about our children?'

'Because we've only just found out that Jill took an overdose.'

That stunned me. 'Why haven't we been told that? After all, she is our children's mother too.'

'Sorry, I assumed you knew.'

'It's not your fault. Social Services have never wanted to tell us anything, so it sounds like you know a lot more than we do!'

'And we've only just found out about all the problems the other children have had. And we were told Jill had no learning difficulties.'

'That's what they've always told us too, but I've watched

her when she attends supervised visits – she's only made it to two so far. There's no way that woman doesn't have learning difficulties. I would say that she has quite severe problems.'

'Well, we're already concerned about Lee. He cries all the time, no matter what we do for him. And he's been very slow in reaching his milestones, so far. We are quite worried about what problems he may have inherited . . . Do any of your children have problems?'

'Well . . .' I wanted to tread carefully here. 'What about the notes Social Services sent you? We haven't had anything, you see. Well, not officially anyway. And they have always denied everything when I've asked. But they were at considerable risk in the home. Anita was—'

'Oh, do you mean she was sexually abused?'

'Where did you get that from?'

'It says so, here in the paperwork they sent me.'

'What do you mean? What does it say?'

'I'll send it to you. Do you have a fax machine?'

I gave him our fax number and, only half an hour later, he faxed a few pages through to us.

'Mike!' I yelled down the stairs from our office. 'You've got to come and see this.'

He came straight up and joined me as we read the faxed notes, so different in their depth and extent of detail to what we had been sent.

'Here it is, in black and white,' I exploded with anger. I was furious. 'What the hell has all this got to do with Michael Warren? He doesn't even know the children. *We* are the ones they should have sent it to, straight away, when they first came. How dare they reveal confidential details like these about a small child to complete strangers? I'm absolutely livid!' I was so angry that I could feel the blood rushing through my brain. 'What happened to my girls, to all the children? Why didn't they tell us?'

Mike put his arm around me and continued to read the rest of the fax.

'You've every right to be cross,' he said. 'It's disgraceful that they sent this information to strangers, who have nothing to do with our four. And I can't believe they kept refusing to send anything to us, no matter how many times you asked them.'

'I'm getting straight on the phone to Social Services on Monday and I'll show them how angry I am!'

Monday morning came and as soon as I was back from the school run, I rang them. No faffing about; straight to the point.

'Can you tell me why you have sent Michael Warren detailed, intimate information about *our* four children, when you have always refused to send anything to me? You even denied that any of it ever happened. How can you justify that, I'd like to know?'

'But you are mistaken, Mrs Merry,' said this infuriatingly calm, patronising voice at the other end. 'We haven't sent any information at all about the four Mackay children in your care to Michael Warren, or anyone else. I can assure you of that.'

'Oh really?'

'Yes, really.'

'Well, I know you did, and he phoned me about it, and I'm hopping mad.'

'Well,' she changed her tone, 'if that is the case, what can you do about it?'

What *can* I do about it? I thought, as I went to bed that night, still far too cross to sleep. I can't do anything! It was all so unfair.

A few days later, and the kids had been off the wall. I'm not joking. I can't remember what it was, but something started them off, and they were all a nightmare. I was called to come up to the school or the nursery every day, twice a day, and their behaviour was more antisocial than ever before, kicking off in the classroom, kicking out at teaching assistants or nursery staff, smashing up toys or equipment, everything you can think of.

As I drove them all home, fighting like crazy in the back, I remember thinking: These kids have got to have some therapy. I've got to get something organised for them, because it's not working without.

And when Mike showed me an article in the newspaper that night about a counsellor specialising in abused children, I wanted to get onto him straight away, but I knew we couldn't afford him without help. That was my light-bulb moment. Yes, there is something we can do about it. I can sue Social Services to get the money for the therapy that they had always denied us for the children, every time I'd asked nicely for it.

Of course I realised it wasn't going to be as simple as that, and maybe it would have to be something we could look into, but the prospect cheered me up no end. And I think that might have rubbed off on the children too, as the rest of the week was much calmer.

Perhaps because of Jill's situation, she hadn't been to visit the children for quite a while, and I was told via the agency that her parents, the children's grandparents, were going to come instead. Well, I knew very little about them, other than the case notes I had been sent that mentioned briefly that the girls had been to stay with them for several days at around the time that Simon was born.

As usual, I said nothing to the kids until the day came, just in case plans were changed and they might be disappointed. None of them had ever mentioned their grandparents, so I was shocked by their reaction when I finally told them on the morning of the visit.

There was a stunned silence for several seconds.

Finally Hamish spoke. 'Do we have to go?'

'Yes, they'll be on their way shortly, so we'll meet them at the family centre.'

'Do we all have to go?' he tried again.

'No.' Anita's face paled. 'I don't want to. Can I stay behind?'

'And me,' added Caroline, her gaze darting from one sibling to another.

Simon of course seemed quite unconcerned.

Their responses took me by surprise, but I had to help

them go through with it. 'It will probably only be a short visit, as one of the social workers is driving them up.'

'Will you be with us too?' asked Anita, her eyes pleading.

'Yes. I'll make sure they let me.'

'OK then.' She sighed.

We arrived just before they did and waited, listening to the sounds as they were brought into the building. The door opened and in walked this middle-aged couple. The woman was a little subdued but the man gave the children a big smile.

Caroline went rigid. Anita had a look of fear. Could she really be afraid of her own grandparents? Then I realised – something must have happened, might perhaps have been going on over time, maybe abuse of some kind, but I wasn't sure, yet . . .

The social worker put the chairs in a circle and we all sat down, the girls either side of me.

Grandmother looked pleased to see the children. 'Look how you've grown,' she smiled with pride.

Grandfather said nothing until the social worker tried to engage him in conversation, with little success. He just looked from Caroline to Anita and back again, while they shuffled uncomfortably on their chairs.

Hamish took the initiative, got up and tried to persuade his grandfather to come with him for a walk outside, but he was having none of it.

'I want to stay here and look at my beautiful girls,' he

insisted. 'Come,' he turned to Caroline. 'Come and sit on my knee and make your grandfather a happy man.'

Caroline grabbed my arm with a grasp so tight it hurt.

'Come along. I won't hurt you.' He paused. 'Anita, my pretty one. You will come and sit with me, won't you?'

The social worker gave her a persuasive look and Anita bravely walked over to be lifted onto her grandfather's knee, where she dangled uncomfortably, cringing while he stroked her ear with one hand and her thigh with the other, while shifting in his chair.

By now I was sure I was right.

The grandfather leaned his head down and whispered in Anita's ear. She looked frightened.

I wondered what he said to her . . . and what part he had played in their lives. It seemed increasingly clear to me that he had abused them both and hoped to do so again.

Meanwhile, the grandmother coaxed Caroline to edge over to the grandfather as well. I noticed the alarmed look on Hamish's face when the grandfather stood up.

'I'm just going to take the girls out to look at the garden,' he said, with them held tightly by the hands, dragging reluctantly behind him and glancing back at me in fear. I made a face at the social worker and went towards the door, where she joined me. Between us, to Hamish's obvious relief, we managed to bar Grandfather's exit with the girls.

'I'm afraid the visit can only be conducted inside this room,' said the social worker.

He looked disappointed, signalled to his wife and they both left.

'I'm sorry,' said the social worker hurriedly to me as she rushed to follow the grandparents out. 'I didn't know it would be like this.'

That night, the three older children had the worst nightmares since the night they arrived, crying out and wailing in their sleep. Anita sleepwalked, so I had to close the stair gates to prevent her falling. I could barely imagine the harm that man did to his own vulnerable and helpless grandchildren. I'm ninety-nine per cent certain he sexually abused Anita and Caroline on several occasions, and no doubt their mother too. That visit put back the kids' recovery for weeks.

13

Telling Tales

'Their expectations of Mum are so low, nothing seems to disturb them.'

Extract from my diary

Once she was dry by day, Caroline was a year late starting at St Mary's First School, with all the settling-in problems we had come to expect from her – almost daily phone calls about one misdemeanour or another. Because of her learning difficulties and unusual behaviour, the head teacher arranged that there would always be a support assistant in Caroline's classroom, to give her some support. The trouble was that Caroline wanted this woman all to herself, and the class teacher had other ideas.

'Mrs Merry,' said the school secretary's voice on the phone, 'Caroline smacked another child today. Now she's run out to the field and is screaming.'

'But it's lesson time, isn't it?'

'Yes.'

'Where is her support assistant?'

'She ran out after her and is with her now. But Caroline

refuses to move, and we are not permitted to restrain children these days, so we can't force her back into the classroom. Do you think you could come and persuade her to calm down and come back inside?'

'All right. I'll be there in fifteen minutes.'

Why do they need me to do everything? I thought. Surely their teachers and assistants are trained to deal with this sort of thing?

'What happened to spark Caroline off this time?' I asked the assistant as I joined them on the school field.

'That's just it, Mrs Merry,' she said, with a puzzled expression. 'I was right there next to her and I don't know why she reacted like this.'

'Were you helping her with something?' I knew that, like the others, Caroline didn't like to be told what to do, and with her it was doubly difficult as she often found instructions impossible to understand.

'Well, she was busy with the coloured pegs in the board, so I was just helping another child who had asked me for a spelling.'

'Oh well, that's probably it then. Maybe she didn't want to share you. I expect she felt you were neglecting her by helping another child.'

'Well, that's rather unreasonable, in a busy classroom.'

'Caroline doesn't see it that way.' I paused. 'Maybe, if we can get her inside, you could take her to the book corner and read a picture book to her, just the two of you?'

'Yes, of course.' She smiled with relief.

I turned to Caroline. 'Come on, let's go in and choose a nice book for Maggie to read to you.'

Caroline hesitated and looked from me to Maggie.

'Come on,' coaxed Maggie, crouching down to Caroline's level and smiling warmly. 'Shall we go and find a Mog book?' It was like luring in a hard-to-catch fish. It has to be the right bait.

I watched them go inside, hand in hand, and drove back home again, wondering what it would be about next time.

A few days later, Social Services rang to say that new visits had been arranged for each of the children's parents. This time it would be their father one day, and their mother the next.

I had to take all four children out of school and we arrived at the required time, but just as I turned into the family centre's car park another car sped out and away into the distance.

'That was Dad,' shrieked Hamish, then stuck his head out of the open window. 'Dad, Dad!'

'It's no good, Hame,' I said. 'He's too far away to hear you.'

I could see Hamish's crestfallen expression in my driving mirror and I felt a surge of sympathy for him, for all of them. The silence was almost painful as I drove round the car park and out again.

'OK, kids, it's not worth going back to school, so who's for an iced doughnut from the bakery?'

The mood lifted immediately. But as they sat in the cafe,

chomping their doughnuts, their resentment resurfaced. Anita was particularly angry.

'Dad always tells lies,' she blurted out, spitting hundreds and thousands across the table.

An elderly couple next to us sipped their teas noisily and exchanged disapproving glances.

'He makes me fucking mad!' she shouted, and now everyone in the place was turning round.

'Yes, he always lets us down,' added Hamish. 'Like the time he said he was taking me to Scotland, and he went without me.'

'Well, never mind. I expect he got the time wrong,' I said, trying to make excuses for him, in an effort to help the children accept what had happened.

'No, he's a wanker. He just didn't want to see us,' snarled Hamish. 'And I didn't want to see him either. I don't care if I never see him again.'

'Me too,' said Caroline, in support of her brother.

'Fucking hell,' added Anita, having the last words.

The next day I took them all back to the family centre to meet their mother for a supervised visit. She wasn't there when we arrived, but she was usually late, so we went in and the children got all the toys out, so they were fine for a while. But the time was passing, and she still didn't show up. After an hour, I decided to call it a day.

'Come on, kids, let's tidy up and go home,' I chivvied them. 'It doesn't look as if Mum can make it today.'

'She's a cunt!' exclaimed Anita. 'She's so lazy that she can't even be fucking bothered to come and see us.'

'She can never get anything right,' added Hamish, almost as angry as Anita. 'She never could do anything for us. She can't look after herself, let alone anyone else.'

'Well, let's go home. It's a lovely afternoon. Why don't we all go to the park by our old house and you can play Poohsticks off the bridge.'

'What's Poohsticks?' asked Caroline.

'Like in *Winnie-the-Pooh*,' I said. 'Come on, I'll show you.'

As we walked across the grass that afternoon, with the younger three scampering in front of us, Hamish confided in me.

'I used to worry when I was at school.'

'What did you worry about?'

'The little ones,' he said, with his serious expression. 'When Anita and me went to school, I knew we were leaving the little ones alone in the house with Mum and her boyfriends. Mum never got up till lunchtime, and I don't think they did either, and there was nobody to look after Caroline and Simon. Nobody to make them breakfast, give them a drink, change their nappies or anything.'

'I see what you mean.'

'I used to sit in the classroom and worry all day. Sometimes Mum still wasn't up when I got home, and they had pulled their nappies off. They had wet and dirtied everywhere. I used to try and clean it up.'

'Do you still worry about the others when you are in your classroom?' I asked.

'No, they're all at school now. And if they are at home ill, you will look after them, won't you?' His eyes pleaded.

'Yes, of course I will.'

We walked on in silence for two or three minutes, but I could almost hear him thinking.

'I like it here best, with you and Mike,' he said. 'Because the food is good.'

'Oh,' I smiled. 'Not my brilliant personality then?'

'Just the food,' he said with a cheeky grin, and ran off to join the others on the playground. Then we all went across to the bridge and I showed them how to play Poohsticks, which caused great hilarity.

On the way back to the car, Anita clung to my arm as we walked, while Hamish kicked a stray tennis ball around for Caroline and Simon.

'I'm glad Mum didn't come today. I didn't like it at Mum's house,' she said. 'It made me unhappy. I don't ever want to go back there.' I could feel her arm trembling, tucked into mine. 'I was always scared.'

'Well you don't have to be scared any more,' I reassured her.

'Promise you won't send us back there?' she pleaded.

'It's not up to me,' I explained. 'So I can't promise, but I'm as sure as I can be that you won't ever be sent back there again.'

The look she gave me was relief, mixed with uncertainty.

'As far as Mike and I are concerned,' I added, 'you can live with us as long as possible.'

Aged seven, Caroline was now at Park School, with the older two. They were all there together for one year. Park School was close to home and the head teacher there was brilliant – the best head teacher any of them had. Mrs Harris really understood them all, as far as anyone could, and always tried to find creative ways to deal with their different problems.

The phone would ring. 'Mrs Merry,' she would say, with a smile in her voice no matter what the kids were up to. 'I wonder if you could come in and have a chat about your three children?'

'Yes, all right, Mrs Harris. I'm on my way.'

'Who is it this time?' I asked as I sat down in her office.

'Where shall I start?' she laughed, almost fondly. 'I'm afraid it's all three of them today. Hamish refuses to sit down in the classroom and spits at everybody. Anita is swearing outrageously at the top of her voice, and Caroline, well . . . she started by pinching Tracey, her support assistant. Then she plunged her hand right down inside her blouse, and later up her skirt.' She paused. 'I know it's just attention-seeking, but you can imagine Tracey's response!'

'Yes.' I tried to suppress my smile. 'It must have been quite a shock for poor Tracey!'

'She's done the same things to some of the dinner ladies too. I could hear the screams from here!'

'I'm so sorry,' I said.

'Don't apologise, Mrs Merry. It's not your fault, and I know it's not really Caroline's fault either.' That lady would have laid down her life for Caroline. 'You are doing a grand job with those children.'

'Thank you,' I said, unused to receiving any praise. 'I'll talk to them all when I get them home.'

'Have you ever thought about counselling?' asked Mrs Harris sympathetically.

'For me or for them?' We laughed.

'Well, I suppose you could do with it too sometimes! But let's start with the children.'

'Have I just? I've thought of little else. They all need some sort of therapy to help them unravel the effects of all that neglect and abuse, to untangle their minds.'

'And maybe help with their behaviour?'

'Yes,' I groaned. 'You must all think they have 666 tattooed behind their ears! It's the cost. We can't afford it for all four of them, and neither Social Services nor the agency will pay. The answer is always no.'

'What about if I write a letter to our educational psychologist, asking for them to go to sessions with a counsellor?'

'That would be brilliant! Could you?'

'Yes, of course. I'll do it today.'

14

A Dry Place on the Mattress

'Not a good visit. Jill whispers to them and wants to take them to the toilet. Nightmares — Anita and Caroline the worst. Anita sleepwalks. Hamish mumbles and cries out.'

Extract from my diary

'We've found a great psychiatrist to work with the children,' said John at the agency. 'I think that letter from the school helped, as the education department are going to pay half.'

'Oh thank you.' I smiled with relief. 'I owe you a hug. That's great news.'

'I think you'll like him, and he's very good with children. He's going to contact you direct to arrange a preliminary meeting.'

'With me?'

'Yes, for some background information. It will only be for a limited time, I'm afraid. But at least it should be a help.'

'I have great hopes. Anything will be a help to these kids.'

A few days later, Dr Siyay arrived. The house was peaceful for once, as the children were all at school and, fingers crossed, nobody would need me for a while. I made him some coffee and we sat together in the living room.

'Now, what can you tell me about the children's parents?' he began.

I told him what I knew of Jill's background in particular, and the children's first few years with her, with him writing notes as I spoke. He must have heard so many horrendous stories over the years, working with abused children, but he made all the right responses, sensitive and sympathetic, and I thought here is someone who will really listen to the kids, and hopefully help them.

Then I told him about some of the things that had happened since they came to us, some of the awful stories they had told us, and their behavioural problems at school.

As I told Dr Siyay all this, I began to wonder whether it was me. Perhaps I'm too old for this. Perhaps things have moved on so much that I'm not as good as I thought I was.

I asked him lots of questions and he answered me as far as I could.

'But I need to start working with each of the children,' he said. 'They need the chance to speak, to be listened to and to have what they say acknowledged and valued, to help them understand themselves better and to unravel some of their most confused thoughts and feelings.'

'Yes, that's just what they need.' I breathed a sigh of relief. Now, at last, I felt that we had help to deal with the past and move forward.

The children all warmed to Dr Siyay and liked going to see him when it was their turn. It did seem to help and they were generally calmer for a while. When, a few weeks after their last sessions, the report came out for each child, I felt relieved that he had understood them all so well. But it also made me realise it had only scratched the surface, and they needed a lot more input than the agency could afford.

'How do you all feel about staying on longer with Mike and I?' I asked them one evening, when they'd finished their tea. 'The agency has told us this will be a long-term placement, if that's what we all want. What do you think? Would you like to stay with us for a long time?'

'Yes, I like it here,' said Caroline.

'I feel safer here,' added Anita.

'Me too,' echoed Caroline. 'I want to stay forever.'

'What do you think, Simon?' I asked, trying to make sure he had his say.

'Yes, OK,' he replied, in his usual detached way. 'I don't really remember before I was here.'

'We all want to stay,' said Hamish. 'But it would be good if Mum visits less often. She's always letting us down. Half the time she doesn't turn up anyway.'

'I can't ask for her not to come,' I said. 'But maybe that will change over time. We'll have to wait and see.'

Mike and I were well aware that our role as foster parents wasn't only to look after the children. That would have been challenging enough. But we had expectations to meet, and that was the additional pressure that sometimes threatened to break my back, not to mention my sanity.

Ofsted, Social Services, our own local authority and the agency, all had expectations that required us to show how much better the kids were doing in our care than in their parental home. To all these organisations, our true job was to help all of them prove that the children's parents had failed to give them the care they needed.

We had to show that they were looking better, eating better, sleeping better . . . All of them could now see that the children could read, knew their numbers and their colours, though Caroline was still a bit wobbly on those. The local authorities were happy with the agency, who were happy with us, and the children were happy. The whole of the first year I'd had to keep a daily diary – a challenge in itself when you're as dyslexic as I am! I also had to keep up with the washing, ironing, cooking, cleaning up after the kids, monitoring their behaviour, reading them stories, taking them to schools . . . and everything else. I was always in demand, and it didn't get any easier as time went on.

'Come on, kids,' Mike would say on a Saturday morning, 'we're going for a walk.' And he would walk them for miles. He'd walk the legs off them. That meant I had a couple of hours, phew! I could listen to the silence – what bliss.

Nobody was saying 'I'm hungry' or 'I've just wet myself'.

'I like doing the fun bits,' Mike always said. Every Saturday or Sunday he would take them somewhere, to the park, to the woods, on a drive, to different places every time.

'Where are you going today?' I asked him one Saturday.

'Do you think they've ever been on a train?' he asked.

'Errrmm.'

'Right, I'll take them on the train to Ashbridge today.'

'You should have seen their faces when the train pulled in to the platform,' said Mike that evening. 'Poor Simon had a hissy fit!'

'I suppose he'd never seen a life-sized train before,' I said, smiling. 'It's a bit different to rolling his toy train along the kitchen floor!'

'Yes, and he really didn't like the noise it made.'

'What about the others?'

'They really enjoyed it.'

He didn't mind how far they went, even to London. One time he took them all the way to Blackpool to see the illuminations.

'Right,' he said on Father's Day, 'do you think they've ever been on a bus? I'm going to take them on the double-decker bus to Birmingham for the day.' Most dads would want the day off, but Mike loved taking the children out – that was his treat and he always spoiled them rotten. They had a great time, and jostled through the front door when they arrived home, worn out and happy, all competing to tell me about their adventures and what fun they'd had. I dreaded to think what junk food they had eaten with Mike, but I tried not to worry about that.

Mike has always been a great dad and a very good husband.

If it was a frazzly day, I would only have to say: 'Do you think you could take the children swimming while I get this done?'

'Yep,' he would say, even if he'd just walked in through the door. He always said 'Yep,' taking them to the fair, the cinema or whatever.

He never once turned round and reproached me with 'Well it's the life you chose' or anything like that. He doesn't pretend to understand the psychological side. That's the bit I'm interested in. He just wants to see them happy. He's been very, very good.

As usual, early one sunny, summer Saturday, Mike was planning where to take the kids for the day.

'The countryside or a beach,' he said. Mike was never really into funfairs or theme parks, so it was usually somewhere he was happy to go.

'Why don't I come with you today?' I said.

'Really? Are you sure?'

'Yes. It's time I came along and we had a big family day out together.'

'Great!' he said with a smile. 'That will be a real treat.'

'Let's go for a picnic, somewhere with a beautiful view.'

Mike immediately got out his road atlas, picked a destination and worked out the route, while I started on making the sandwiches.

The children came rattling down the stairs and breakfast was the usual scrum.

'Where are we going today?' Hamish asked Mike through a mouthful of food.

'We're going on a picnic,' I replied.

'Are you coming too?' asked Anita.

'Yes. We're all going on a picnic together.'

'Hooray . . . we're going on a picnic . . .' The children cheered and hyped themselves up for the outing.

We loaded up the car with all the food, enough for an army, and we squeezed in a football, cricket bats and stumps, a kite, rackets, balls and God knows what else.

Mike chose a pretty drive that he knew I would like, through stone-built villages and country lanes, towards Ashbridge. As we drove along a ridge, he pulled into a stony lay-by, opening onto a lovely wide expanse of moorland. We found a flat spot and I handed all the tins and containers out of the car to Mike, who passed them along the line of children to Hamish at the end, where we had spread the rugs. He lovingly set out all the food and we sat down to eat.

'What a lovely day!' I said. 'Lots of blue sky, sunshine, a slight breeze and just one wispy, white cloud on the horizon. What do you think it looks like?'

'Cotton-wool?' ventured Hamish.

'A cat with its paws in the air,' suggested Anita.

'A rabbit!' shouted Caroline, entering into the spirit of things.

'What do you think, Simon?'

'I think it looks like a cloud,' he shrugged, and we all laughed.

We played games to start with; everything in quick succession, as they all had the concentration span of a dragonfly, flitting from one thing to the next. Then they tucked in to the food. No knives and forks today, so they really stuffed themselves with gusto.

When the food was all gone, we took some photos. Then the children ran around and played some more games with Mike, while I packed it all away.

Finally, when we'd been there God knows how long, I called out to them all.

'Come on, it's time to go home.'

Mike, Anita, Caroline and Simon packed all the games things back into the car, but Hamish wandered around with his chin on his chest, kicking the ground in a temper. I went over to him.

'What's the matter, Hame?'

He wouldn't reply and refused to speak to anybody, only climbing into the back of the car at the last minute and sitting in a sulk all the way home.

That evening, I put the younger three to bed first, then came back to find Hamish in the bathroom, brushing his teeth.

'What's the matter?' I asked him as he rinsed his mouth out.

'You promised.'

'What?'

'You promised we were going on a picnic,' he said.

'We have been on a picnic.'

'No, we haven't.'

'Yes, we have. We've been on a picnic today. You were there. You ate the food.'

'But we didn't go on anything.'

I suddenly understood his confusion.

'Aah,' I said. 'It wasn't going on a ride or anything. We

just went on an outing. We went on a picnic. That's what people call it when you eat sandwiches and things outdoors on rugs.'

Of course, Mike had previously taken them on all sorts of rides, on buses, on trains, on donkeys, on fairground rides . . . This was one of those times when I realised how their limited vocabularies and speech-patterns could still affect their understanding and enjoyment of things that everyone else takes for granted.

One night, when I was tucking Anita into bed, she gently smoothed her hand across the soft cotton of the duvet cover with a smile and a happy sigh.

'I love the sheets,' she said as she lay down.

'Oh yes? What do you like about them?' I asked, thinking she meant the colour.

'We didn't have a bed each. We had a mattress for all of us, and we never had sheets or a duvet, just a filthy blanket.'

'A mattress on the floor?'

'Yes, and I always used to try and find a dry bit.'

I couldn't get that image out of my head for days. Even now, it still makes me shudder.

'I like tidying up,' said Caroline one day, as she helped Hamish and Anita to put all the toys away in their boxes and cupboards in the playroom, then wiped clean the blackboard we had put on the wall for them all to draw on.

'Good. You can go up and tidy your bedrooms too, if you

like.' It was encouraging to see them all, even Simon, getting some pleasure from making their surroundings clean and tidy. The two older ones in particular were becoming quite fussy about putting their clothes away neatly in their wardrobes and drawers.

All four of them now washed their hands and faces and cleaned their teeth without needing to be reminded. And Caroline was at last getting over her fear of the bathroom. This was definite progress!

We hadn't seen or heard of Jill for a while, but out of the blue we had a call to say she was coming to visit the children again.

'She probably won't come,' said Hamish with a scowl.

'I hope she doesn't,' added Anita.

As usual, we arrived in good time and settled down in the family room. I knew the children had mixed feelings about this, but I hoped she would actually turn up this time.

She arrived on time . . . with Kevin, and I could hear an argument in the reception area. As soon as the children heard Kevin's voice, they drew closer to me and listened with anxious expressions – fearful even.

'I've come to see the kids with Jill,' insisted Kevin. His gravelly voice had a startling effect on all the children. Hamish in particular resumed his protective mantle.

'You can't let him in here,' he pleaded with me.

'I want Kevin to come in with me,' Jill's shrill voice resounded. 'He wants to see my kids. They will want to see him.'

'Don't worry,' I tried to reassure them. 'I'm sure he won't be allowed in.' Well, I was nearly sure, but there was only the social worker and me, so I hoped we could stop him.

'I'm sorry, Mrs Mackay. You know the rules. If your friend does not leave the building immediately, I will call the police.'

There was a pause when we couldn't hear them speaking, and then the front door opened and closed. I went to look out of the window and Kevin was sitting on a bench outside the patio doors. I checked they were locked.

Jill sidled in with a forlorn expression, her hair lank and her clothes shabby, emphasised by their contrast with her bright-pink plastic shoulder bag.

'Why did you have to bring Kevin with you?' asked Hamish, keeping a watchful eye on the man they all feared, his back to the building, smoking a roll-up and tapping his foot impatiently on the flagstones.

'He helped me come on the train,' replied Jill with a distracted glance towards the patio doors. 'He wants to see you.'

As before, Jill sat on a chair and more or less ignored the children as she fiddled with her phone, texting.

At one point, Caroline went up to her with a picture book. At least Jill didn't push her away this time. Instead, she took Caroline's hand and walked her across the room to the play area, and whispered to both of the girls. Anita immediately cast an imploring glance in my direction, as Jill tried to steer the two girls towards the door. I looked at the social worker, who glanced at me and we both hurried across to intercept them.

'No, I don't want to,' wailed Anita, trying to pull away from her mother's grasp.

Caroline looked confused and Hamish came running over to try, as always, to protect his sisters from their own mother and her dangerous friend.

'Leave them alone, Mum,' he pleaded.

'I'm only taking them out to the toilet,' Jill said, trying to open the door.

'I'm afraid you cannot take the children out of the room, Mrs Mackay,' said the social worker. 'Trisha, can you take them, if they want to go?'

'OK. Who wants to go first?'

'Can we both come?' asked Anita.

We went across the entrance area.

'I don't really need the toilet,' she said when we got there.

'OK. Let's go back then.'

'No. I don't want to be with Mum.' She was trembling as she spoke. 'She wants to take us to see Kevin.'

'Oh . . .'

'I don't like Kevin,' wailed Caroline.

'I hate Kevin,' added Anita. 'He hurt me.'

'Me too. I don't want him to hurt us again.'

'We're all frightened of him. He tried to take away Mum's baby.'

By the time we got back into the family room, Jill had gone.

That night, both Anita and Caroline sleepwalked and had terrible, screaming nightmares all through the night.

Hamish mumbled and cried out in his sleep. Being deaf, Mike didn't hear a thing, but I always had the baby monitors on, so I heard every distressing sound. I can almost hear it still.

15

Fire! Fire!

'Anita gained in confidence but she still had many other problems. She was over-friendly to strangers and had one experiment with fire before she left.'

Anita's school report

One Saturday, the children got ready for Mike to take them off for the day, as usual.

'Right, Trisha,' he said. 'We're off now.'

'Here are your lunch boxes,' I said to the kids, handing them over to pack in their backpacks. 'Have a good day.'

Then I turned to Mike. 'Please don't buy them any sweets or fizzy drinks. Please do not buy them any gunge, rubbish, or whatever.' Those were my last words to him as they piled into the car.

I knew Mike would go to Tesco's and pick up his papers first, and then they were all allowed to choose a small bag of sweets each. I suspected it of course, but I never let on.

I was revelling in the prospect of a whole day of peace and quiet, to do the chores uninterrupted and maybe have some time to read. But only half an hour after they left, the phone rang.

'Oh my God, Trisha!' It was Mike's anguished voice at the other end. 'You won't believe what . . . I've just been asked into the manager's office.'

'What for?'

'I thought I'd won a prize – millionth shopper or something, but it was nothing like that. He was very angry and he's made all the children pull their pockets out.'

'Right . . .'

'Hamish had a small pack of Jaffa Cakes. Simon had his pockets full of Pokemon cards, stuffed to the gunnels. Caroline had been the lookout, which she wasn't very good at, and she just had a small packet of sweets.'

'What about Anita?' I asked, knowing that of all of them, she was the most likely to steal.

'Well, that was the strange thing. The manager didn't find anything at all in her pockets.'

'Did he look in her pants?'

'No.' Mike laughed. 'He didn't want to get into that kind of trouble!'

'But I bet that's where she's stashed her haul.'

'Well, I'll have to leave that to you to find out.'

'Did any of them say anything?'

'Yes, Anita said Simon was taking the Pokemon cards for Red Nose Day.'

'What's that got to do with it?'

'She said he was going to sell them at school to raise money for charity.'

'Right,' I said to Mike. 'I'm coming straight down to the store, big guns blazing!'

Luckily, the manager knew Mike well as a customer, so he just wanted us to make sure it didn't happen again. Out of the children's hearing, I told him my plan and he let them go with no more than a telling-off, this time.

As soon as we got back home, I lined them up in the hall and put on my cold, angry voice.

'Right. All put a backpack on please. Put in your pyjamas, your toothbrush, your flannel, your toothpaste and one small toy. I want you back down here in five minutes.'

The look of confusion on their faces! But they knew I was cross and, for once, they meekly did as they were told.

During the couple of minutes they were packing their bags, I told Mike what I intended to do.

'I don't think I'll be able to keep a straight face,' he said.

'OK, then you stay here and I'll take them down on my own.'

'Have you got everything?' I asked them as they lined up again. 'Now, into the car.'

They all piled in and off we went.

'Where are we going?' asked Hamish in a little voice.

'The police station.' In the mirror, I saw them giving each other sideways glances, with apprehension on their faces, but nothing more was said.

We pulled up in Middle Street, outside the police station, and went in.

'Can I speak to the policeman please?' I said to the woman behind the counter. 'The policeman in charge of Tesco's stealing.' I gave her a wink, unseen by the children.

'Oh, dear me,' she said with a serious face, looking at all

of them in turn. 'Right. Are you the ones that have been stealing in Tesco's?'

'Yes,' they all said in unison, their heads bowed.

'Right, OK,' she went. 'Go and sit down.'

They all looked petrified, so I knew it was having the desired effect. But I was slightly concerned, thinking: I hope I haven't gone a bit too far.

As we sat in silence in the foyer, a security door barrelled open and two big policemen came over to us and stood, jangling their keys.

'Are these the children?' asked one of the policemen.

'Yes,' I nodded.

'What is your name?' they asked me.

'Mrs Merry.'

'Your names?' he asked the children, and they said all their names in turn.

'Right, come with us.'

I thought, oh, he is just going to have a word with them, you know. So we all followed him back through the door, which he locked behind us.

'Right,' he said, giving the children a stern look. 'If you steal again, this is where you'll be having your fingerprints taken. This is where you'll have your photograph done.'

'Are we allowed to smile?' asked Anita.

'Do you have a number?' added Hamish.

Quite interested they all were by this time. Curious about the details. The officers could see something more was needed, so they led us all down the corridor until we got to the overnight cells.

'Cor, it smells of wee,' sniffed Hamish.

'Yes, it does,' said the main officer. 'Prisoners have to stay in overnight.'

'Oh,' exclaimed Caroline.

So the policeman said: 'Right, I'm going to open the door.' He looked at the children and pointed at Hamish. 'You're the oldest, you can go in first.'

I was a bit worried now, watching Hamish going in and the cell-door clanging shut behind him. He couldn't bear to be enclosed in small spaces. Maybe this was going a bit too far.

Anita went into the next cell, quite gingerly, and then the policeman shut the door. I was beginning to panic now. That's enough, I thought. It seemed ages, but it wasn't more than a couple of minutes, with Caroline and Simon waiting next to me in the cold corridor, looking as anxious as I felt.

When the police officer opened the doors, Anita was very pale, and Hamish couldn't get out of his cell quickly enough. Next he put seven-year-old Caroline in and he just shut the door for two or three seconds and Simon swapped places, but without the door being shut. Even so, he was near to tears. I felt like Cruella de Vil for having put the younger ones through that. I hadn't expected this dose of medicine to go so far.

'Did that frighten you?' asked the officer.

'Yes,' sniffed Simon. 'You haven't made a space for the food to come under.'

The officers laughed and the second one turned to me. 'I think he's been watching too many old films!'

Finally, the first officer gave them a good pep talk about the perils of stealing.

'Even if it was for Red Nose Day,' added the second guy.

'Right,' said the first one. 'Do not let it happen again.'

When we got back home, my grown-up daughter Jane was there with Mike and she greeted us at the door.

The children couldn't wait to tell her and Mike what had gone on.

'I hope you've learnt your lesson,' said Jane.

'Yes, we have,' squeaked Simon, near to tears. 'We have, because we've been banned now from Tesco's and we've got to go to Sainsbury's and we don't like Sainsbury's.'

That broke the tension at last and we all had a good laugh together. Even the children saw the funny side of it.

It wasn't quite true, but we kept up the pretence for a while, to stress the seriousness of their actions. For quite some months after, Mike would pull up in the car park. 'You can't come in,' he would say. 'You can't come in. I'm just popping in to get the papers.' And of course they would knock seven bells out of one another when they were left together in the car. Then Mike would come back and have to sort them out.

I think in the end it was Mike who absent-mindedly said one day: 'Oh come on, we'll all go in.'

'No, we can't go in,' said Anita.

'We're banned,' Hamish reminded him.

'No, it's all right. You can come in,' explained Mike. 'We only said that.'

'Oh, can we really?' asked Simon. They couldn't believe we had been teasing them all this time, but they took it very well.

Anita was now stealing from school on a daily basis. If it was there, she would take it. She'd steal clothes, money, whatever she found; it didn't matter what it was, anything, hair clips, make-up . . . She had boxes and boxes of stolen property upstairs, and when I discovered it I asked her about it.

'Why do you take all these things, Anita?'

She just looked at me and shrugged.

'There must be a reason. Some of these things belonged to your friends. Why did you steal them?'

'I don't know,' she said. 'It just happens.'

I think half the time she just took it because it was there. And, nine times out of ten I think she threw it away after she'd taken it, because she knew she didn't need it, and often she didn't even like it. I was always being called up to the school and the head was always as patient as she could possibly be with Anita, but we were at a loss to know how to stop her.

One morning, about two hours after seeing Mike drive all the children off to school, the phone rang. Here we go again, I thought. Another problem at school. Who was it this time?

I picked up the phone.

'Mrs Merry, can you come up? Anita's set fire to the school.'

Of course I had an immediate vision of flames rising up through the roof. I dashed out to my car and drove as fast as I safely could.

As I rounded the last bend, I expected the school to be in ashes, but I couldn't even see any smoke. What an anti-climax. So perhaps Anita hadn't caused too much damage. In fact, when I got there I found she'd just scorched some floor-tiles and the door jamb in the toilets.

After a fireman gave Anita a stern telling-off, during which she looked suitably subdued for once, we had to see the head teacher, who told her off again and banned her from swimming for a week.

'I hope you have learned your lesson, Anita.'

I agreed to take Anita home for the rest of the day, till everything got back to normal. We had a silent drive home. I needed her to realise how serious this was.

'Tell me exactly what happened,' I said to her as we sat opposite each other at the kitchen table.

'Well, I was in the front of the car, on the way to school,' she began. 'When I saw a lighter in the space between the seats. I remember looking at it and wondering how it works. Something in me was saying: "If you ask Dad, he won't let you." So I thought I'll just take it, right?'

'Didn't Dad notice?'

'No, he was looking at the road, so I sneaked it into my school bag.'

'And then what did you do?'

'I remember sitting in class with this niggling feeling – I wanted to go and light this lighter. I really had this urge.

And I didn't know why. So I made an excuse to go to the toilet and I set light to some of the toilet paper. But it was like tissue and it caught fire too fast. I didn't like it burning so quickly. It only lasted a few seconds before it died out.'

'So how did it burn the door jamb?'

'I was really annoyed that it didn't stay alight, so I went out and got some leaves.'

'A lot of leaves?'

'Two handfuls. I didn't really think of the fire burning anything else except the leaves. I piled them up together on the toilet floor and set fire to them. It made a *psshhh* sound. The flames suddenly shot up. I panicked and ran for it, through the outside door, chucking the lighter behind some bushes.'

'Wasn't that the lighter with Mike's name on it?'

'Yes, but I forgot about that. Then the fire alarm went off. It rang really loudly. I thought crap, what if they find out it's me? We all lined up across the playground and then we were told the fire was out and we could all go back to our classrooms.'

'Did somebody find the lighter?'

'Yes, because twenty minutes later, the head teacher walked in, holding it up. My heart nearly stopped. I thought crap, Mum's going to kill me!' She gave me a look. 'You won't, will you?'

'I might,' I said. 'I'm cross enough. But it was Mike's lighter. What do you think he will say?'

'He won't be as cross as you!'

'You're quite right. I'm angry that you took his lighter in the first place, and I'm even angrier that you were stupid enough to use it like that.'

She sat and waited for the fireworks.

'I'm very disappointed in you, Anita. Do you realise how dangerous this was?'

'Yes.'

'You could have caused thousands of pounds of damage. And, even worse, you could have killed somebody.'

'Yes, I know it was stupid. I'm sorry.' She hung her head. I think she really was quite shocked, but I needed to do something to make her see how important this was.

'There's only one thing I can do with you, young lady. You're coming with me down to the police station and you're going to apologise for setting light to the school.'

At the police station, Anita was quite subdued. She did apologise and they gave her a very serious telling off. I think that was more of a frightener to her than the first time, after the Tesco's theft.

'What a day that was!' I said to Mike as we sat after dinner that night. 'I really thought the school would be a gonner.'

'Even Anita couldn't have talked her way out of that one,' he said with a grin. 'It will be something to laugh about in years to come.'

And it has been.

16

Over My Dead Body!

'Review meeting. What a shock!'

Extract from my diary

As foster parents, we were always the last to hear anything, and we were rarely consulted about any potential change of plan. But I suppose the signs were there.

The children had been with us for two or three years now and they were costing Social Services about £6,000 per month. They paid the agency and the agency paid some of that over to us. Because they had been such a hard-to-place family with so many problems, we were given a good fostering allowance, well above the norm, but of course our bills were huge. Food alone cost more than £300 per week. And we'd had to buy all of them several sets of new clothes.

The washing machine and tumble dryer were on permanently with all the nappies and almost daily changes of sheets, and I couldn't begin to tell you what the electricity bill came to. We needed to swap our previous family car for a people-carrier, which consumed petrol at an alarming rate, and of course there were all the outings Mike took them on to keep them occupied and give me time to get things done.

We were called to attend a review meeting and, as usual, I went on my own. Mike was deaf and his hearing aid wasn't discerning enough to help him cope with round-table discussions, so he left all that to me. I think I was in shock when I drove back home that afternoon, but I had to go and get the children from school and do all the usual things, so I didn't have time to sit down and really think about it until after the children had gone to bed.

'I need to explain what might happen,' I said to Mike. 'From what they were saying at the meeting today, I think the time has run out for the children, financially.'

'What does that mean?'

'Social Services can no longer afford to pay that much and they are now looking for cheaper options.'

'How can they do that?'

'Well, they say that the children will have to come out of the system because they cost too much to foster for any longer.'

'But that's ridiculous.'

'Yes, they're pulling the plug, or trying to. They're pushing to get the children adopted.'

'Oh. Did they ask you what you thought about that idea?'

'Of course not. I soon realised I wasn't there to contribute to the discussion. Their decision had already been made in some anonymous office where they don't know anything about children, or care about their needs.' I paused. 'To be fair, I can see it's a very high cost to the local authority.'

'But they should have thought about that years ago,' said Mike. 'When they could have intervened and avoided the children having so many problems.'

'Well, we always knew their time with us might be limited.'

'Yes, but they need more than two years for us to set them on the right road.'

'They might need a lifetime for that!'

'So what will they do?' he asked.

'I suppose they will try to have them adopted.'

'Together?'

'I can't see that happening.'

'But they have to stay together.'

'We know that, but try telling the accountants!'

'I can't see anyone adopting them separately either,' said Mike. 'Aren't they too old already?'

'Then it would be children's homes.'

'Separately?'

'I expect so. Where would they find four spare places at once?'

'That would be awful. They would go wild.' He scratched his head. 'How long have we got?'

'As long as we can persuade them to let the children stay here, or as long as it takes to get them adopted or placed.'

'Have they suggested paying us less?'

'No. They would want it to be a lot less . . . or nothing. How could we manage that?'

'I don't know. But surely they have to keep the children together?'

'They don't have to do anything. The decision is entirely in their hands.'

'I suppose we couldn't adopt them?'

'No, we're much too old. We'd have to be at least twenty years younger for them to even consider us.'

'So it all comes down to money!' groaned Mike.

Just as there had to be court orders that the children should be brought to us, firstly as an emergency placement, then for longer-term care orders, so any change would have to go back to the courts for legal agreement.

Social Services appointed a guardian ad litem for the children. Her name was Liz and it was her role to ensure, as far as she could, that the best interests of the children were taken into account in any decisions about their future and to advise the courts accordingly.

I remember when she first came round and introduced herself. I liked her straight away and she'd obviously done her homework. She'd even visited Jill's house sometime before, when the children still lived there, and she told me a lot of things about what went on that the local authority had refused to reveal.

'I've been to some houses in my time, Mrs Merry,' she said. 'You couldn't even sit on the settee. The children had no nappies on and they'd messed and wet everywhere.'

'Yes, Hamish told me about that. He used to worry about the younger ones, with no one to look after them when he was at school.' I gave her a look. 'How awful.'

'Yes, absolutely awful,' she nodded emphatically.

She was very sympathetic to the situation, and had some understanding of the children's individual needs. Of course, I filled her in on their progress since coming to us.

'It seems as if you've both done a brilliant job so far. The children are very lucky to have you.'

'You do know I've got a lot wrong along the way?' I said, almost automatically, then realised how badly misconstrued that could be. 'I mean . . .'

'Don't worry,' she laughed. 'I know you were being modest, so I shall ignore that comment. You might be only human, but it looks to me that you've done extremely well with these children – that's what Steve at Social Services told me. And the agency was full of your praises, both of you.'

Well, you don't get many compliments in this job, so it was good to hear.

'Would you like a coffee?'

We sat down and started to go through everything. She had a lot of questions and I answered as best I could. Then it was my turn to ask her some things that were preying on our minds, starting with the biggest question of all.

'What do you think will happen to these kids?'

'Do you want me to be frank?'

'Yes.'

'I think they will be split up. The social workers are going to advertise for adoptive families for them, but nobody would take them all together, so they will be advertised separately.'

'Do you think that will work?'

'It doesn't look good for them,' she sighed. 'To be honest, you can forget Hamish, at nine, coming up to a difficult age. From what I've read and what you've told me, Anita will be almost impossible to place, because of her behaviour. Caroline would also be very difficult to place, in my opinion, with her learning difficulties. Simon is the only one that's saleable.' She paused, then must have seen the shocked look on my face. 'I'm sorry to be so blunt,' she explained with a shrug. 'But that's how it is.'

'And what if nobody comes forward?'

'Children's homes.'

'That's what we thought. It's what we dread. Even a change of any kind at this stage would probably break them. But children's homes . . .'

'Yes, I know.'

A few days later, Steve turned up with a camera.

'I've got to take some photos of the children for this adoption magazine,' he said.

'You mean their photos will be part of the advertisements?'

'Yes, it helps to see happy, smiling faces. It makes them more likely to read the text.'

'Sounds like a meat market to me! It's the worst thing for these children. They've hardly been here two years and there's still a lot of work to be done. You want to take them away and split them up?'

'It's not my choice, Trisha.'

'No, I know that. But who else can I moan at?'

It was a cold day, but we took the children out into the

garden to get some natural shots. Then we tried them indoors as well, playing at the kitchen table. Finally he felt he'd got enough smiling shots to choose from. I didn't tell the children at that point why Steve was taking photos, but Anita, usually the most difficult one, loved preening herself for the camera and giving it her best smile, so all the others followed suit and nobody asked why.

'So how do the adverts work?' I asked Steve, away from the children.

'They go in the magazine and we hope that brings forward some interested people.'

'Do you really believe that?'

'Well . . .' he said shifting uncomfortably. 'It will come out next week and after that I'll come down for another visit and fill you in on any responses we get. We'll let you see any applications, so that you can make comments if you wish.'

'Are you saying your bosses will take our opinions into account?'

'I can't say for sure, but they usually share information with carers, to try and avoid making any big mistakes in placements, so I think that means they will include your responses in the decision-making process.'

'Good. I expect we'll have plenty to say!'

Three weeks later, Steve returned with a thin sheaf of papers. 'They're all for Simon,' he said.

'Can I see them?'

Steve pulled out a crumpled sheet of paper. 'Well, this man has come forward.'

'What is he like?'

Steve made a face as he started to read a note fixed to their form. 'No . . .' He placed it on the bottom of the pile. 'You can't put anyone here.'

I didn't even ask why, but I guessed.

'There's this family in Liverpool . . .' He placed their form on the table to where we could both read it, and then got out a social worker's notes following a visit to their house.

'But it says here that their house is in a very grubby state, with cat-pooh everywhere.'

'Yes. We've offered to clean their house before they can be eligible to adopt anyone.'

'What good would that do? It would soon go back to what it was,' I fumed. 'You must be mad! You've taken them away from a filthy, dangerous home, you've brought them here, and now you want to take them back to that kind of squalor? The world has gone mad!'

'Point taken,' he said, putting that application away. 'What about this one? It's a woman on her own with just one son.'

I began to read the notes. 'But it says here that she runs a chip shop, her son has severe disabilities and she is his sole carer. How is she going to manage all that *and* adopt a five-year-old disadvantaged boy who's probably on the autistic spectrum? What do you think she wants him for? Will he end up being their skivvy?'

Steve sighed, slipped that application under the others and picked another off the top. 'This is the only other one we've had so far,' he said.

I read the beginning of a letter that said: 'Yes, we'll have them all, if you build an extension on our house and buy us a minibus and pay us at least £500 per week for each of them and . . .' I didn't read any further.

'How dare they see our children as a meal ticket! They must be blinded by the pound signs in their eyes. That's nearly double what we get as foster parents. Adoptive parents don't get any allowance, do they?'

'Not unless they qualify for the usual state benefits.'

'Surely the panel wouldn't take any of these people seriously?'

'I honestly can't say.' Steve looked almost as depressed as I felt.

'I'm not being rude, but these people are the dregs. I know the local authority just wants to get our children off their books and—'

'I know,' said Steve. 'It's going to be an uphill climb.'

'I don't care what metaphor you use. This isn't right. These are children. I know they're not high on the local authority's list of priorities, but this is their future, good, bad or worse.'

'We did approach their grandparents,' he said.

'Over my dead body! I'm ninety-nine per cent certain that animal has abused both the girls, and almost certainly their mother too.'

'You don't need to worry, because they said no.'

'I bet that was their grandmother's answer, not his.'

'Well, we always have to go through family members first.'

'No matter how dangerous?' I was tanking mad. 'Hasn't enough harm been done to these kids already? You might as well give them back to a paedophile ring.'

'Ooh, I think that's going a bit far.'

'It's not! Believe me.' I paused to let my blood pressure drop from the top of my head. 'Somebody needs to stand up for them.' I gave him a challenging stare.

Steve turned his head away, with a look of defeat. 'I wish I could be that person,' he said. 'But I can't. I've tried it before. Why should it be any different this time?'

'Well, if you can't do anything, I bloody well will. I'll kick up the biggest stink Social Services has ever known if they don't find the right family for these vulnerable children.'

He gave me a long look. 'There's only one way that's going to happen,' he said.

I returned his gaze, hearing but at that moment failing to understand his meaning.

Just then the kids came home, collected by Mike who had taken the afternoon off work. They all ran in helter-skelter, as usual, school bags and shoes in all directions, then into the kitchen to see what snacks they could have.

'Hello, Steve,' said Mike, following them in. 'I'll take the biscuit tin downstairs with the children,' he said, always willing to help, never complaining.

'He's a good man, Mike,' smiled Steve.

'Yes, he's been a wonderful support all these years. I couldn't have done any of it without him.'

'Well, it's time I went. I'm already too late to miss the

rush-hour traffic!' He put the sheaf of papers away in his briefcase. 'I'll keep you posted.'

'Yes, make sure you do.'

'And if you have any further thoughts . . .'

'I'll have my say. You can be sure of that.'

The following morning, the guardian ad litem came.

'I wanted to find out how the children are coping with the stress of everything that's going on,' she said. 'It must be a very worrying time for all of you.'

'I don't think they've noticed anything different,' I laughed. 'Their life has been stress from the day they were born, so I haven't bothered them with all this yet. They're just enjoying the extra attention. But Mike and I are reeling, and I'm absolutely furious at the totally unsuitable options being considered.'

She nodded sympathetically as we sat down in the living room.

'I dread to think what will happen to them in the end. If they get split up, you might as well throw away the key. And, if they end up in a children's home, it will be like passing a death sentence on them.'

'Well there's only one way to avoid that,' she said.

'That's exactly what Steve said yesterday, but I didn't know what he meant.'

'Why don't you and Mike adopt them?'

That silenced me. It was several seconds before I picked my jaw up off the floor as my thoughts raced in confusion.

'You must be joking!' I replied. 'Have you gone off your head?'

She laughed. 'No, I'm serious. That way you could assure their future and everyone would be happy.'

'But we're too old,' I protested. 'We hadn't even thought of that. Everyone knows you have to be under forty to adopt even one child, let alone four!'

'Yes,' she nodded. 'That is the general rule, but there can be exceptions.'

'How?'

'You can just apply to adopt them. Simple as that. But you would need to have a big enough house for them each to have their own bedroom.'

Nearby, in Victoria Road, there was a four-storey Georgian townhouse for sale. It had been on the market for quite a while. Mike and I had looked at it a couple of times, but we decided we couldn't afford it. It was very, very run-down, with parts of it falling down, but it had seven bedrooms.

Right, I thought . . .

So, when Mike came home from work that evening I was keen to tell him.

'Have you had a nice day?' he asked, as usual.

'Yes, I had a lovely day today.'

'What did you do?'

'I've bought 27 Victoria Road.'

He gulped. 'Has it got a roof and windows?'

'Yes . . . at the front.'

We both broke into a fit of hysterical laughter. And Mike didn't even know why, yet.

'The guardian ad litem came today,' I told Mike after dinner.

'Oh yes. How did that go?'

'She was fine, but it was all rather depressing . . . until it took a strange turn!'

'How do you mean?' He gave me a quizzical look.

'She said why don't we adopt the children ourselves?'

'But we're much too old,' shrugged Mike. 'We knew that.'

'She said they might consider making an exception.'

We sat and talked through all the angles we could think of to this new suggestion. It was potentially the ideal solution, yet we hadn't even thought of it before, so there was a lot to consider. If we had talked it all through clinically there would have been so many possible barriers from a selfish point of view. But neither of us thought of it like that. Emotionally, we could only focus on the more obvious factors that might affect the children as well as ourselves. Their future was uppermost for us and there was no question what our decision should be as far as they were concerned.

'Do you think we will have the energy?' I asked. 'To keep going for the next fifteen years, coping with all their ups and downs?'

'That would take me through to nearly eighty. And I'm creaking now!' laughed Mike. 'But we're both healthy enough, touch wood. And, anyway, you've always got enough drive for the both of us.'

'Yes, but just think. If their behaviour is a problem now,

at five, six, eight and nine, what's it going to be like from fourteen to eighteen?'

'That's true, but you're the behaviour expert. I'm just the entertainments manager, so that will have to be your decision.'

'Well, I suppose we've been through it enough times with other foster children, as well as our older adopted family when they were teenagers.'

'And that stretched your abilities from time to time,' Mike reminded me with a grin.

'Perhaps our ages may not be a barrier to adopting – we'll have to wait and see. But would it be fair on the children? We'll be as old as most of their friends' grandparents. They might not like that when they're teenagers.'

'Yes, but teenagers will always find something to complain about. If not age, it would be something else.'

'That's true!'

'So, do you think they would accept us to adopt the children?'

'I think it looks like a strong possibility. After all, that would get the children, the expense and the responsibility off their hands in one go.'

'And they would all be ours instead!'

'Yes,' I said with a hollow laugh.

'It will be a struggle to afford it all . . . and a new house that's almost falling down!'

'I know, but I'll find a way to earn some money. I could start our own fostering agency. After all, I should know enough about it by now! And I'm sure Jane would help me.'

'It will be a challenge, but we'll cope with the expense somehow.'

'If we do get the go-ahead to adopt them, we'll be in for a bumpy road ahead. Do you remember what Jane said when we adopted her?'

'No. What was that?'

'She said, "You always told me you loved me, but once you adopted me, I wanted to see how much . . ."'

'Ah, yes. And I seem to recall that she did push the boundaries.'

'I'm sure they all will.'

'The main thing is to remember the alternative,' said Mike. 'And we can't let that happen.'

'No,' I agreed, vehemently. 'There's no way I would let that happen, when it looks as if we may hold the key to a better future. What do you think?'

'Well, it's a chance for any couple to take.'

'Yes, but if anything does happen to us, we have a close and supportive family, and lots of great friends.'

'Yes, they'd all rally round.'

'And I'm sure the children are learning from how we all are with each other, how a strong family works together. We're none of us perfect. We can fall out with each other, then make up again. We can get angry and walk away, but it doesn't last for long.'

'Yes, we are certainly lucky with our family, but they are lucky with us too,' said Mike.

'All the way along, we've both done the best we could for all our foster and adopted children. We haven't always got it right,' I conceded. 'And they haven't always got it right either. But, as I always say, we've done it all out of love.'

'So we're saying yes?' He looked hopeful.

I nodded. 'We're saying yes. I'll call the guardian ad litem tomorrow.'

17

The Freeing Order

'The contact with your birth family seemed to be unsettling for you all . . . A goodbye meeting took place.'

Extract from a letter to Anita

'You must be mad!' erupted Jane when I told her we'd decided to apply to adopt the four children. 'Look at their behaviour now. It's not going to get any better.'

Then I phoned my other adopted daughter Sally and it was a similar, shocked reaction: 'Do you really want to do this . . . at your time of life?'

Our adopted son Daniel was in Russia, and out of contact, so I couldn't let him know at that time. But Anna, our older foster daughter, who is one of the family, had a different reaction. 'I can understand why you want to adopt them . . .' but she sounded concerned for us too.

The move into our new, seven-bedroom house gave us a lot of extra space, so I set up an office and put my idea into action by starting up my own fostering agency. Whether we would be allowed to adopt the children or not, it was something I was well qualified to do and all my experience over the years gave me a head start. Now that Jane's children were getting older, she came and joined me as the business grew.

In fact, the agency was doing so well that it needed more of my time and I now had the worry of how I would cope if the adoption did go through and I had to work full-time. I had a chat with Mike about it one evening.

'Well, don't worry,' he said, in his usual measured way. 'We could take on a daily cleaner, and have the laundry done for us . . .'

'Yes, I suppose so.' Part of me was relieved, but I also had a niggle of guilt there.

'And I'll be retiring soon,' added Mike. 'So I can do the school runs. I'll go and buy a chauffeur's cap to wear!'

We filled in all the adoption paperwork to start off the official process, knowing it could take a very long time to get through all the stages, if it ever got that far. I always had the feeling that someone was going to come along at some point and say 'No'.

But as the weeks turned into months and things slowly edged forward, I reached the stage where I knew I would fight tooth and claw to keep these children, and woe betide anyone who tried to stop me! And, like many experienced foster parents, I had developed a certain ego that says 'Nobody's going to look after these kids better than I can.'

For Mike and me, the thing that gave us the most hope for the adoption becoming a reality was getting our Form F done. As part of that we each had to have a session with a psychologist, to judge whether we were stable enough as a couple, with a supportive enough family and a strong enough capability to look after these vulnerable children for the rest of their childhoods, no matter what.

I compared notes with Mike afterwards.

'Did he ask you about us – how we get on with each other?' I asked him.

'Yeah. I don't find it easy talking to strangers about our marriage.'

'Me neither. But I thought he was very fair. He didn't make it feel like he was prying or anything.'

'No, he seemed all right.'

'What did you tell him about us?'

'Quite a bit, when he asked. Oh, and I told him you were my ideal partner.'

'What do you mean, "were"?' I laughed.

'Go on then, what did you say about me?'

'I said they shouldn't underestimate you.'

'Oh yeah?'

'And that whenever we have a problem, we always talk it through together.'

'I told him the only thing we argue about is the Christmas decorations . . . every year!' Mike said it with a groan, then we both broke into laughter.

'It's true. Every year since we got married, we've had a row about the Christmas decorations. It's become a tradition now!'

The Form F was completed, ending with a strong recommendation that we should be approved as adopters of the four children. Phew! It was sent off to go before the panel, who were a group of people with a lot of experience in deciding about suitable adoptive parents. They would read everything about us and discuss it in detail together, then interview both of us as well, before making the final decision as to whether the adoption could go ahead.

While all this was going on, behind the scenes, we were in lengthy discussions with Social Services to have some sort of financial arrangement, to replace at least some of our generous foster carers' allowance. They finally agreed, along with leasing us a new people-carrier. I desperately wanted them to pay for long-term therapy for each of the children, but I didn't dare make any more demands . . . it was all such a delicate balance, and they could have turned around at any moment and taken the children away from us completely, if we pushed them too hard.

We'd had a rough ride for more than a year already, while all this adoption process was going on, not to mention the house-move and all the work we had to do on it, and the continuing phone calls from schools and . . . So it was such a relief when we finally heard that we'd been accepted! It felt like a stamp of approval. All of these ten or twenty people along the way had agreed that they thought we could do a good job. At last we knew we could do it, and everybody said we could do it well. But then, of course, there's always that niggling doubt . . .

As Mike said: 'Now we've got to prove it!'

'And we'll have to tell the children what we've done.'

'How do you think they'll take it?'

'I'm not sure. I just hope they won't be too upset at the prospect of being stuck with us for life!'

A couple of days later, I called the children together around the dining-room table to tell them the news and discuss it all with them.

'Are you going to join us?' I asked Mike.

'No. You'll soon get fed up with me saying "pardon" whenever I can't hear properly. You can tell me later how it went. Just tell the kids I agree with everything you say, as usual!' He laughed before going off to catch up with his newspaper.

They all sat down, still in their school uniforms, wondering what this was all about.

'Do you remember when I asked you if you would be happy to stay longer with us?'

'Yes,' replied Hamish in a solemn voice. 'And I said I didn't want to go back.'

'I don't want to go back either,' added Anita.

'What about you two?' I asked Caroline and Simon. 'Are you happy to stay here?'

'I like it here,' smiled Caroline, and Simon just nodded agreement.

'And do you remember that day when Steve came and took photos of you?'

'Oh yes,' grinned Anita. 'I wore my pretty dress.'

'What were the photos for?' asked Hamish, as if he could sense the way this conversation was going. 'Why didn't he send them to us?'

'He took them to show people who might want to adopt you,' I said carefully. 'But we didn't want anyone else to adopt you, so we applied to adopt you ourselves. And now we've been told we can. Would you like us to become your proper parents?' I looked round the group, with all their faces breaking into wide smiles.

'Forever?' asked Hamish, as if in disbelief.

'Yes, forever. Even when you've grown up and left home, we would still be your parents, like we are to Jane, Sally and Daniel.'

'And Anna,' added Anita.

'Yes. We couldn't adopt Anna because she still wanted to stay with her real mother sometimes. But we always include her in our family, don't we?'

'But what about Jill and Gary?' asked Hamish. 'Won't they mind?'

'They've been told you are going to be adopted and they have signed the forms agreeing to that. I think they know they were not very good at looking after you themselves, so they have said yes to your being adopted and looked after the way you need.'

'But what if they change their minds and come looking for us? I don't want them to know we live here,' he pleaded with a frown.

'No, it's OK. Nobody will let them know where you are, without your permission.'

'Really?'

'Yes, really.' That seemed to reassure him, for now anyway.

'So we won't have to go and live anywhere else?'

'No, you can stay here.'

'All of us?'

'Yes, all of you. We've waited till now to tell you because we wanted to get through the application stages first. But now it looks like it's all going ahead, once the judge signs the agreements, and we will be your mum and dad.'

'Can we call you Mum and Dad?' asked Anita.

'You can if you like, or you can call us Trisha and Mike if you prefer.'

'Will we have to call you that?' asked Hamish, frowning again. 'Can't we call you Nan and Grandad, like Laura and Brett do?'

'Yes, if you want to. We're not fussed about our names.'

'Can we stay in this house forever?' asked Anita.

'Yes, you can all stay in this house if the judge says "yes" but maybe not forever, because we might move to another house one day. Wherever we live, we would all be together. Would you like that?'

'Yes, please,' said Caroline, unsure what it was all about, but certain she wanted to stay together.

'But what will happen to Mum?' asked Anita, thinking it all through. 'Will somebody feed her? Is she going to miss us?'

'I think your mum will be very sad. But she knows it's the best thing because she can't look after you. And I'm sure the social worker will go in and look after her.' They hadn't seen her for months now, as she rarely turned up for visits and they had petered out.

* * *

Everything was going so well in this final stage of the process . . . perhaps too well.

One Sunday, while Hamish and Anita were sorting something out in the garden with Mike, the two younger ones were sat with me at the kitchen table, doing some colouring while I sewed somebody's buttons back on.

Suddenly, the calm atmosphere was broken by a wail from Caroline.

'Simon has taken my red pen!'

'It's my pen,' protested Simon. 'I had it first.'

'It was my turn.'

Simon looked up and stuck his tongue out at Caroline.

She reached across and tore his colouring in two.

'Get off!' He scribbled with the red pen on the back of her hand.

Caroline now completely lost her temper, swore at Simon and aimed her two middle fingers straight at his eye. He put his hand up to try to protect himself.

'Don't do that, darling,' I said. 'Because you'll hurt him.'

She looked at me, then she looked at Simon.

'I hate him,' she growled and suddenly lunged for his other eye.

'No, no, no, you mustn't do that!' I moved to protect Simon, but he ducked, then spat a great gob of saliva across the table into her face.

This time she really went for him, both fingers rigid, with all her might.

Instinctively I put my hand up in between and it just caught her fingers. 'No!' I said again. 'You do not do that to eyes.'

Simon, realising his narrow escape, started to cry. Caroline, her fury thwarted, started crying as well out of frustration. I sat down again and they each got down from their chairs and came over to me for a cuddle. That was it – fight over.

The next day I dropped the children off at their schools as usual, and about an hour later there was a knock at the door. It was a social worker, so I showed her in.

'Mrs Merry. Caroline has made a complaint at school that you smacked her for no reason.'

'Really?' I was angry. 'Let's call her teacher and find out what this is all about.' I didn't wait for her agreement. I knew all the school numbers by heart.

Sure enough, the secretary took the phone to Caroline's teacher, who told me that Caroline had been crying when she came into school.

'I asked her what was the matter, and she said you had smacked her very hard and it made her cry. I asked her why you had smacked her and she said no reason. So I'm sorry, Mrs Merry, but our school policy is to report anything like this, so I had no choice.'

'Even if it wasn't true? You've told me yourself that Caroline often tells you lies.'

'Well, I couldn't know for sure whether it was true—'

'You could have rung me first!'

'Our policy is always to believe the child, so I had no alternative.'

I thanked her coldly and put the phone down.

'I know what this is about,' I said to the social worker as

I sat down with her in the living room. 'I'll tell you exactly what happened and you can make your own judgement.'

I recounted the whole episode of Caroline's finger-jabbing, describing every stage of their fight, what I said and how I reacted.

'So you see,' I explained, 'I put my hand out to protect Simon as Caroline lunged at him and it caught Caroline's outstretched fingers.'

'Oh, right,' was all she said. 'I will report back to my superior and we will let you know how we will proceed.' She got up to go.

'When will you let me know?' I asked, anxious that this seemed to be escalating too far, and the final stage of the adoption was only weeks away. I was only too aware how this could impact on all our hopes and plans.

A few days later, the senior social worker called round to interview me. I went through it all with her, blow by blow, and finished with the catching of Caroline's fingers.

There was a pause while she wrote some notes.

'Are you aware of these children's problems?' I asked her.

'Do you think you need more help?' she replied.

What a loaded question. I was damned if I did and damned if I didn't. So I said nothing as I thought it through.

She just gave me a long, withering look. 'I think you need a break, Mrs Merry.' Another ambiguous statement. I felt a sense of dread, knowing where this could be going.

I showed her out and dropped into a heap on the sofa. This seemingly innocent accusation by Caroline could

scupper everything, for her and the others. It really frightened me. I felt in more of a turmoil than I'd ever experienced
before. But then my sensible side kicked in and I realised
that I could over-analyse all this. Yes, perhaps that was what
I was doing.

Apparently she went back and spoke to the school again,
the doctor and I don't know who else, but it was so near the
end of the adoption procedure that it was too late and the
issue too comparatively insignificant to stop it now. We
were on a roll, thank goodness!

The final requirement before we could officially adopt the
children was the freeing order. This is a chance for the children and their birth family to say goodbye. Normally, it's
supposed to be done in easy stages, over as long a time as
can be arranged, to smooth the process – usually a month to
six weeks. But, despite it being two years since our application, the end part of it was all so quick that the freeing order
had to be done and dusted in a day.

So a meeting was arranged, to include everyone at once,
even though the children hadn't seen some of these people
for a long time.

There was birth dad, birth mum, mum's first husband,
who none of them knew, their elder half-sibling Mandy,
who had severe learning difficulties, their grandma and
their grandad.

I had to take our four along to that meeting, stay, then
take them back home again. But even more arduous was the
need for me to explain all this to the children themselves, so

that they all understood what it was about, and to prepare them for the emotional impact it might have on them. I had to try to keep them as calm as possible, despite the significance of what they were about to experience. I also had to encourage them to talk to everyone when they got there – an almost impossible task for the younger ones in such a large and daunting gathering.

In the days leading up to the freeing-order meeting, they were increasingly anxious and asked me to explain the purpose of the meeting over and over again. I'm not sure even then whether the younger ones took in what it meant.

It was a horrendous situation and an absolutely horrendous day. I don't think it was any easier for the adults than it was for the children, perhaps even more stressful emotionally. What Jill's first husband was doing there was as baffling to him as to anyone, but at least he came with their daughter Mandy, who Hamish and Anita did remember as she came to live with them for a short while, when they were little.

What made the whole situation even more difficult to bear was that it was all these people in one small room, with no toys or play area to break the tension for the children.

It was hard for Mandy too. It was years since she had seen her mother, let alone Hamish and Anita, and she couldn't understand what was going on.

Their birth dad came, but all he did was chain-smoke and drink his lager. He went out then back in repeatedly, smoking all the while, but never interacted with any of the children, other than his initial 'Hello, kids.'

Jill, their birth mum, did exchange a few words with

Hamish and Anita, but would not even acknowledge Caroline, who was desperately trying to attract her attention, in all the most inappropriate ways – 'Here I am' – trying to get Jill to notice her. Finally Caroline burst into tears, inconsolable. It was so frustrating to see the damage they were doing to this little girl and be helpless to do anything.

Grandma and Grandad were there, and Grandad was going over to talk to her. I wasn't sure that was a good thing. He whispered something to her and her face froze. He took her by the hand and led her back, stroking her hair and arms and more or less all over as he sat down, placing her in front of him, with one hand on her bottom and the other on her tummy, holding her hard into himself, which she clearly found uncomfortable. She squirmed and he smiled. She tried to get away, but he held her even tighter, pulling her in harder. She squirmed all the more. His breathing quickened . . .

I turned to the social worker who was supposed to be leading this meeting and shot her frantic looks. She looked anxiously from me to Caroline and to the grandfather, back and forth, seemingly incapable of doing anything to rescue the poor child.

I was desperate to stop this, but Liz, the guardian ad litem, who was sitting next to me, put her hand on my arm, as if to warn me. I was horrified, but I knew I was not allowed to intervene. This was intolerable.

Fortunately, Jill changed places with her mother, to sit next to Grandad, and leant forward to give him a coquettish smile. My immediate thought was that there was something very wrong here. It looked almost as if Jill was jealous of his attentions towards her least favourite child.

Grandad suddenly let go of Caroline, who ran to me, as if for safety. I gave her a hug and she clung to my sleeve. Meanwhile, Grandad stroked Jill's cheek and her ears, gazing into her eyes. She clearly enjoyed this, turned her body towards him and put her hand on his, directing his hand down her neck . . .

I looked at the grandmother, who was also watching them, but with what looked like a resigned expression. I wondered if perhaps I was reading too much into all this. Perhaps I'd got it all wrong, but I couldn't ignore the signs.

The social worker cleared her throat and asked Jill something about her journey, so the spell was broken, for the time being anyway.

While all this had been going on, Simon just sat alone in the corner, ignored, not spoken to or even picked up, now that he was no longer a toddler.

By now, with nothing to do, the other three were just bouncing off the walls. The social worker made no effort to re-engage them with the adults and the whole meeting became the nightmare I had dreaded.

I turned to Liz. 'Who in their right mind put this together? It beggars belief. Absolutely beggars belief.'

She nodded, turned her head away from the group and grimaced at me.

It was cruel, expecting four vulnerable, confused and emotional children to say goodbye to all those adults, lumped together, all in the space of a couple of hours, not to mention all the complicated relationships.

And what was particularly difficult for me was that I had been helpless to do anything to improve the situation. They kept looking towards me for help, and I could do nothing. By the end of the meeting, all the related adults were in tears and the children looked stressed to bursting point. I couldn't wait to get them out of it and as far away as possible.

As I was driving them down the Northend Road, I remembered we'd be passing one of those ball-park places, so I turned in and parked. Whenever I had taken them there before, they had gone wild. I thought it would be especially good for them today because they could scream, shout, jump and make as much noise as they felt like.

We went in, and yes, they were over the top in one way, but they all looked shell-shocked, in an alien environment, unable to let out their feelings. They had been cooped up in a small room, without any food, both of which Hamish in particular does not do well, surrounded by people, some of them virtual strangers and most of whom completely failed to communicate with them, and they had long ago eaten the snacks I had taken in the car. The four of them just stood there, surrounded by other children's fun and noise, too traumatised to take part.

They knew it was coming up to teatime and that was now their one reference point, so we all climbed back into the car and went home.

After tea, I tried to get them talking about the meeting,

because I felt it might help them to get it out in the open. I thought I had prepared them so well for this day, but it seemed to me now that I hadn't done nearly enough. This was the last time they would see their birth family, at least until they were adults, but I don't think the enormity of it had really taken root.

It was an awful situation and, as before, there was no counselling offered to them, which I felt was very harsh. It had been a significant experience for them, but in all the wrong ways, and we were left to pick up the pieces.

18

Choosing Names

'I have contacted Dan Tillman regarding your request for name changes.'
Extract from a social worker's letter to the children

'Come on, kids. We need to have a discussion.' I gathered them round the dining-room table one Sunday morning.

'What about?' asked Hamish with an anxious look.

'Don't worry. Nobody's done anything wrong.' Well, that wasn't quite true of course, because there wasn't even half a day without one of them messing up! But it wasn't the point of the meeting. 'I want to explain to you about the last part of the adoption.'

'When will that be?' asked Anita.

'I don't know. We haven't been given a date yet. But on that day, we will all go and see a judge, who will give each of you a piece of paper that says this is your new mummy and daddy.' I paused to let that sink in. 'And that's when you can change your name if you like.'

'But how can we change our names?' puzzled Hamish.

'Well, being adopted means having a new start. And that

means having new names as well, if you want. But you don't have to. Or you could change it just a bit, so you could be Hamish Mackay Merry if you don't want to lose your old names.'

'I don't want to be Hamish and I don't want to be Mackay.'

'Well, what names are you going to have then?'

'Can we choose anything we like?'

'For your first name, yes.'

He pondered for a few moments, while we all waited with mounting interest.

Eventually I thought perhaps he might need a bit of help. 'It's probably a good idea to choose something similar to your old name,' I said. 'You don't want to be Hamish one day and Benjamin the next!'

He looked anxious.

'The English name for Hamish is James,' I suggested.

'I like James,' he decided. 'I could be Jamie.'

'Yes, Jamie is good.'

He smiled.

'What about you, An?' I gulped, hoping she didn't choose something too glamorous or outrageous that she might regret later.

'I'm going to be Anastasia,' she said, with a toss of her long, shining hair.

'That would be fine, An. But it's quite a mouthful. What about Anna, or Stacey?'

'Yes,' she agreed. 'But Anna is too much like Anita. I like Stacey.' She smiled brightly. 'Stacey,' she repeated. 'I really like it. I want to be Stacey. And I can have Anastasia as my middle name. Stacey Anastasia.'

'Are you absolutely sure?'

'Yes.'

'And what about you, Caroline?' I was really worried about her name. She was already called a lot of different names because of her speech problems, so if they didn't see it written down, one person might call her Carla, another might say Carlynne, or Colleen . . . Poor thing, she was already confused enough about her identity, with so many different names and pronunciations. I didn't think she would cope with a completely different name.

'Caroline, a lot of your friends call you Carrie, don't they?' I said. 'So you could change your name to Carrie if you like,' I suggested. 'What do you think about having Carrie as your proper name?'

'OK,' she nodded. 'Can I be Carrie Stephanie?'

I hesitated only a split second, because she couldn't pronounce her Ss, but she wouldn't need to say it much. 'Yes, that would be lovely.'

Finally I turned to Simon. 'What about your name? Would you like a new name too?'

'Yes.'

'Any ideas?'

'No.' He hunched his shoulders. 'Can you choose?'

'What about Sam? That's a good name.'

Simon nodded and said it to himself.

'Now we have to decide on your last name. Do you want to join the two names and have Mackay-Merry?'

'I don't want Mackay,' said Hamish.

'No, no, no, not Mackay,' agreed Anita.

'Why can't we just have Merry? I want to be Jamie Merry.'

'Yes. Let's all have Merry,' they agreed.

So that was decided.

'Can we start with our new names straight away?' asked Anita.

'No, we'll have to wait till we sign the papers,' I explained. 'The schools are not supposed to change your names until then, so we'd better do the same.'

Hamish screwed up his face. 'But I start my new school soon. Can't I start with my new name? People always pick on me with my old name being so different.'

'I'll go along and see your new head teacher,' I agreed. 'I expect they will do it if they're allowed to. Then they won't have to change all their records just a few weeks later.'

I spoke to our local Social Services and they agreed to sign a letter, giving permission for the secondary school to register Hamish in his new name, Jamie Merry. Next, I went to see the headmistress at the secondary school.

'We're adopting all the children,' I explained to her. 'The eldest will be coming here this September and the adoption should be finalised only a month or two later.'

'Yes?'

'And Social Services have signed this letter for you to register him with his new name, Jamie Merry.' I handed her the short letter and she quickly read it through.

'Right,' she nodded. 'That will be fine. I'll pass this on

to the office and they will make all the necessary arrangements.'

September came around and Hamish went into school on the first day with a cheery wave. But he came out close to tears.

'All the boys made fun of me,' he wailed. 'They called me "Haggis" and "Hag-boy", and made loony faces at me.' He buried his head in his hands while I drove away, furious that the school had been so insensitive as to ignore my request, despite the local authority's official permission.

The next morning, I went into the school, all guns blazing. I didn't ask anyone; I just marched straight into the headmistress's office.

'You said you would make sure that my boy's records would be changed and you would use his new name. But you broke your word and let us down badly.'

'I'm sorry, Mrs . . . ?'

'Merry.'

'Oh well, you know, Mrs Merry, all our paperwork . . . the office, you know . . .' I had caught her off-guard and she was flustered.

'This boy was so excited about his first day at his new school, expecting to be Jamie Merry, only to find he is still Hamish Mackay. Some of the other children called him names and bullied him. He had a terrible day, and it need not have happened.' I was on a roll now. 'Why didn't you pass on that letter and amend your paperwork as you said you would?'

'To "Jamie"?'

'Well, yes!'

'I . . . I'm not sure . . .'

'It's not for me to tell you your job, but I am very disappointed.' I marched straight out again.

I carried on fuming to myself all the way home. Wasn't it bad enough that the poor lad had wrinklies like us for his parents? We couldn't change that, but I had done all I could to ensure that we could avoid this situation, and the school could not do this one simple thing to help us protect a child from being bullied and upset! I felt like shouting out Anita's favourite phrase.

One day an official form came in the post, with a compliment slip from Social Services, asking me to sign it. I read it all through. It was asking me to keep the contact going with their birth parents, but they had made it clear to me several times lately that they didn't ever want to see their mum again and Hamish in particular was scared that she might come looking for him. I didn't feel it was right for me to sign away the children's rights to decide. I didn't want to sign it, so I called the number to tell them.

'You must sign the letterbox contact form, Mrs Merry,' said a snooty voice at the other end of the phone.

'I can't sign it on behalf of the children, because this is not what they want.'

'It's just about keeping the contact channel open,' she explained. 'The parents have got feelings too, you know.'

I wasn't making any progress there, so I rang our solicitor.

'Just sign it,' he advised. 'Because it's not worth the paper it's written on.'

'OK.' So I signed it and sent it off.

Finally the date came through for us all to go to court and meet the judge who would hopefully confirm the decision made by the professionals.

It was time for one more round-the-table meeting with the kids to make sure they understood, as I explained what would happen on the day itself.

'And then the judge will probably want to talk to each of you.'

'What for?' asked Hamish.

'To ask you if you understand what adoption is and if you're happy to be adopted.'

'I can't wait!' exclaimed Anita.

'What can't you wait for, to change your name or to be our child?'

'Both,' she laughed.

'Then, when the judge is sure you all understand what adoption is and are happy about it, he or she will ask me to sign the papers for each of you.'

'What do the papers say?' asked Hamish.

'They put your old name and your new name. They say that you are now becoming the daughter or son of Mike and Trisha Merry. Do you think you will be happy for me to sign that for you?'

'Yes. I wish you could do it today,' sang out Anita.

'Well, it won't be long to wait now. Then you will be part of our family for the rest of your lives, or at least until you are grown up. Will that be OK?'

'Yes,' they all said.

'When you have signed the papers and adopted us,' Anita said with a grin, 'then we can be as naughty as we like.'

'Er, no,' I laughed. 'That's not the way it works. If you do something naughty, we will be just the same with you as we are now.'

'But you can't send us back if you adopt us.'

'That's true. But we will never want to send you back. We love you all too much to do that. That's why we're adopting you. And we will always be honest with you, no matter what. Honesty is very important for you too. We all have to trust each other. If you can't trust me, who can you trust? When we sit here together and talk about things, we must all be honest and say what's really happened, or how we really feel.'

'I feel happy!' Caroline smiled.

'Good. How do the rest of you feel about the adoption? Hamish?'

'Yes, I'm glad too. I want to belong, and I don't ever want to be hungry again.'

'I'm excited because I'm going to have a proper family,' added Anita. 'I love being adopted.'

'What about you, Simon?' I asked. 'Do you understand what being adopted means?'

'Yes.'

'And how do you feel about it?'

'Good.'

The adoption day went very well. I signed the documents and took our copies away, one for each child and one for us. It all happened so quickly that it was almost an anticlimax, except that we were all so happy as we left the court building.

'Let's go and have lunch out,' suggested Mike. 'To celebrate being one family. Where do you want to go?'

'The place with the Knickerbocker Glory,' Stacey called out, and everyone agreed.

A few months after the adoption day, Social Services phoned me.

'Mrs Mackay is having another baby by the paedophile.'

'Right . . .'

'And she wants to know how the children are getting on.'

'Yes?'

'She would like to see them again.'

'I'm sorry, but a) the children don't want that, and b) I don't know whether I do.' I was quite adamant in not letting this happen, so I changed the subject. 'Why is she having another baby to be taken away?'

'That's nothing to do with you.'

'Next you'll be asking for them to see the paedophile too . . . and then Mrs Mackay's first husband who they didn't even know until the freeing-order meeting.'

'There's no need to take that tone, Mrs Merry.'

'Well, I think there is. If the children don't want to have any contact, it's not going to happen.'

'You signed the letterbox form.'

'Well, take me to court!'

19

Christmas Capers

'Carrie was the one inclined to go to her mum. But mum pushed her away.'

Extract from my diary

Every school holiday, all four of the kids were off the walls with energy and mischief, not to mention the bickering and spitefulness that went on every day, sometimes all day. Anyone with children will identify with this to an extent, but these four won the gold medal for family infighting. And it was even worse when we took them anywhere.

There were four holiday play centres in town. I can't remember what the first one was called, but they enjoyed their days there. The trouble was, all the other children suffered the effects of their invasion. I don't think any of the staff were used to handling children like ours, so they ran riot and took everything over, pushing all the other kids out of the way, taking their toys, getting paint all over everyone, knocking kids over by coming down the slide with arms and legs outstretched, spitting at them, swearing, snatching their food, scribbling on their colourings – everything you can think of . . . and more.

Every day the play-leader rang to complain about one or other of the children's latest misdemeanours and I had to go up there and remove them for the rest of the day. After two weeks I had their final call.

'Your children really are very, very difficult, Mrs Merry.'

'Really? I didn't know that!'

'Yes, I'm sorry, Mrs Merry. But we are just not able to cope with them any longer, so I'm afraid we will have to exclude them. We've tried to do our best with them, and on occasions we have enjoyed their lively company, but we are now losing other children because of your four.'

I looked up the local listings and found another play centre. I think it was called 'Bridge House'. I took them there for a while, but it was a similar story. So now they had all been banned from two play centres.

Right, I thought. I'm going to try the church children's club and play centre. Perhaps they'll be more patient and forgiving there. So off we all went with high hopes . . . and high spirits too, of course. This one was run by members of the congregation. Most of them, being more mature, were very kind and rather more tolerant than the youngsters that ran the first two play centres, so I was optimistic that this would be different.

Well, it did seem to go better for the first few days. Nobody phoned me, but I did notice the increasingly frazzled expressions on the helpers' faces each time I collected the kids. They were more long-suffering than the previous two places, but in the end the phone call came.

'So they're all banned?' I asked. 'Permanently?'

'Yes, I'm afraid so. But you could try St Mark's sports centre,' added the woman. 'I believe they have spaces in their holiday scheme.'

So I booked them into St John's and the first morning I took them everyone was very welcoming. It was a bright and airy place with lots of space and several sporting activities on offer, as well as a large play area, with a number of smiling helpers, so I hoped it would work out this time.

'Would you like to buy a raffle ticket?' asked a sports coach, standing by a child's bike on a stand – a beautiful, big, sporty, shiny yellow bike.

'Can we have a ticket each?' asked Jamie. They were all looking at it enviously, and eight-year-old Sam couldn't take his eyes off it.

'Why not?' I said, smiling at the coach and giving him the £4.

Sadly, things went downhill from there. The looks from other parents when I dropped them off there in the mornings, the phone calls for me to collect them early, the stories of complaints . . . I knew the day would come, and it did.

So now, all four of the children had been banned from every play centre in the city, and the eldest was still just twelve years old.

'We were only naughty,' said Sam on the way home.

Fortunately, it was near the end of the holidays, and the weather was good enough for them to run wild in the garden. Then they all went back to school and things moved on, so I was surprised one day to receive a phone call from St Mark's.

'Is this Mrs Merry?' he asked.

'Yes.'

'And you have a son called Sam Merry?' I could tell from the way he spoke through gritted teeth that he wasn't comfortable making this call.

'That's right. I'm really sorry that my children were so naughty you had to ban them,' I said, assuming this was a belated call from him to explain what happened.

'No, I'm not ringing about that, Mrs Merry.' I could hear him take in a sharp breath. 'Sam's won the bike.'

Well, I'd forgotten all about that. But Sam hadn't. He was thrilled when I told him later – the most enthusiastic I think I've ever seen him.

I could tell this was probably the last person they would have wanted to win their raffle, but at least they were honest enough not to draw it again.

I couldn't face the embarrassment of collecting the bike myself, so I had to send Mike. The irony was that because Sam had been banned, he couldn't go with Mike to collect his prize.

Christmas always had a long lead-in at our house. It started at the beginning of September with making the mincemeat, then later in September we had fun making the Christmas pudding. They all helped me weigh and measure the different ingredients, taking turns to stir the mixture and make a wish.

The first week in December is when we put the Christmas trees up. This is when Mike and I almost come to blows, every year.

'Why does it have to be so early?' he always asked, as if it was a new question.

'Because it's our family tradition. It's good for the children to have traditions, and it gives us a longer time to enjoy it all.'

'Well, why can't we just have one tree?'

'Because that would only be in one room.'

We always had one tree in the breakfast room, one tree in the sitting room and one in the dining room. And the children decorated them all. We used to have a competition to see who could decorate theirs best. They had boxes and boxes of decorations to choose from, but they usually all ended up fighting over one length of tinsel!

These are the things I used to do with my grandmother when I was little, and you never forget that. I think it's important to offer children traditional things – all the things they had never experienced before.

For these children, it was two extremes. The environment they came from, they had nothing – no toys, no decorations, hardly any food. They couldn't remember Christmas before they came to us.

'Oh, we used to send packages in for them at Christmas,' Steve told me once. 'With toys and crackers and food.' I asked Jamie about that and he made a face.

'Dad used to sell them,' he shrugged. 'And even after he went, all the things that Social Services gave us got sold by Mum or her boyfriends.'

To come from that level of deprivation, into a household

where there seems so much . . . Perhaps I made the mistake of thinking that, by overcompensating, it would make things better for them. Now, looking back, I don't think it did. It just confused them, and possibly made it even harder for them to cope.

I remember once hearing a psychiatrist talking about ways to handle a child's bad behaviour.

'You may find,' he said, 'that by taking some things away from the child, it might stop the temper tantrums.'

On one occasion, when Jamie had just thrown a very big wobbly that frightened us all, I calmed him down and told him about that.

'There are various ways I could deal with your anger, and one of them is that I might have to take something away from you.'

'OK,' he muttered, kicking the chair leg and avoiding my gaze.

'How would that make you feel?'

He shrugged. 'All I had when I was young, was my mum, and they took me away from her,' he said. 'So what can you take away that beats that?'

He was right, of course. Good, bad or indifferent, she was his mother. I mulled it over for a minute or two, as we sat in silence.

'Right, Jame,' I said to him. 'I've thought about it, and this time I'm not going to. But next time there will have to be some action. If I don't take something away, I might have to keep you in, or stop you watching television, or . . . There has to be a sanction, something that will help you see how important it is not to get so angry that you frighten everyone like you did today. OK?'

With his head down, he gave a slight nod.

'If you lose control like that at school, you might have all kinds of people coming in and what we don't need is all the Social Services and everyone playing the heavy with you or with us.'

I've often found that children can say things which absolutely knock you off your perch, just like Jamie did that day.

He's never grown out of that sensitivity to anything someone might say to him, at home or at school, which he mistakes as a personal criticism and it sets off a tantrum. He always had to be the leader, the father figure to his siblings, so it's understandable that he doesn't take criticism well. But despite everything, I still really love him. Funny boy. He wants to get things right.

Something I had always done with foster children as well as those we had adopted, was to put up a photo of their parents, or at least their mother, somewhere in the house. Usually it was a positive thing, but occasionally it had quite the opposite effect.

I had scanned and printed a photo of Jill and pinned it up on the drawing board where they could all see it. It had been up so long that I didn't think they were taking any notice of it, until I saw all the little pinpricks where they had been stabbing her eyes. I quietly took down that photo and replaced it with another and within hours they had stabbed her eyes out completely. I didn't see whether it was one or all of them doing it, but each time I just replaced the damaged photo with another copy. In the end it stopped. I suppose they got fed up with stabbing it every time.

I did ask Stacey about it once, when we were chatting in the kitchen.

'Well . . .' she replied in a cold voice, 'she was a prostitute . . .'

That silenced me for a moment. I had no idea she even knew that word. 'Well, how do you know she was?'

'If a woman goes upstairs with different men, what is it?'

I realised how slow I had been to see how attuned these children's perception of their mother could be. They may not fully understand what they witness . . . but they take in enough to process it in their own immature way. And from that, they are taken into the care system, where everything is sanitised – their history wiped clean. This is now your new home; like it or lump it. So forget how bad that was because you're going to be OK now . . . Well, it doesn't work like that.

Despite everything, Carrie's feelings towards her mother still niggled at her. It was about three years since the freeing-order meeting, and I think she was the only one who had been concerned that she might never see her any more.

'I think I'd like to see my mum again,' she said to me one day.

'Do you really want to see her?'

She pondered for a moment. 'Yes.'

'Are you sure?' It worried me that of all the children, it

should be Jill's least favourite child who had changed her mind. 'You haven't seen her for quite a while now.'

'I know.'

'Do you want me to ring up and ask?'

'Yes, please.'

The following morning, I asked her again. 'Do you really want to see your mum?'

'Yes, please.'

So I called the letterbox contact line and told them.

'Oh,' said the familiar snooty voice. 'I'll ask Jill if that's what she wants.'

'Not long ago you told me she wanted to see the children.'

'Yes, she wanted to see all of them.'

'But maybe not Carrie on her own?' I didn't like the way this conversation was going. I feared for Carrie and wished I hadn't acted on her wish, but I couldn't ignore it.

'I will ask Jill and let you know.' The line went dead.

Only a few minutes later, the phone rang.

'I asked Jill and she said no, she didn't want to see Carrie again.'

'But why?'

'That's all I can tell you, Mrs Merry. Goodbye.'

So now I had to think how I was going to break this news to Carrie.

'Mummy feels that her life is OK at the moment,' I explained to her later that morning. 'And she doesn't feel it's a good time to meet at the moment. She thinks it would upset you and upset her.'

But this was a child with learning difficulties and a very young cognitive age. It was all too much for her to take in and cope with. She was distraught and I could do nothing to console her.

20

Knitting with Fog

'A lot of troubles.'

Extract from my diary

We had lived in our house since before we adopted the children. But my fostering agency became so successful it grew out of its first basement offices in Victoria Road and now needed to take over the whole house. So we looked around for another large house, this time without any neighbours to complain about the children's noise and their various antics.

As soon as we saw this beautiful old farmhouse at the end of a long drive, in rolling countryside a few miles out of the city, we knew it was the place for us. We were surrounded by fields and a long way from anywhere, but there was a bus that plied the country lanes and passed the end of our drive, on the way into town, so we felt it was perfect. Somewhere for the children to breathe fresh air and run riot to their hearts' content.

It came as a complete surprise to me when people expressed criticisms and suspicions about our move.

'Why are you bringing the children here? It's very remote,' sneered one health visitor.

'Because it's such an idyllic place to bring children up in,' I replied. 'And because of their background, they can be quite difficult, so it gives them the freedom to be themselves without having to worry about annoying the neighbours.' But I saw what she wasn't saying and I'd have loved to tell her: No, we're not going to beat them up, we're not going to sexually abuse them, we're not going to torture them!

'Well, if they're that difficult, why did you adopt them?'

'Because we wanted to, and because we love them.'

'Who chooses to live so far away from anywhere?' asked a teacher.

'We chose it as a family,' I replied, as sweetly as possible, wanting to ask why it mattered to him. 'We had a family meeting and everyone agreed.'

I suppose that it might have looked a bit odd to some people. But it was right for us.

The move had come at a time when all four children were being bullied in school, and three of them were causing various degrees of mayhem as well. After a period of relative calm, I was constantly in demand again.

Carrie, aged ten, had a superb support worker at her school, but her attention-seeking led her to making unfair and usually untrue accusations against me, her support worker Tracey or anyone else, pitting us all against each other, to gain any kind of attention to herself. Mrs Harris fully understood Carrie and did everything she could to smooth out all these situations.

'My mum beat me up last night,' she would tell her support worker one day, and then that evening she would tell me, 'Tracey hit me today.'

'Oh,' I'd say. 'I had better come into school and see Mrs Harris about that then.'

So the next morning I'd go into school and see Mrs Harris. Carrie was called in to join us and confronted with the things she'd said.

'I didn't say that,' she insisted. 'Mum didn't beat me.' And later: 'Tracey didn't hit me.' But she was now in the head teacher's study, with all our attention on her. Just what she wanted.

The next day, and every day, it would be something else. 'Mum smacked me,' she told them one time, and another time, 'Mum wouldn't let me out of my room', or 'Mum didn't give me anything to eat'. Whatever it was, I'd be called in.

The same happened when she came home from school. If her support assistant so much as looked at another child, Carrie would be enraged that she wasn't focusing entirely on her, so she always tried to make trouble. It would be 'Tracey pulled my hair today', or 'Tracey stabbed my arm with a pencil', or 'Tracey wouldn't let me have my lunch' . . . I became a constant visitor in poor Mrs Harris's office, and she was always so calm and so patient about it all. That woman was a saint. Tracey was very long-suffering too.

I tried to explain to Carrie at home. 'If you say things that aren't true about Tracey, she might leave and then you won't have anyone to help you. You might even have to leave the school yourself, for telling lies about people.' But I could see that, with her learning difficulties, Carrie just didn't understand that actions have consequences.

Fortunately, Mrs Harris and Tracey agreed with me that there was no malice in her. Everything she did was a claim for attention and we rode the storms together.

This was the best school the kids went to and Mrs Harris was the best head teacher. She organised speech therapy, reading tests and all sorts for them. Sam made four years' progress in his reading in one year there.

But when it was time for Carrie to move to the next school, that's when things became really bad for her. Because of her low cognitive age and her speech defect, she was always getting picked on, kicked or sat on in the play-ground and came home from school in tears most days. I used to tell her teacher and it might get better for a bit, but not for long.

Every day they were ringing me about Carrie. 'She's spitting at other children . . . she's making rude gestures . . . she's forgotten her homework.'

'This child has learning difficulties. She's got a ten-minute attention span,' I would say. 'That's why she often loses her way between classrooms, or forgets what you've asked her to do. Her homework was out for her to bring this morning, but she must have forgotten to put it in her bag.'

On one particular occasion, I dropped off the others and then took her to the doctor for something in the morning and we got to the school at breaktime. She found her friends, but then another girl came up to her.

'Oh, there you are, Carrie,' she said. 'Vicky's looking for you because she wants to start a fight with you.'

'I was really scared,' Carrie told me later. 'Vicky is a bad bully and she always spites me.'

'So what happened?' I asked.

'Vicky came over to me and she kept hitting me. I didn't want to hit her because she is smaller than me. I didn't want to get told off.' I took that with a pinch of salt.

Apparently, quite a crowd gathered. Sam saw it and tried to intervene, which got him into another fight, and the older children on the adjoining playground went to look. Big brother Jamie saw it was Carrie and Sam and jumped over the wall to rescue them. Fortunately he managed to stop the fights that day.

The school phoned me up and I had to go and collect Carrie and Sam early. That was when I decided to take Carrie out of that school and look for one more suitable for her, somewhere that would cater better for her learning difficulties.

I tried every school and special unit I could find, but nobody was willing to take her at that stage, so I just had to keep her at home for the rest of the year and teach her myself.

When she did get a place for the following September, it was in a small special needs unit at a private school, where she started at a year below her actual age, which was much better for her.

But that wasn't the end of it. One day Carrie ran away across the meadow to the next farm and found somebody to speak to. She apparently told them I had beaten her with a stick on the set-aside field. Well, we'd been out looking for her and came back to find the police, social workers, everybody waiting for us. I showed them all into the house and a policewoman undressed Carrie to see the wounds she'd complained of.

'What did you find?' I asked her.

'Nothing,' she said in a surprised voice. 'There's not a mark on her.'

'Well, I did tell you she wasn't telling the truth. It's not really her fault. She had a difficult background until they all came here. She never had enough attention when she was small, so she's been trying to make up for it ever since.'

'So did your mum, Trisha, hit you?' asked the social worker again, just to make sure.

'No,' muttered Carrie, looking down at the floor.

Eventually they left us to ourselves again, to another 'normal' evening of madness and mayhem.

That night, after the children had all gone up to bed at last, Mike and I flumped into our chairs in the living room. We talked about the incident with Carrie and I told him about Jamie's temper tantrum when they came in and Stacey's latest misdemeanour at school.

'The trouble is, I daren't even sit down to have a coffee or the phone will ring from Stacey's school and tell me she's stolen the class's dinner money, or exposed herself to a teacher . . .'

There were times, and that was one of them, when Mike and I looked at each other and both gave out a long, slow breath.

'I hope this is the bumpiest it's going to be,' I said.

'Hope is all we can do,' he agreed.

After years of social workers, health visitors, agency workers and the like before we adopted the children, it was quite
a relief to have them to ourselves at last, now that we'd
adopted them, but it does suddenly hit you that you really
are on your own.

As the children's behaviour worsened and their rebel-
liousness increased, I was nearly ready to give up some
days, things were so bad. There seemed no end to it all. It
felt like whatever I did, somebody would tell me I was
wrong. I talked to lots of the experienced agency staff as
well as a couple of psychologists I knew and asked for
their suggestions about how to deal with the children's
problems, but they all gave conflicting advice, so I was
even more confused.

I was knitting with fog with these kids. I tried everything
the experts suggested. I felt like I was holding a pair of
scales all the time. On the one hand, if I did this, or on the
other hand . . . Was this really just teenage hormones, as
some people suggested, or was it me doing things wrong?

That's when I decided to join an adoption support group.
I went in and sat in this room with about twenty-five other
people, all of whom seemed to have adoption breakdowns.

They were all moaning that they hadn't been given
enough information. Some of them had young people with
schizophrenia, others had children who were heavily into
drugs and all sorts. My God, they made my four sound like

angels! I remember sitting near this lady called Morag who ran the group and she had circles round her eyes and half-way down her cheeks. She looked as if she'd just been bombed.

A social worker stood up. 'Right, what you all need is respite, and you need some training sessions, and you need help with . . .'

We sat around the room, lapping this up. 'Ah, lovely. At last – just what we need.'

'Of course, if we had the funding, this is what we would do, but . . .'

There was a loud, collective sigh of frustration around the room.

'Why have we come here?' asked one woman. 'If all we're going to be told is this is what you could have if we could afford it, but we can't?'

I became quite hostile and this social worker didn't seem to understand why. Morag was bravely trying to cool our anger.

Then somebody who vaguely knew me called out: 'Don't talk about social workers to Trisha. She's likely to get up and thump you!' Somebody else said something about Social Services telling lies.

'Huhh,' I said. 'Don't even get me on that. And don't get me started on why one person who needs it most can't have information when everybody else has that information, but won't admit to it.'

By this time, everyone was laughing, so at least it broke the tension. The woman sitting next to me turned towards me.

'Have you adopted them?'

'Yes.'

'Problems?'

'Yes, you could say that.'

'I'm a solicitor,' she said. 'And I work on behalf of adopted children. If ever you need me . . .' She gave me her card and I put it in my bag.

That evening I told Mike where I'd been. 'I don't think I'll be going there again,' I said.

'Why?'

'I don't think I've ever seen so much misery in one room!'

Stacey, reaching puberty at twelve, was now going out of control. I don't think she could handle how she felt. She wrote letters saying she wanted to have sex with as many people as she could. She ran off to a girlfriend's house one night and didn't come back till the next night. This happened quite a few times after that.

One day she came back from her dance class with a pair of see-through tights on, but no knickers or skirt. Everybody could see.

There was something new every day, sometimes more than once a day. She was either sitting next to a boy on the school bus with her blouse undone, or she was stealing money from people's pockets in the cloakroom, or stuff from their lockers. She drew sexually insulting notes and passed them round her class, and she drew sexually explicit graffiti all round the school. And every time I was called in to help them deal with it or to bring her home. It got so much that we arranged for her to see a therapist for a few sessions. I went to see him myself and told him what was going on.

'This is out of my league,' I said. 'What should I do about it?'

'Oh, she might grow out of it. It's just a reaction to something she's seen.'

It was all causing huge problems at Stacey's school.

'You can't go to school looking like that, Stacey,' I would say, when she was plastered with make-up and had an old blouse on that was so tight it was bursting.

Or if she was meeting her friends, she would have pulled her V-necked sweater right down to leave nothing to the imagination, thinking I wouldn't notice. When I stopped her, she took it personally.

'Don't you want me to go out looking pretty?'

'But Stace, you can't go out like that, and you've got no knickers on, have you?'

The school was constantly ringing me up to complain about her, and people were phoning me and saying: 'I saw your Stacey in town. God, didn't she look terrible?'

The incident that I remember the best was all about a skirt. I bought Stacey a new school skirt, which had to be no more than two inches above the knee. I made sure that it was actually knee-length, so there would be no argument.

She put on her new skirt and looked very demure as she came down to breakfast in it. She still had that skirt on when she left for school, but within the hour I had Mrs Hacket on the phone from the school office.

'Mrs Merry, can you come in?'

'Right,' I said.

I went in to see Mrs Baker, the headmistress, and noticed straight away the disapproving expression on her face, like a bad smell.

'Good morning, Mrs Merry,' she began, pointing me to a seat next to Mrs Hacket. 'We were just wondering why you allowed Stacey to come to school in such inappropriate school uniform.' 'No, I didn't. She's wearing the knee-length skirt I bought her in the school shop.'

'That's no skirt,' she said. 'Mrs Hacket tells me it's a boob-tube.'

'No. I'm sorry but that can't be right. I saw her walk down the road to school in her knee-length skirt.'

'Well, all I know is that Mrs Hacket followed her down the corridor and she said it was so short she could see the cheeks of Stacey's bottom. And when she turned round, it apparently left nothing to the imagination at the front.'

'No, you definitely must have the wrong girl. I bought her skirt myself from the school shop.'

But after a lot of toing and froing, I discovered that she had indeed changed out of her skirt and into a tiny, elasticated boob-tube as soon as she got to school.

'It was in her locker,' said Mrs Hacket. 'So that confirms it, I think, don't you? And while I was there, I noticed a load of make-up in there too. Do you let her bring make-up to school?'

'Certainly not,' I said.

'Then she must be stealing it.'

'Oh, I don't think so. She has plenty of make-up of her own at home.'

'But not at school,' said the head. 'Until she stole it.'

The trouble was, Stacey now had such a high profile in that school, because she had so often stolen and broken the rules, that she was automatically the one they would suspect. In this case they were right, but it was a different story when they suspended her for stealing money and phones from her classmates' bags when she arrived late at a drama lesson, following a lecture from another teacher about her bad behaviour.

As soon as the others noticed their things were missing, they all looked at Stacey.

She was hauled up before the head of year and made to write a statement about what she was doing when she arrived late. As usual, she couldn't resist embroidering her story and making it sound much more dramatic, so that didn't help her case either. The head of year didn't believe her and suspended her for the rest of the week.

Of course, I wasn't sure whether to believe her or not, but she was adamant that she hadn't done it this time.

'You know the story about the boy who cried "wolf"?' I asked her, and explained how it related to her. 'That's the trouble, Stace. Even if you didn't do it, they're all going to think you did.'

'Hang on a minute,' Stacey said. 'They put a CCTV camera where everyone left their coats and bags. Maybe that will show who did it.'

I phoned up the school and asked if somebody could check the CCTV footage for the time Stacey was supposed to have been stealing all these things. The next thing I knew there was a phone call from the head of year to say it had been someone else, so Stacey could come back to school.

'Don't you think you owe Stacey an apology?' I suggested.

He mumbled something and put the phone down.

The next day, Stacey came home with a supposed letter of apology from this man. It was very brief:

Dear Stacey,
Because of your past behaviours, I'm sure you can understand
why I made the judgement I did.
Mr Archer.

'Not much of an apology, is it, Mum?' grinned Stacey.

I went into the school to see Mr Archer the following morning, all guns blazing.

'Surely you should have checked the CCTV before suspending Stacey? You should have looked at the evidence.'

He looked me in the face. 'Well, of course she's a trouble-maker.'

'But that's beside the point. She hasn't actually done anything this time.'

'Only because somebody else beat her to it.'

'That's not fair.'

'The trouble with you, Mrs Merry, is you're too

overprotective. It doesn't matter what any of your children do, you'll always believe they couldn't have done it.'

'Well, she didn't do it this time,' I said abruptly and flounced out, slamming his door, which gave me some satisfaction.

21

Just a Joke

'Their secondary school must take some responsibility for the children not doing better. They were all bullied at school.'
Extract from a psychologist's report

When she was thirteen I moved Stacey to a small, private Christian school, because I thought it might be better for her. But her lying and her stealing only accelerated all the more. We had complaints about her unauthorised absences, even though I'd dropped her off at school every morning. More than once we were called into the school because she had been found in a classroom with a group of lads in a state of undress.

At home, Stacey constantly overrode the others. 'No, I'm going in with Dad to get the fish and chips on Friday night,' she insisted, and the others just backed down.

But it was her effect on Sam that was the most worrying. Stacey has always admitted to being a drama queen and she certainly made the most of any opportunity to act up and shock the other three. She often tried to frighten them in different ways.

On at least a couple of occasions, Stacey walked into

Sam's bedroom with nothing on but her knickers and said to him: 'What are you going to do about it?'

He was horrified, poor lad. No wonder he was such a mixed-up kid.

Not long after I found out about this, a friend of mine came up from Cheltenham to stay for a few days. Alison is a play therapist and was interested in all the tales of woe I told her about the children. While I was cooking, I suggested she go and look round the house as we'd just finished doing it all up and the children each had their own bedrooms.

'Go and look at Sam's art in his bedroom,' I said. He loved drawing and painting and had put some of his artwork up on display.

She came back into the kitchen with a serious expression that made me stop what I was doing.

'Sam needs help, Trisha,' she said.

'Well, his drawing is quite good,' I replied, completely misunderstanding what she meant.

'No, have you seen his play?'

She made me go up with her and have a look.

All the bedrooms were big and he had a pasting table down one side of his. He had a King Arthur's Castle model, with dragons and all sorts of other extras. So we'd given him this pasting table to do all the enactments on. He had a lot of Lego, with the Lego people, and his model farm.

When we had climbed the two flights of stairs to his room, I saw some of the farm set out on the pasting table.

'Ahh, he's always loved this farm,' I told Alison,

thinking it was some kind of security for him that he still played with it.

'Have you really looked at how he's set it out?' she asked.

'No. Why?'

'Look how he's got the farm hedging around the edge, with four Lego children and two adults inside. And then he's got two more people over here with the dragons, down on the ground. And look at this group of people, quite a lot of them, on this side. He's put lots of animals around them, all lying on their sides.' She paused. 'And over here' – she pointed at a separate group – 'these people are surrounded by lots of dead animals, big, small, all sorts of animals. And there's the same thing in the opposite corner.'

She had me worried now. I had never really looked at all this before, but now I was beginning to catch on to what she was talking about. I dreaded what else she was going to tell me.

'Now,' she said, pointing at the first group, surrounded by hedges, 'this is Sam and his family, in here, protected by this. And over here are the baddies. They've all been killed now. These people over here . . .' she explained, 'they're the baddies now.'

I looked at it all and I thought, yes, I can see . . . I knew nothing about play therapy, so I'd always fondly thought it was just Sam playing imaginary games. A part of me still wondered, was she reading too much into this? Something that may not be there at all?

But I've read up on it since and I've learned that there are certain patterns that follow people's experiences, like people who've been in concentration camps always keeping their larders full of food throughout their lives, just in case.

I knew Sam had kept his Pokemon cards – just the monstery ones. He still had nightmares most nights, as they all did from time to time. He was always afraid of the dark and had to have the light on all night. He never did talk about his emotions.

It was chilling, seeing what Alison made of Sam's play with the farm. I'd always thought that, being the youngest, he had been the least affected by his early life, but now it seemed he too, like the others, may have been the subject of these paedophile predators' abuse, and still kept the after-effects locked up inside him.

It made me all the more desperate to get therapy organised for all of them.

As all the children's problems continued and their behaviours escalated, their need for some sort of counselling therapy seemed more acute than ever. But for all four of them I knew the costs would be way beyond our means, so I had to try to think of a way to fund the therapy. Then I remembered that solicitor I'd met at the adoption support group, so I found her card and rang her number.

'Can I come and see you?'

We arranged an appointment and I went along to her office.

'What are the chances of suing their local authority?' I asked. 'Because these children desperately need therapy. They're wrecking their lives. Their wrecking everyone's chances at school, they're wrecking our home life, and we can't go on like this.'

'Do you have any evidence of the local authority's negligence?'

I told her about the different sets of case notes and Michael Warren being given information about my children that they had refused to give me. I explained the background of how they had neglected the children's welfare and safety for so long.

She agreed to take on the case and secured a pot of funding to pay for it, so we thought it was all going ahead. She interviewed us and put together a file of evidence to apply for a court case. All we had to do was wait for a date for the case to begin and then it would be all systems go.

Meanwhile, with the other three causing their own problems at school, I had not really given much thought lately to Sam's situation. He had done very well at his primary school, and he never complained, even though I had the feeling he was still being bullied for his detached manner. He never really took part in things, in class or with the other children. He didn't want to do group activities and he refused to be in any plays they put on. It was all part of his autistic tendency that I'd never had diagnosed. He had a hard enough time with it, I thought, without having a label.

It was Sam's first year at secondary school, and at that time this school was renowned for its bullying. One day he came home a gibbering wreck, with a terrible tale to tell. He was in such a state that it took us a long time to get it out of him, but what it came down to was that a group of boys had held him by the ankles from a third-floor balustrade, hanging upside down over the open stairwell.

Had it been Carrie telling me this, I wouldn't have believed it. Or Stacey, with all her dramatic fantasising. But the thing about any kind of autism is that the person cannot tell lies. Everything has to be literal. So I knew that, with Sam, there was no embroidering of the truth. He was telling me as it was.

I called the school number straight away, but it was too late, the call went to voicemail. I was livid. All the more so because there was no one I could talk to till the morning, so I took my frustrations out on everything inanimate, banging down the saucepans on the stove to get rid of my pent-up anger.

'What's the matter, Trisha?' asked Mike as we tidied up after the kids had gone to bed. 'I've been dodging bullets all evening.'

So I told him everything Sam had said. 'He was so upset, poor lamb,' I said.

'Petrified, I should think,' nodded Mike.

'I can't get that image out of my head. Him being dangled over that twenty-foot drop. How could they do that? It makes me shudder.'

I called the school first thing in the morning. 'I need to talk to the headmistress,' I said in my sternest voice. 'It's very urgent.'

'I'm afraid she's in a meeting at the moment. She won't be free till half past nine.'

'Right, I'll come in and see her then.'

'Well . . .' the secretary hesitated. 'I'm not sure if—'

'I want to make a formal complaint.'

'I see,' she said sounding surprised. 'I'll let her know you're coming, Mrs Merry.'

Then I rang Ken Piper, an adviser who goes to tribunals. He was as shocked as I had been to hear what had happened to poor Sam.

Mr Piper came into the school with me and when we got to the meeting room there was the headmistress, the assistant head and the chair of the board of governors. The secretary must have alerted them all.

'I want to make a formal complaint,' I began. 'Yesterday, my son Sam was held over the stairwell by his ankles by a group of children in your school.'

'It was a joke, Mrs Merry,' grinned the assistant head. 'I heard about it and spoke to the children involved, so I know it was just a joke.'

I saw red. 'Well, a good job they didn't drop him, then. Because, what would that have been? A farce?'

'Oh no, they wouldn't have dropped him.'

'I don't think you have any understanding of my children's needs.'

Mr Piper sat next to me, his long legs sticking out, his paperwork on his knees, and he looked shocked at the assistant head's response. Meanwhile, the headmistress said nothing. She was inscrutable.

'You have no idea about my children. You do not understand complex children's behaviour.'

The chair of governors was sat there, silent, next to the head.

'On the contrary, Mrs Merry and Mr Piper,' said the assistant head. 'We're well used to oddballs like your children.'

Still neither of the others said a word.

'Come along, Mrs Merry,' said Ken, 'I think we have heard all we need to hear. It's from the top down. Indicative.'

And we walked out together.

We stood by my car and he said: 'You've got a case here, Mrs Merry.'

I sighed with the weight of everything that kept hitting me. 'But I'm already fighting the local authority about their neglect of the children, and trying my best to cope with everything else that happens with teenage children. I can't, I just can't fight the school as well.' It was true. I felt it was all too much. I could not have gone to a tribunal just then. I couldn't. But I wished I had.

The only thing I could do was take Sam out of that school and find him somewhere more suitable, smaller and more caring. So he went to a private all-through school with a brilliant art department.

'Sam is a gifted artist, you know,' said his art teacher at the first parents' evening, and I was so glad that we moved him when we did.

But it didn't solve everything.

22

The Runaway

'A child who has been damaged in the past will sometimes actively spoil things to confirm their own unacceptability.'

Therapist's comment

Something strange was going on. We all noticed it. When any of us went to top up our mobile phones, we found large sums of credit already there.

'I've heard of gremlins getting into gadgets,' said Mike. 'But this is the other extreme.'

'A phone fairy, or something?' I suggested.

'Well, I don't know what it is, but I like it.'

'Perhaps the phone companies are giving out more generous freebies these days?'

'What's in it for them?'

'Maybe they're lulling us into a false sense of security . . . and then they'll strike with huge increases.'

Then I discovered it wasn't just us.

'There's something very odd happening to my phone,' said Jane one day. 'The credit keeps going up, but I haven't paid anything into it. Laura and Brett's phones are just the same. What do you think it can be?'

'Join the club. It's happening to us too.'

It was all quite a mystery . . . until my credit card bill arrived. That's when I saw all the payments to our phone providers, and for a lot more numbers than just the family. I called the bank, but they didn't know how it had happened.

'There does seem to have been a lot of irregular activity on your account, Mrs Merry. I have a note here that somebody in the fraud department did try to ring you, and left a message, twice. But you didn't call back.'

'Really? I don't remember that,' I said. 'But now I realise that so much money has gone . . . How did it happen?'

'All the mobile phone payments were made on your card,' they said. 'With your pin number.'

I checked my statement again, with a calculator, and all the phone payments added up to about two thousand pounds. I looked to see if one had received more than any of the others, but nothing jumped out at me. I just couldn't understand who would have done this.

'So,' I said to Mike. 'Somebody must have taken my card out of my bag, found out my pin code and used it to do the topping up.'

'But why?'

'Yes, it does seem very strange. Usually, fraudsters only benefit themselves, and most of the payments were for family phones.'

'Who do you think it could be?' he asked. The two of us sat there, puzzling it all through, and suddenly the penny dropped.

'Who's the most likely person in our family to think up a

devious way to gain credit on her own phone, without attracting suspicion?'

He looked at me with an open mouth. 'You mean Stacey?'

'Yes. Who else would pull a trick like this?' We had to laugh, but we weren't going to tell her that. And it was actually very serious. I couldn't afford to lose two thousand pounds.

When I confronted Stacey about it the next day, she openly admitted it; brazen as you like.

'Well, I have a lot of friends.' She shrugged. 'I needed to call them, but I never had enough credit on my phone. And you always say how important it is to have our phones with us when we go out, in case of emergency, so I didn't think you'd mind,' she said, smiling sweetly. 'I added some to their phones too.'

'But how did you get my pin number?'

'Oh I've known that for ages. I watched you use it at the checkout in Tesco's.'

'But why top up all our phones as well?'

'So that you wouldn't know it was me, of course,' she smirked. 'Don't you think that's quite clever?'

'Clever's not the word I'd use, Miss Stacey,' I said. 'It's a huge amount of money you've taken from me. But never again! I've cancelled this card and you can bet your bottom dollar I won't be telling you my new pin number!'

The value of money didn't seem to be on the kids' agenda. I suppose they had come from somewhere that had no money for anything they needed, to a home where everything they could possibly want, and more, was generously provided for them.

That combined with their disruptive behaviour and wrecking skills made an uncomfortable equation. I don't think most people realised just how destructive they all were, to each other, to us as a family, to school, to their clothes, to their toys. They would be given something and within hours it would be broken or lost.

'Where's your phone?' I asked Sam.

'Oh, it got lost somewhere.'

'But I only bought you that yesterday. It cost a hundred pounds, Sam.'

'I'm really sorry,' he mumbled. 'I don't know what happened.'

At least he apologised. I didn't usually get that from the others.

Shopping with Stacey one day for a new bra, she caught sight of a short denim skirt.

'Look at this skirt, Mum. Isn't it lovely?'

'It looks OK,' I said, checking the price ticket. 'It's far too expensive, love – £70,' I gulped. 'And there's hardly any material in it!'

'But it's so cool,' she said. 'All my friends have denim skirts, and I've wanted one for ages, but I never saw one I liked. But I really love this one. It's exactly what I always wanted.'

'What about getting the next size up?' I suggested, holding it up against her. 'That's much better. The length is more attractive, and you'll be able to wear it for longer.'

'But it doesn't show off my legs,' she wailed.

'Sometimes, it's better not to show off too much, Stace. Leave some things to the imagination.'

Judging from her withering expression, she thought I was too old-fashioned to have any opinion worth listening to.

'You just don't understand!'

But that was the problem, I understood only too well. Stacey was the ultimate believer in 'If you've got it, flaunt it.'

As usual, she was so persuasive that she had to have it as there was no other denim skirt in the world as good as this one. I reluctantly paid over the £70.

The next day I went into her room to put her laundry away and there, scrunched up on her bed, was the £70 denim skirt, with a wide ragged strip cut off, so that it was now shorter than a pelmet.

I picked it up and took it away. My first thought was to confront her with it immediately, but something told me to hang on to it for a few years, for the day when she was earning her own money and would understand the value of it. Perhaps then she would realise how disappointed I was.

Jamie had never stolen from us, or from anyone as far as I knew, since his food-stealing days were over. I don't believe he lied much either. His main Achilles heels had always been his anxiety and his anger.

However, as a teenager he became more and more obstreperous, and by the time he was fifteen Jamie was in total rebellion, running away for odd nights at friends' houses, not telling us where he was, getting up to all sorts of things we didn't know about. But he always turned up within twenty-four hours. Until one day.

We had found out that he was now smoking weed and drinking alcohol, though goodness knows where he got it all from. School maybe, or the youth club.

Thinking about it now, I suppose it takes a lot of guts for someone like me to ring up Social Services and say 'I'm struggling with this.' But that's what I did. I didn't want to go blundering in and get it wrong, but I knew we had to deal with this as a family. We couldn't just overlook his drug and drink problems, but I wanted some advice about the best way to approach it.

'Well, Mrs Merry,' said a detached voice at the other end of the phone. 'Why didn't you stop this before it started? Why haven't you talked it all through with him and engaged him in other things with you? Why don't you—?'

'Hang on, hang on,' I said, exasperated. 'Who will look after the other three, all of whom have their own individual needs, while I spend all my time with Jamie?'

'Well, how long have you allowed him to be on drink and drugs?'

'No, you've got it wrong. We haven't allowed it. We've only just discovered he's doing it.'

'You should have stopped him doing it.'

'If I tried to stop him, just like that, he would kick off and run away for good, so how would that help him? Anyway, we couldn't stop him if we didn't know.'

'Why didn't you know?'

'Look,' I said, as calmly as I could, 'all I want to do is find the best way to help him now. Do you have any suggestions?'

'Get a therapist,' she said.

I don't think I had ever felt more alone than I did that day, with no useful support from anyone, except of course Mike and my adopted family. The authorities just didn't have either the expertise or the money to help and being an adoptive parent is a lonely place when you can see it all crumbling in front of you.

I talked it through with Mike that evening and we decided what I would say when I broached it to Jamie. So the next day I sat down with him at the kitchen table while Mike took the others out to walk the dogs. But he seemed very wary and I think he knew. As soon as I started to speak, he flew into a rage and stormed out of the house.

That was it. He just went and, of course, we didn't panic. He'd come back like he always did. He might be a bit the worse for wear, but hopefully with no real harm done.

However, this time he didn't come back.

The following day we had a phone call from a woman with a raspy voice called Mrs Edwards.

'Jamie's staying here, Mrs Merry. He's told me all about it.'

'Right, OK.' I was so surprised that I didn't really know what to say. God knows what he had told her, so what could I say? I wasn't about to argue with a stranger about whatever accusations he might have made about us.

'You should never have children if you don't know how to look after them,' she admonished me. 'You've got to understand them. He's very unhappy, you know. He's in the same class as my grandson, and I've adopted my grandson, so I know all about adoption and how it works.'

'Do you?' I asked, with a mixture of irony and indignation. 'And if you want me to get in touch with Social Services, I will do that as well. They will need to know, Mrs Edwards, because Jamie is under sixteen and you need to have a CRB check, and you would need to inform me officially if you are thinking of fostering or adopting him privately. I would want to know that everything is done properly and the local authority needs to be fully involved.'

'Oh, I knew this would be your response,' she said in a superior voice, with more than a hint of annoyance, as she hung up.

A couple of days went by, and she called again. This time she spoke in a very irate voice.

'Mrs Merry, Jamie tells me he has no clothes, so I'm going to have to go out and buy him some.'

'Oh, don't do that,' I replied calmly. 'I'll bring his clothes over to you.'

She gave me her address and I went upstairs to Jamie's bedroom to pack some of them up for him in black bags, so that I could carry them straight out to the car.

Now, this lady lived in a narrow street at the back of Church Road, just round the corner from where we lived when the children first came to us. I pulled up outside her tiny Victorian cottage, and went to knock on her front door.

'Hello,' I said in a cheery voice as she opened the door a crack. 'I'm Jamie's mum.'

'Oh yes,' she said, opening the door wider. 'Have you brought Jamie's clothes?'

I nodded and went back to get out the first black sack, which I brought to her door and popped it down just inside.

'Thank you,' she said with evident resentment.

'No, that's just the first bag,' I said calmly as I went back and brought two more black bags, then two more, and two more.

Her eyes widened with every delivery. 'What's all this?'

'Oh, that's the contents of Jamie's two wardrobes,' I explained. 'I haven't emptied his chest of drawers yet. I'll bring all that tomorrow.'

'I can't have all this,' she said, running her fingers through her thin grey hair. 'He told me he had no clothes.'

'Well, as you can see, that wasn't quite true.'

True to my word, I took almost everything else round to her the following day.

She looked horrified. 'I can't take all that in,' she wailed. 'I haven't got room.'

'Well, I'll just leave them on your doorstep then, I said, trying to keep a straight face. 'Now, what do you want me to do with his weekend cases?' I asked her. 'And all his gadgets and other stuff?'

'Don't you bring them here, Mrs Merry, whatever you do. I can't take any more.'

'Well, perhaps this might teach you a lesson,' I said, as

kindly as I could in the circumstances. 'Please do not believe everything disgruntled teenagers tell you.'

'Well!' she huffed.

I didn't hear anything for a while, but at least I knew where he was, and when I checked with the school, he was still going there, so I thought I'd let him come to his senses and perhaps he would eventually come back as if nothing had happened.

But a few weeks later, I had another phone call from Mrs Edwards.

'I don't know whether you are aware, but your Jamie is smoking stuff.'

'Yes, we knew that he was drinking and smoking weed. That's why he left, when we tried to broach the subject with him. That's what all this is about, his act of rebellion, staying with you, not contacting us and everything.'

There was a short silence at the other end. 'Well, I don't want my grandson to be involved in this,' she said.

I don't know whether she turfed him out or whether he just left, but soon after that I discovered that this lady's grandson was the dealer Jamie had bought the drugs from.

Throughout this time, I texted him once a week, saying 'Are you OK?'. If he wanted to reply he did, but I didn't push him. A couple of times he rang me out of the blue.

'Shall we go for a coffee?' he would ask cheerily.

I found out that he spent the next few weeks sofa-hopping, and then finally went to the YMCA. But that didn't last long as they have rules and Jamie has never been one for rules.

'If you go out in the evening, you must come back by eleven,' they said. 'You'll be kicked out if you don't.'

Well of course he didn't come back and they threw him out. He did some more sofa-hopping, wheedled his way back into Mrs Edwards's house for a couple of nights, got back into the YMCA and finally joined a house-share in the city, which he could just about afford on his housing benefit.

The one good thing amongst all this was that he kept going to school. They excluded him permanently, about three months before his GCSEs, for his disruptive behaviour and telling the teachers what to do, but they let him go back and sit his exams.

'Hi, Mum,' Jamie rang me with a cheery voice. 'I've just finished all my exams.'

'Well done, Jay.' I was relieved he'd managed to go back for that. He must be maturing a bit.

'I think I surprised everybody when I turned up on time, clean and sober, for all my exams! I thought you'd be proud of me.'

'Yes, that's great. I am proud of you for taking your exams and even more because it took some guts to go back to school to do them after you'd been expelled. So well done. How did the exams go?'

'They weren't too bad.'

'Well, you probably missed a lot, with missing out on so much school.'

'Yes, I know. But I think it was mostly revision the last few months.'

'Well, at least you had a go.'

On the day the results were due, Jamie went in to collect them and phoned me from outside the school.

'I made my head of year cry,' he announced.

'Oh no!'

'Don't worry, it's all right. It was in a good way,' he explained. 'When I opened the envelope and showed her my results, she was so happy that she had tears in her eyes.'

'The suspense is killing me, Jay. What did you get?'

'I actually passed four of them,' he said. 'Four grade Cs. Isn't that great?'

'Yes, after all your troubles, I reckon that's a real achievement. Just wait till I tell Dad. He'll be so glad.'

At around this time, Jamie met his girlfriend and they settled down together. He never came back to live with us, but he would often pop back for meals and family occasions, so we were all back on an even keel . . . or so we thought.

23

Making a Statement

'I felt everybody was against me, being a teenager.'
Stacey's comment, years later

The agency had grown to such a size that it was now almost running itself. Mike had long been retired and I wanted to join him. The children were more demanding now than for quite a few years, and I felt it would help if I was free to spend more time with them and with Mike too.

Another successful fostering agency made a very good bid for ours and we agreed terms with them. Jane and our accountant dealt with all the paperwork side of things.

I don't know how long it was happening before I realised for sure, but I often had less money in my purse than I thought. It was just ten and twenty pound notes to begin with, and I couldn't be sure that I hadn't spent them myself.

But finally one day I knew, because I'd been to the bank and drawn out a large amount, three thousand pounds, for a particular reason. When I went to my bag the next morning and got out my purse, the whole lot was missing. I was shocked. Could I not even leave my bag unattended in my own home? I had my suspicions, of course, but I didn't want to risk doing anything hasty, just in case I was wrong.

Meanwhile, some of fifteen-year-old Stacey's secrets were surfacing, as the younger ones reminisced about our holidays for example.

'Do you remember that caravan holiday?' asked Carrie.

'Which one?' I said. 'We had lots of caravan holidays.'

'The one that was in Devon or near there. Stacey used to wait till you and Dad were asleep, then climb out of the caravan window and go into town with a very short skirt on.'

'I never knew that!'

'Yes,' Stacey laughed. 'I just wanted a bit of fun.'

Even then, Stacey, as well as being the funniest, was the most outrageous. I think there must have been a lot of things going on that I didn't know about, but money was always the thing that held her back . . . until she took the leap into larger scale theft and fraud.

The head teacher phoned us.

'Mrs Merry, can you come up to the school, please? I think we have a problem.'

When I got to the head teacher's study, there was Stacey, looking subdued, together with the head, the deputy, her form tutor and another teacher I didn't know. Oh dear, I thought.

'Mrs Merry,' said the deputy head. 'Are you aware of the school rules about jewellery?'

'Yes. I know it's not allowed.'

'That's right.' She turned to Stacey's form tutor. 'Mr Bailey?'

'Yes,' he said. 'This morning, at registration time, I noticed that Stacey had quite a large ring on her finger, a five-stoned diamond ring. Well, they looked like diamonds, and I knew that it would be quite valuable if they were. So I had to confront her about it.'

I was shocked. An image of the antique five-stone diamond ring, left to me by my grandmother, came into my mind. I hadn't worn it in years. I just kept it in my jewellery box. It was one of two rings, the other with three diamonds, that I was going to give to Sally and Jane when they each turned forty.

'What did Stacey say?' I asked him, trying not to show what I was thinking.

'She said: "My mum's given it to me."' He paused. 'Is that right, Mrs Merry?'

I hesitated to answer, but I looked at Stacey, and her unconcerned face.

'No.' I shook my head slowly, sadly. 'I do have a five-stoned diamond ring. But I didn't give it to Stacey. I'm hoping it's still in my jewellery box at home.'

'Well, I wanted to show it to you, so that you could tell us if it was yours,' said Mr Bailey. 'But unfortunately, it was off Stacey's finger in a trice and nowhere to be seen. We even searched her pockets, her bag and her desk, but there was no sign of it, only minutes after it had been on her finger.'

The head turned to Stacey. 'Can you tell us where it is?'

'I don't know,' she replied with a straight face. 'I took it off, and then it got lost. I must have dropped it. Maybe somebody else picked it up and stole it.'

'But that's not all,' added Mr Bailey, turning to the other teacher.

'A couple of days ago, I told Stacey off for wearing jewellery too,' she said. 'That was a three-stone diamond-type ring. Do you have one of those, Mrs Merry?'

'Yes, I do.' I felt like I'd been punched in the stomach. How could Stacey do this to me? I knew that stealing was like a disease or addiction to her, but it had always been small things until the phone topping-up fiasco. And now this . . .

'I told her off about it and made her take it off, so she put in her pocket to take home. At least, that's what I thought.'

'Well, she didn't give it to me,' I said, then turned to face Stacey. 'Did you put it back in my jewellery box?' I asked her.

'You don't even know I took it,' she protested, the tears welling up on demand. 'Or the other ring. Why are you accusing me?'

'Well,' I answered, the anger building up inside me. 'If they're not both in my jewellery box when I get home, I'll know, won't I?'

She looked down at the carpet and said nothing.

Of course, they were missing when I got back, along with a third family heirloom ring, and I knew she must have taken them all. The evidence against her for the first two was undeniable.

When Stacey arrived home that evening, I questioned her about what she'd done with the rings. She insisted she'd lost them and whatever I said I couldn't make her change her story. But I knew those two rings were together worth about eight thousand pounds. And the other a few more. This was serious theft.

'What do you think she did with them?' asked Mike after I'd told him the story.

'I really don't know,' I shrugged. 'But I'm very disappointed that she stole so much, both the money and the rings, and God knows what else, from her own mother.' By now I was pretty sure it must have been Stacey that stole that cash from my purse as well, but I didn't want to heap anything else on her just at that point, so I kept that quiet for now.

'Maybe she's pawned them,' he suggested. 'She must have known she could get money on those rings.'

I was horrified. 'But she'd never have got their full value.'

'I'll see if I can track them down,' he said.

But, if she did pawn them, it wasn't locally and we never found them. I did look into trying to make a claim on our insurance, but that wasn't possible because they were taken by a family member.

On the day Stacey turned sixteen, there was a birthday card from her grandfather. It was the first time she'd ever had a card from him. She opened it and read what was written inside with a poker face.

'What does it say?' I asked her.

'He wants me to go away for the weekend with him.'

'And your grandma?'

'No, just him, just the two of us, in a flat he's rented.'

'Oh.' I had a bad feeling about this. 'Why do you think he wants to be alone with you for the weekend?' It seemed a remote possibility that he just wanted to treat her, and I was far more concerned that it was to do with her age, being sixteen.

'I don't know.' She looked down at the floor. 'What do you think?'

'Well, you're sixteen now.'

'Yes, I know.' She looked puzzled.

'It's up to you, Stace. You're old enough now to make up your own mind about your grandfather, and whether you want to go for a weekend alone with him.' I paused. 'If you do want to go, that's fine. I won't try to stop you, as long as you're happy to go . . . but personally, I've got to be honest, I don't trust the man. Think about it. Why does he want you to himself?'

'Yes, Mum. That's what I was thinking. And my gut instinct is I don't want to go.'

'OK. That's fine. It's your decision.'

'I'll write and tell him no.'

Here was my chance to try to find out whether my hunch had been right about that man. 'What memories do you have of him when you were little?'

'Not much,' she said. 'I remember he used to give me a special chocolate drink at bedtimes when Caroline and I went to stay for a week with him, when Sam was born. He used to stand over me while I drank it. Then he would smile and say, "That's because you've been good." And I know he made me sleep in a bed with him, in a separate bedroom, and he gave me that chocolate drink. I don't remember anything else. I don't know what happened. Maybe I've blanked it out. I think I've blanked most of that week out.'

It was now a few months since the phone top-ups swindle, but one day I had a letter from the bank. Not knowing what it was, I assumed it would be a statement, and left it to open later. When I finally got around to it the next day, it was much more serious than that.

My heart lurched as I began to read it through.

> *We have not written till now, because the person who defrauded your account is known to you, and you stated at the time that you did not wish us to take any action to retrieve the funds. However, our head office has asked us to let you know that this is a case of fraud and if you won't take it any further we will have to pursue the legal route ourselves . . .*

I rang them immediately and spoke to somebody in their fraud department.

'Do you have to prosecute her?' I asked bluntly. 'Please don't. She's so young, still a schoolgirl, and it would give her a criminal record for life. She wants to be a social worker when she grows up, and this might make it impossible.'

'I realise the implications, Mrs Merry. But we have to follow the bank's procedures in this case, as in any other.'

'Is there anything I could do to stop you?'

'Yes, you could sue her yourself.'

'But, surely that would have the same effect?'

'That's true. Can you hold on a moment, Mrs Merry, while I consult my supervisor about this?' I waited for what seemed like ages while the inane music played. 'Are you still there, Mrs Merry?'

'Yes.'

'Sorry to keep you waiting, but I am told that in this unusual situation, with your daughter still being at school, the bank would refrain from taking any further action in this case as long as you take her to a police station to admit her guilt and make a statement.'

It sounded a very serious thing to have to do. 'Wouldn't that still go on her record?'

'I don't believe it would give her a criminal record of any kind, if she just makes the admission in a statement. You can check that with the police. Making this admission would satisfy our head office, in these circumstances, and that way you would not need to have any charges made against her.'

'Thank you.'

'Is that what you wish to do?'

'Yes, I'll take her down on Saturday,' I said, feeling a mixture of relief and trepidation. I had no idea how she would take this, but it had to be done.

I realised of course, that unless we sued Stacey for fraud, the bank wouldn't replace my stolen funds. It was a great loss to me, and we couldn't afford to overlook it, but it was a hard place to be in and I had to put Stacey's future first.

So I confronted her straight away.

'Why did you do it, Stacey?' I asked her. 'The rings, and the money, and there was cash too from my purse, wasn't there?'

'I needed the money, Mum,' she said. 'And I didn't think you'd notice.'

I explained about the bank wanting to sue her.

'The only way for you to avoid having to go to court and being prosecuted, with a criminal record,' I explained to her calmly, 'is to come down to the police station with me on Saturday morning and admit that you did it.'

'What, just tell them I did it?'

'And sign a statement to say that you did it. That way the bank will be happy, I won't make any charge against you and your record will be clean.' I paused. 'But you have to get a hold of yourself, Stacey. You have to stop all this stealing. I can't trust you any more, and I hate that. You've hit me very hard financially, and even worse, you stole away my family history in those rings. They were full of precious memories of my grandmother and other relatives. Their financial value is a considerable loss, but the stealing away of their sentimental value is something I can never get back.' I paused. 'Please stop stealing, Stace.'

She hung her head and said nothing.

Saturday came and I drove Stacey to the police station. I sat with her while the policewoman wrote down what Stacey told her, then gave it to Stacey to read and sign, which she did very belligerently.

'Well done,' I said, squeezing her hand, but she withdrew

it within an instant and, without even looking at me, stood up and strode out of the little office, down the corridor and out of the front doors to the car.

She had been subdued and resentful inside the police station, but as soon as we got back in the car, she kicked off big time, shouting and ranting all the way home.

I made a pot of tea and poured us both a mug.

I tried to talk with her about her plans for the weekend, but she refused to play this game, seething silently as she sipped her tea.

'When I've had my pocket-money on Saturday, I'm leaving this dump,' she announced, just as Mike came in, unaware of exactly what had gone on.

'Oh well,' he joked. 'I'll give it to you early, then!'

She slammed her mug down on the table, with tea going in all directions, stood up and stomped out of the kitchen, past Sam and Carrie in the hall, without saying a word, and straight out of the front door.

We all watched her striding down the long drive into the distance.

'Don't worry,' I said to the kids. 'She's just going walkabout. She's taken nothing with her, so I'm sure she'll be back later.'

But, of course, I was wrong. She didn't come back that night. She didn't answer her phone when I rang her and in the end, I was so tired, I just had to go to bed, hoping she would creep in overnight.

As I began to drift off to sleep, all the troubles I'd had with Stacey for so long, all the heartache and all her frequent, screaming nightmares of her childhood abuse flashed through my mind. I had struggled with her behaviour for so many years, just to get through each day. But no matter what, Mike and I had always been there for her, sticking up for her. We'd never had a night out together since we'd taken the four of them in. We couldn't leave them with babysitters; they'd never have coped. But that was all part of the deal. We'd never regretted it, never complained. And we still didn't, because we loved them all.

24

The Pit Bull

'This report is not factually accurate. She has names wrong, dates and relationships. She was appalling to the kids. And she was on our side?'

My written comment to our solicitor

I got up early the next morning, as usual, and checked in Stacey's room, but her bed hadn't been slept in. I remember coming down the stairs thinking: Oh my God. I don't know where Stacey is, whether she's hurt – she could be anywhere.

Then I thought back to the previous day, the police station. Oh no, she's going to have this on her file, and she's thinking of going into social work when she leaves school.

I later found out that she'd reported me to Social Services for frogmarching her down to the police station and forcing her to go in. That wasn't true as she'd come of her own accord, but they probably wouldn't have believed me. I was very mithered about that. And then I began to wonder whether perhaps it was all a mistake and the money hadn't been taken after all. But, of course, I knew it had.

That was the last we saw or heard of Stacey for a while, and it worried me sick. Why didn't she answer her phone? Where could she have gone? How would she manage?

The pile of paperwork for the sale of the agency rose to mountainous proportions. We agreed a six-figure price for the lot, offices and all. Then they decided they didn't want the two offices. We all signed and they paid us a deposit. We had to pay to get out of the office leases, so that didn't leave us with much. But we should soon receive the other part of the purchase price, to sort all our finances out at last.

I phoned around various people and discovered that Stacey had gone straight to stay at the home of her boyfriend's parents, but weeks went by and still no response to any of my texts or calls.

First Jamie had gone, and now Stacey. It was this second escape from our clutches, as some people called it, that set the tongues wagging. Just when we were at our lowest, and needed support as a family, we were overrun with professionals. We had tried every conflicting suggestion already, and look where it had got us. Even one or two of our friends were now making comments – 'Maybe it was something you did' or 'Well, they wouldn't have run away over nothing.'

I gave them all the same answer: 'They've run away because I won't let them take drink and drugs in this house. Is that so unreasonable?' Of course I knew it was a lot more than that, but I was too tired to argue any more. I just thought, *before you judge me, look at yourself*.

* * *

Finally, after a few months, we found out where she was.

Jamie phoned me. 'I saw Stacey,' he said. 'I hardly recognised her and she pretended she hadn't seen me.'

'Where? Is she all right? Was she with anybody?' I had so many questions and wanted so much to go to her.

'One of her friends told me that she's heavily into drugs.'

'Oh no!' My heart sank.

'And she's sleeping around. She's homeless and dossing down wherever she can.'

'Where did you see her? I must go and find her.'

'No, Mum, I don't think you'll do any good.'

'But I have to do something.'

'Well, this friend says she moves about, so I have no idea where she might be now.'

'If you see her again, tell her we love her and to come home.'

'I'll try.'

'I'm glad you phoned, Jay. At least I know you are settling down now,' I said. 'But I still worry about you.'

The children's case against the Council was still simmering away in the background and one day I had a call from Katy our solicitor in the case to update me on progress, which seemed to be grinding on very slowly.

'But don't worry, Trisha,' she assured me. 'There are a lot of stages to go through, but we're making progress. That's why I've called you. Do you remember when I said we would need to prepare a psychiatrist's report on each of the children for the judge?'

'Yes.'

'Well, I've found a lady in London, Dr Boteral. I haven't used her before, but I know she has experience in this type of case.'

'Good. Will she come to see the children here?'

'No. That would be too expensive, I'm afraid, so she's given me a couple of dates for you all to go to London.'

'Will she want to interview me too?'

'I don't know, but probably not as the children are all old enough to answer her questions and speak for themselves, but I assumed you'd want to accompany them?'

'Yes, of course . . . but did I tell you that both Jamie and Stacey have left home?'

'Have they?' She sounded surprised. 'They're still quite young, aren't they?'

'Yes. Jamie is seventeen and Stacey is sixteen. They both rebelled in a big way. Jamie had a bit of a wild time for a while, but he seems more settled now, in his own place. But Stacey went overboard and we don't know where she is.'

'Do you think any of her friends would know? We do need to include Stacey in this. It seems she was the one who was the most abused.'

'Yes, I think that's right.'

'Can you try and track her down?'

'No promises, I'm afraid. But I'll do my best.'

So we agreed on a date.

The next thing was to find a way to get a message to Stacey. Jamie was my first thought. He had a mobile phone number for her, but when I tried it the number had been discontinued. I called round some of her old friends and finally found one that said she had Stacey's current email address. So I gave her all the details, the date, the time and where to meet us.

'Please make sure you tell her this is part of the legal process and the case can't continue without her,' I said. 'The solicitor arranged this, and all four of them have to be involved. Tell her it will be a great help to her as well to win the case. She will understand what I mean.'

As the date came nearer, we waited to hear news that Stacey would come. If not, I'd have to call Katy and cancel the visit.

Finally, Stacey's friend texted me to say she'd meet us at the station.

On the morning of our trip to London, Carrie, Sam and I all dressed up in smart clothes and went to the station to meet Jamie and Stacey.

Jamie was there waiting for us, with a shirt and tie on.

'You look great, Jay,' I said.

'I feel a bit stiff and starchy with this tie on,' he grinned, loosening it. 'Where's Stacey? She is coming, isn't she?'

'Well she agreed to, so I hope she does.' I didn't let on, but I wondered whether she would. It would take guts for her to come and join us like this. But one thing I knew: of all of them, Stacey, who could be so fragile in some circumstances, was perhaps the toughest at facing up to things, so I hoped she'd keep her word.

'Just going to the toilet,' Jamie said anxiously as he crossed the waiting area. I could always gauge how nervous Jamie was by how often he went to the loo.

The train was up on the board, with three minutes to go. We were all getting tense, waiting for Stacey, with so little time left.

Finally, just in time, a young girl slouched along towards us.

'That's Stacey,' gasped Carrie.

What a shock! I didn't even recognise her at first. Of course, I hadn't seen her since she walked out that day, several months ago. She was overweight, in a mishmash of clothes. She looked like an alcoholic, her face was bloated and the most terrible colour. She stank and her hair looked dreadful. This wasn't the Stacey we knew.

'Hello,' she mumbled without eye contact, keeping her distance.

'Hello, Stace,' I said. 'I'm glad you made it in time.'

We dashed onto the platform, just as the train pulled in, all of us together, and on our way to London.

It was a difficult journey.

We arrived at the tall, Edwardian, grey-stone building on time and a slim, rather frosty-faced woman greeted us, with the thin hint of a smile on her lips, but her grey eyes were cold and steely. I immediately felt this was the wrong person to be talking to my kids. I knew I had to trust in her professionalism and her reputation as a child psychiatrist, but I suddenly felt very protective of the children.

Dr Boteral began by speaking to all of us together. She asked a few questions, but right from the start, I didn't like her manner. She seemed oblivious to the children's individual needs and, unless I was imagining it, openly hostile towards me. She had the sympathy of a sideboard.

As always, Jamie found it difficult to sit still and listen for long. Within moments he was fidgeting and anxious. He stood up and she gave him a look.

'Sit down,' she barked at him.

Jamie never takes kindly to orders. 'I need to go to the toilet,' he said.

'Not now. You stay with the others until I've finished.'

'Well I won't be long,' he said.

'He does need to go to the toilet quite a lot, I'm afraid,' I excused him.

She gave me a stare. 'Well not today. He'll just have to wait,' she said crossly.

Poor Jamie crumpled back into his seat, moody and unresponsive for the rest of our joint meeting. Then she wanted to see the children individually. They had previously asked me to go in with them, so I asked her if that was all right.

'Oh, if you must!' She almost spat it out. 'But I'll have them each on their own first, then you can join us at the end of each session.'

She started with Jamie and by the time I got in there, his anger was ready to explode. I don't know what she said to him but I could see it hadn't gone well. He dashed out.

'Why did you let him go?' she asked.

'Because he always needs to go to the toilet more often when he's upset and he hasn't had a cigarette since he arrived, so he had to go.'

'Huh,' she snorted. 'What nonsense!'

Stacey was next. When I was called in to join them I found her in tears. Now Stacey had the natural talent of an actress, and could cry at the drop of a hat, but on this day I knew her tears were genuine. I sat next to her on the sofa, took her hand and gave it a squeeze. For that moment, it was as if she was still my little girl and she had never been away.

Dr Boteral, like a pit bull on the attack, wasted no time.

'Is that for Stacey's benefit?' she asked, looking pointedly at our clasped hands. 'Or mine?'

'Stacey's,' I said, as calmly as I could, to conceal my anger at her insinuation.

'So why did you run away?' she asked, and before Stacey could answer she continued, 'Was your grandmother cruel to you?'

'D-d-do you mean Trisha?' she asked through her tears.

'Who else?'

'She's not my grandmother.'

'Well, whatever she is. Tell me how she made you run away.'

I'm sure Stacey could normally have come up with lots of things I'd done wrong in her eyes, but in the face of this unexpectedly forthright challenge, she was speechless.

'All right,' shrugged Dr Boteral. 'If you won't answer, I'll ask her.'

She tossed her head and turned to me. 'Why are you refusing to have Stacey back?'

'Excuse me,' I said in my bolshy voice, 'but if you had properly read the notes, you would know that Stacey left for her own reasons, following some things she herself had done. And neither I nor my husband have ever refused to have her back. She hasn't asked us. In fact we have worried about her every day since she left.'

As I paused, I noticed the woman's scornful look.

'But she did hurt us all by some of the things she did and several of the extended family would find it difficult to accept her back without any apology. I would have Stacey back and I'm sure my husband would too – he's always stuck up for her, no matter what.'

'I see,' said Dr Boteral, narrowing her eyes and making a scrawled note on her pad.

Stacey gave no impression of having really taken in what I'd said, still tearful from whatever had happened before I came in.

Next it was Carrie's turn. This woman gave her a half-smile, as if to a small child, then asked her a complex two-part question expressed in such convoluted language that I knew Carrie would not be able to understand. And Carrie gave me a look to prove it.

'What Dr Boteral means,' I began to explain, 'is do you—'

'Shut up!' interrupted the psychiatrist. 'I'm talking to Carrie, not you.'

'But please remember, she has the mental age of a small child. She doesn't understand—'

'Nonsense! I'm sure she can answer for herself.'

Carrie did try to answer the question, but didn't know how, so faltered after a few words.

'Come on,' urged Dr Boteral. 'Spit it out.'

At that point, Carrie burst into tears and we had to stop the interview.

Sam's session was apparently much the same. He was so young when all the neglect and abuse happened that he genuinely had no memory of it. The things that went on had damaged him, but he couldn't explain them. Dr Boteral was on the warpath when she called me in, almost shouting that he'd refused to cooperate with her and haranguing me for his poor communication skills.

At the end, she asked to talk to me on my own.

'It's all your fault,' she confronted me. 'You shouldn't have taken in children with problems if you weren't up to dealing with them.'

'Well, to start with, we didn't know they had so many problems. Nobody said anything about all the abuse they had suffered, nor the severity of their neglect. We weren't told about any of that.'

'So why did you take them in? Why did they bring them over a hundred miles to you?'

'They told us it was because we had more experience than anyone else to look after families of difficult children.'

'Huh!' she exclaimed. 'Well, they got that wrong, didn't they?'

By now I felt she was on the attack, deliberately maligning me.

'No one human being can get things right every time,' I said in my own defence. 'And I'm sure I've got a lot wrong along the way, but I know I got a lot right too.' I stood up. 'Goodbye, Dr Boteral,' I said and walked out.

I had been led to believe that we were going to see a respected child psychiatrist who understood children and their carers. But it was clear she didn't have a clue and, even worse, had set out today to attack and undermine us all.

As we went out of that building and down the steps I was fearful of what would happen next. Here I was in the big city, with four disturbed children who were now knotted up with repressed rage and frustration. What if they all ran off in different directions? Which one should I run after first?

Somehow we all arrived back at Euston together. Perhaps it was the promise of a good tuck-in that did it. They filled themselves with hamburgers, at least two each, and I loaded up on more snacks to keep them going.

The train journey back was more tense and stressful than it had been going. Jamie was full of anger. 'She wouldn't even let me out to go to the toilet or have a smoke.'

Stacey just sat and seethed in a muttering sulk all the way back, cross with us all.

Carrie was on edge.

'I found her very scary,' she said to me. 'She was judging all of us. She made us feel like it was all our fault.'

'Well put, Carrie. That's exactly how I feel.' The others

nodded too. It was the one point of agreement of the whole day.

I dreaded to think what that dragon's report would be like, but I didn't think it would be good . . . and she was supposed to be on our side!

25

A Devastating Allegation

'Thank you for your co-operation in this matter.'
Extract from the Local Constabulary letter

A week or two passed by and we put that awful experience with Dr Boteral behind us. The sale of the agency was due to go through any day now, so when the phone rang I thought it might be our solicitor. But it was the police.

'Mrs Merry?'

'Yes.'

'Is your husband Michael at home?'

'Yes, I'll just get him for you.' I walked through the house in search of Mike, with the phone still held to my ear. 'What's it about?' I asked nervously, thinking that something might have happened to either Jamie or Stacey.

Just then I found Mike and, because he is so hard of hearing on the phone, we put it on speaker.

'Hello, Mike Merry here,' he said.

'Could you please come down to the police station at your earliest convenience?' asked the voice.

'Yes, of course. No problem. What's it about?'

'Oh, your daughter's made an allegation against you,' said the voice.

'Right,' he said. 'I'll come down tomorrow morning, shall I?' He didn't at first show any concern about this. Why should he?

'It must be some mix-up or other,' he said, putting the phone down.

Quite by chance, our solicitor for the business called straight after that. So I told her.

'I don't know what Stacey's been up to now,' I said. 'But she's made an allegation against Mike.'

'What kind of allegation?'

'Oh, I don't know. He didn't ask. But he's going down to the police station in the morning.'

'Which solicitor is going with him?' she asked.

'Oh, we don't need a solicitor,' I answered confidently. 'It will just be Stacey trying to make a bit of a drama I expect. Mike will go down and sort it all out.'

'No, he won't,' she said with a serious voice.

'But he's never done anything wrong,' I insisted. 'I'm telling you now, he's never done anything.'

'That's not the point. He mustn't go on his own. I'll come with him. Tell him I'll meet him outside the entrance at ten o'clock.'

I had to go and collect something near the police station, so I went with him to meet the solicitor.

'I've spoken to the police to find out what the allegation was about,' she said.

'Was it Stacey?' I asked.

'Yes, and it's a very serious allegation, I'm afraid.'

Mike's face drained of colour. I suddenly felt a bit wobbly and had to hold on to the wall.

'I need you to remember, Mike. Do not say a word.'

'But that will make me look guilty,' he protested. 'I'm not guilty.'

'No, but it's not up to you to prove your innocence. They've got to prove what they're accusing you of. It's not your place to do their work for them. Let them do their job, and they'll find nothing.'

I could see that Mike was very uncomfortable with that.

'We'd better go in,' she said to Mike. 'I don't think they'll want you there, Trisha.'

'No, that's OK. I've got some errands to do.'

I stood in the big glass doorway and watched them go to the counter, and then on towards the interview rooms. I felt so anxious for poor Mike, who never did Stacey any harm. He always stuck up for her when she was in trouble. It must all be a big misunderstanding. I felt a bit calmer now, thinking it through.

'How did it go?' I asked him when he got back at lunchtime, looking ten years older. 'What was it all about?'

He just stood and gazed at me, then started to tremble.

'Here, sit down.' I pulled out a chair for him and we sat down together at the breakfast-room table, my hand on his to steady him.

'She's accused me . . .' His voice wavered as he tried to compose himself enough to continue. 'She accused me of . . . sexually abusing her,' he said, almost in a whisper. 'How could she do that to me?' He looked like he was going to break down.

'No!' I shouted out loud, distraught. 'That's an evil lie. The worst thing she could think of. What a monstrous thing to do!' I could hardly take it in.

Mike shook his head slowly from side to side, silent, his shoulders slouched and his eyes imploring.

'I can't believe she has done this to you, to us. I expect it's just her way of getting back at me, as usual. It's never you she wants to hurt. It's me. She probably thought the best way to hurt me was to attack you. She knew I would be much more upset if she put her sword into you.'

We sat, each immersed in our own damaging thoughts for a while. But the more I turned it over in my mind, the more angry I became.

'When is this supposed to have happened?'

'Lots of times,' he said. 'According to Stacey.' He leaned his elbow on the table, with his hand to his forehead. 'On Friday nights apparently, when she came with me to get the fish and chips.'

'But that's ridiculous,' I protested.

'I know. That's exactly what I said, but the solicitor stopped me saying anything else.'

'So it's Stacey's word against yours?'

'Yes.'

'Well, nobody will believe her story. Everyone knows what a liar she is. It's written all over her school reports and her notes. And, of course, none of our friends or family will believe her.'

'But you know the saying,' he replied wearily. 'There's no smoke without fire.'

'I know a hundred per cent that it is definitely not true in your case, and I'm sure nobody will even think it.'

'But she wrote a statement about it, saying I had tried to abuse Carrie as well.'

'That just proves even more what lies she has told them. There is no way that could have happened without Carrie blurting it out. We all know that.'

'But the police don't. They want to see me again when they've investigated the allegation. Of course, they won't find any evidence, but I have to go for more questioning in a month's time.'

We sat together in silence, horrified by the enormity of what Stacey had done. Mike had always been a calm, strong, dependable influence throughout our long and happy marriage. And the same in all our lives. He had a great sense of fun. Now that had all been cruelly stripped away to leave a disillusioned, vulnerable shadow of himself.

'How dare she do this to you?' I said. 'You've always been such a wonderful father, a brilliant dad to her and to all of them, and you've never moaned about her lying and stealing, or anything else. Not once, no matter how far she pushed you.'

'I did tease her that time, when she walked out, remember?'

'Oh yes, but she's always laughed when you've teased

her before. She was looking for a trigger that day, an excuse to make her go. I'm sure she's not getting back at you for that. It's me she wants to harm.' I tried to stop the tears, but I couldn't.

'But you know what this means? I can't ever be alone with any of the kids or our grandchildren again.'

'That's ridiculous. Of course you can. Just be your normal self and play with them like you usually do.'

'But I can't, don't you see?'

The spark had gone out of him. His eyes were dull and he looked like he was in pain. He certainly was emotionally. We both were. Completely devastated.

'I can't put myself in the situation of being with any children, ever again.'

This was such an outrageous accusation. I knew with absolute certainty that Mike could never have done anything remotely connected to what Stacey had alleged. Not in a million years.

A few days went by, in which we were both under a huge amount of stress. I think Mike spent most of that first fortnight in a daze, numb with shock. On the other hand, I was fuming, full of outrage on his behalf.

'Do you think it will get in the papers?' asked Mike one day.

'I hope not!'

'There's no truth in it at all, but I wouldn't want our friends to read about this.'

'Don't worry,' I reassured him. 'None of them would believe it.'

But we were both anxious all the same. It preyed on our minds and we could think of nothing else.

Out of the blue one morning, I received a letter from Katy, the solicitor for the children, telling us that Dr Boteral's report had come in and she would send it to us, but it was too late because the money had all been spent and there wasn't enough left to take the children's case to court. I couldn't believe it. This was apparently something to do with changes in legal aid, which meant there was about a hundred thousand pounds less than originally promised.

I rang her. 'What are we going to do now?'

'There isn't anything you can do.' She sounded very huffy with me.

'Well, it's not our fault. How could this happen? After all that time and work, why hasn't it got to court? How can it be dropped now?'

She didn't have an answer and, with everything else that was happening at the time, I just felt . . . I can't do this any more.

After two weeks, Mike received an unexpected phone call, telling him the police interview had been cancelled, followed up by an official letter from the Local Constabulary:

13th July 2009

Dear Mr Merry,
As discussed on the telephone today, the matter that was being investigated for which you were interviewed on 1st July 2009,

has now been reviewed by the Crown Prosecution Service and
their decision is to take no further action against you.

You will therefore no longer be required to attend the police
station on 3rd August 2009. I have updated your solicitor
accordingly.

Thank you again for your cooperation with this matter.
Yours Sincerely,
PC 954 Nina Temple
Child Protection Unit

'Thank God,' I said. 'They've seen sense. What a huge relief. Now we can all try and put this behind us.' I wasn't sure we could, though I tried to be upbeat for Mike.

'But it doesn't say I am innocent,' he said in a small voice. 'It just says they're taking no further action. That leaves it all in the air, doesn't it? It means I'll never be given the chance to clear my name.'

'Oh!' I hadn't realised, but of course he was right. It was open-ended. 'She's got us either way, hasn't she?'

One evening, a few days later, Mike hardly touched any of his dinner, and he looked very pale.

'Are you feeling all right, love?' I asked him.

'Not too good,' he admitted. 'I think I'll go up and have an early night. I expect I'll be better in the morning.'

He must have fallen asleep, but a couple of hours later I heard him calling me.

'What's the matter?' I asked as I went into the bedroom.

But as soon as I saw him I could see how bad he looked, and he was clutching his chest.

'I can't breathe,' he rasped.

'Is it your lungs?' He'd always had a weak chest due to a problem with one of his lungs when he was young.

'No, I don't think so,' he whispered between laboured breaths. 'Pain . . . down my arms . . . tight chest.' He sounded very groggy.

'Shall I call the doctor?' I wasn't sure how bad it was. 'Or perhaps I'll call Jane – she'll know what to do.'

He nodded, gulping in mouthfuls of air.

'Call 999,' said Jane as soon as I told her. 'He needs an ambulance. Tell them it's an emergency.'

The ambulance arrived surprisingly quickly and the paramedics were wonderful. They knew exactly what they were doing. They got him on a stretcher and into the back. It was the early hours of the morning by then.

'He's had a heart attack,' said one of the crew in a calm, sympathetic voice. 'We've got things under control and we're monitoring him closely, so we'll go straight off now.'

'Hop in,' said the other one. 'You can come with him if you want to.'

'I can't,' I said. 'I've got children asleep in the house. I can't leave them alone.'

So off they went without me. A heart attack – from the stress of the allegation no doubt. The resentment and fear started to eat away at me. As I stood at the top of the drive in the moonlight, watching the white ambulance disappear into the darkness at the other end, Sam and Carrie both came outside to join me.

'What was all the noise?' asked Sam, stifling a yawn. All the comings and goings must have woken the kids and by the time they got up to see what was happening Mike was already on his way to hospital.

'Where's Dad?' asked Carrie.

'Come back inside and I'll tell you.' I put my arms round each of them and took them into the breakfast room. 'Dad wasn't feeling too good. He's had a bit of a turn, so they've taken him to hospital to keep an eye on him,' I explained, not wanting to alarm them too much at this time of night. 'Let's all have a hot drink, then back to bed.'

When they'd gone, bleary-eyed, back upstairs, I sat in the breakfast room on my own. I felt bad that I hadn't gone with him. But how could I? Mike knew that. Everyone knew how these kids could kick off, even when it was just Carrie and Sam. And they still had frequent nightmares, even after all these years. I couldn't leave them on their own.

I thought of Mike back in those days when those four waifs had first come to us. Fit and well he had been, full of fun, and then how pale and grey he had looked that evening, how he had struggled to breathe, and his hand on his chest. What's happening now? I thought. Please God he hasn't got any worse. Or maybe he has. What if he dies? He's going to die . . .

It was all Stacey's fault. That was what broke him, the man who had always stuck up for her. She might as well have knifed him in the back. I'm not a vengeful person, but right then, that night, I felt I could never forgive her for bringing Mike to this. If he died, it would be her fault.

I don't know how long I sat there in the darkness, with only the moonlight streaming in through the window. I was cold and alone, worrying about Mike. I knew I couldn't go to bed. I couldn't sleep. I didn't dare to, in case Mike died. If I went to sleep he might die. I had to stay awake and will him to stay alive, to get better. It was a long, lonely night, going over memories, thinking of other people I loved who had gone off in ambulances. I never saw some of them again. Would Mike still be alive in the morning?

Thank God, I needn't have worried so much. As soon as I'd dropped the kids off at their schools, I went in to see Mike in Intensive Care. He had an oxygen mask on to help with his breathing and that was much better now. He had various other bits and pieces on him – a drip in his arm, a cannula in the back of his hand and pads stuck to his chest, with various monitors and beepers and numbers flashing. Well, that's how I remember it anyway. It all looked very daunting, but he had a much healthier colour now and he gave me a lovely smile when he saw me, so I did feel better for being there, for seeing him myself.

Gradually throughout that first day, the others came to join me and we all sat around his bed – Jane, Brett and Laura, our grown-up foster daughter Anna, Carrie, Sam and me. My other daughter Sally came up from Portsmouth as well.

He was soon out of Intensive Care and making good

progress, which was a great relief. I knew he was on the mend when he started joking with the nurses. But I couldn't stop feeling it was all Stacey's fault. We could have lost Mike because of her malicious accusation and we all knew it.

'I don't ever want to see Stacey again,' said Jane, 'not after what she's done to Dad.'

Everyone agreed. And as for me, I couldn't bring myself to forgive her, no matter how hard I tried. She could have killed Mike, and damn nearly did.

Finally he was allowed home to convalesce and soon began to resume his old routines, with regular walks to follow doctors' orders.

One afternoon, while he was upstairs resting, the phone rang. It was Jane in a panic.

'Mum, the solicitor's just phoned. The agency buyers are not going to pay us.'

'But they've got to pay us.'

'In this paperwork it says that if eight or more carers left in one year, they wouldn't pay us.'

'Well, that's never happened.'

'Yes it has,' she explained in a brittle voice. 'Our carers' contracts had to go through to them before completion of the sale, and they immediately sacked eight of them.'

'But they can't do that!' It was my turn to panic now. This money was going towards all my children and grand-children's university fees. The remainder of the deposit would only just cover the legal and financial fees of the sale, nothing more.

'Well, they have done it, and the solicitor says there's nothing we can do about it. Only the carers themselves can take the combined agency to tribunal, but even if they do, that will be too late to help us.'

I was confused. I couldn't believe it. 'So, are you saying we won't get any of the rest of the money at all?'

'Not a penny.'

'They've swindled us out of the lot?'

'Yes, I'm afraid so.'

All my plans for the family and for our retirement fell apart that day.

As I sat with Mike and the kids watching something on the telly that evening, a pall of tiredness came over me and I couldn't keep my eyes open, so I went up to bed early and slept through till about half-past five, as usual, though I still felt heavy with fatigue.

I got up and went through the motions, getting Carrie and Sam's breakfasts and seeing Mike off with them to drop them at their schools, then loading the dishwasher, worrying about Jamie and Stacey. Yes, despite everything, I wanted her to be safe.

My mind was constantly buzzing with everything that seemed to be going wrong. I remembered Stacey's thefts from me, Jamie running away from home, the solicitor ringing to say the children's court case couldn't go ahead, our being swindled and losing all that money from the sale of the agency, and of course there was Mike still slowly recuperating, but forever blighted by Stacey's devastating allegation.

There were a hundred and one things I needed to do, but first I decided to give Anna a ring as we hadn't seen her for a week.

I remember keying in her number and looking at the clock, nine fifteen, as I waited for her to pick up her phone.

'Hello, sweetheart,' I said, 'I don't know whether you were thinking of coming up today . . . you could come for lunch if you like.'

'Oh, thanks. I might do, Mum . . .'

That's all I remember. Everything went blank from that moment. But later Anna told me I had groaned like a wounded animal and let out a long wail which set the puppy barking, then she heard my phone clatter onto the flag-stoned floor.

26

Repercussions

'Stacey caused a lot of problems when she made an allegation against Mr Merry.'

Psychologist's report

Anna drove straight over, ran into the house and found me unconscious on the kitchen floor with Poppy our golden Labrador lying beside me.

She called for an ambulance and they came very quickly. They raced me into A & E, and straight through to Intensive Care. They thought at the time that I might have had both a heart attack and a stroke. I don't do things by halves!

While I was still unconscious, they did various tests and investigations and kept me in Intensive Care, where I finally woke up a couple of days later. I remember coming round gradually in a hospital bed, with a drip in my arm and all these people sat around me, crying. Oh my God! I didn't know what was going on or why I was there, so I opened my mouth to ask but no words came out. I must have looked like a goldfish.

I was totally confused and couldn't work things out. I

remember seeing all these strangers looking at me and trying to shoo them out.

With a great effort, I finally managed to say the words: 'Go away!'

I don't remember whether they did go that day, or what happened. I just remember my head was throbbing and my brain felt as if it was full of wet cotton wool. When I tried to move my arms, they felt heavy and wouldn't respond how I wanted them to. I knew how to move them. I could move them, but they were uncoordinated.

The next morning when Mike came in, I recognised him this time, and I remembered his name. Then soon after, Jane arrived, crying. I recognised her as my daughter, but I had trouble getting her name out.

'J-J-Jane.'

Then my other daughter Sally came in but, try as I might, I couldn't remember her name. I knew she was my daughter and I was panicking. How can I not remember her name? I didn't want her to know I couldn't remember it, but then it came to me.

Val and Dennis, old friends of mine, came in to visit me that afternoon. They each came straight over and gave me a hug. I couldn't remember them at all and I felt really embarrassed that this strange man had his arm round me. The next time they came, two or three days later, I did recognise them, and we laughed about it.

When Anna visited, I was delighted.

'I'm so glad you came.' I worked hard to say the words and my speech sounded stilted, but at least I could say a little of what was in my heart. 'Thank you for finding me and getting me to hospital quickly.'

'Well, thank goodness you rang me, because it happened while we were talking on the phone. That's how I knew to come straight away. I don't know whether you remember, but you had just invited me to lunch, and then you started to groan, followed by the most awful, wailing, screaming noise.'

'Really?'

'Yes,' she shuddered. 'I shall never forget it.'

I manoeuvred my free hand onto hers. 'Thank you for saving my life.'

A hospital doctor came to see me after a few days and told me the results of my tests. 'You've had a stroke, Mrs Merry,' he said. 'But, fortunately, it didn't paralyse you.'

Yes, I could move everything, but I couldn't walk properly. My legs felt as if I'd lain on them badly for a few hours. They were heavy and numb and wouldn't do quite what I wanted, and they were like that all the time that first week before gradually starting to get better. It felt like my brain wasn't connected to my body. My balance wasn't good either and I had to hold on to something or someone to get about.

The staff moved me into the unit next to Intensive Care, but it was so awful being in hospital. I had to leave as soon as I could. They hadn't washed me or given me a bath or even combed my hair, and I couldn't eat most of the food they brought me.

Trisha Merry

'I've got to go home,' I said to Mike one visiting time. I don't care if I have to walk all the way, I can't stay another night in this place.'

'But you're not ready to go home yet,' he said.

'I'll be even less ready if I have to stay here any longer.'

'But you can't go while you're attached to that drip.'

'Tell them I want to go home and ask them to take the drip out. If they don't come and do it, I'll take it out myself.'

. Sally was staying at the house, so she brought in some clothes when she came to visit later that day. She helped me to get dressed and gathered up all my get-well cards to take home.

A young doctor came in to see me. 'I hear you want to go home, Mrs Merry,' she said. 'I'm afraid we are not able to discharge you yet as we don't feel you're well enough to leave. That's why you're in this special care unit.'

'Well, if you won't discharge me, I'll discharge myself,' I insisted.

Mike was reluctant to aid and abet me in flouting medical opinion but of course he was happy that I would be at home with him. So he helped me down to the car and drove me away. I can't remember the journey until he turned into our long drive, leading past some farm buildings and up to our house in the distance.

That's when I started panicking again. I didn't remember the house, and when we got inside I didn't know where to go. It was frightening not being able to remember the way around my own house. It was like a stranger's house to me that first day. I didn't know where anything was or how to do the everyday things I'd always taken for granted. I couldn't even have made a cake.

I still couldn't walk properly. It felt very odd because I knew what to do, but I couldn't quite do it. The family were wonderful, looking after me so well and helping me to get moving again. My speech was still rather halting and it took quite a while for me to remember all the words and names I should have known.

The other change in me that seemed to have been brought on by this stroke was how vindictive I increasingly felt towards Stacey for the despicable way she treated Mike, which brought on his heart attack and must have contributed to my stroke too. I didn't want to be so vehement about her, but I couldn't seem to control my anger in those early days after I came home from the hospital. Of course, Stacey probably didn't even know we'd both been so ill.

About three months after I came home, a letter came through with a hospital appointment for me the following week. In the meantime, I started to remember how to do things. One day I went out and sat in the car. I looked at everything and tried it out. My memory was coming back so I went for a drive. I knew I had to be careful, but I was overjoyed that my brain was working better now and I remembered how to drive.

At the hospital, I had scans and tests in the morning. Then a cheeky young medic explained to me what it all meant.

'Your blood-pressure is that of someone in their thirties, your pulse-rate is fantastic and there is no furring in your arteries whatsoever. Look at your blood vessels compared to mine . . .' He showed me the two scans. 'Whatever you're doing, keep doing it.'

'OK. That's good to know.'

'We've scanned every part of your brain and everything looks fine. So although you had all the indicators of a stroke when you were brought into Intensive Care, I don't think you've had a stroke, Mrs Merry.' He paused. 'Have you had a lot of stress lately?'

'A tad!' I laughed. 'Stress in spades.'

'I would think you've had a total protective close-down. A burnout. It happens to people in very stressful jobs and those who've experienced traumas. Your brain couldn't cope any more, so it shut down to have a rest.'

At least I didn't have to worry about having another stroke, but it took me several months to regain full health and mobility. And my memory has never fully come back to what it used to be.

Mike had recovered well from his heart attack, but now that I was better, he wouldn't go out. He wouldn't go to Tesco's or anywhere. He didn't want anyone to see him and he refused to go anywhere there might be children.

Even at home, he was quieter, more withdrawn. Where he would have joked and teased before, now he became more detached in most family conversations. If I walked out of a room where Carrie and Sam were, he walked out too. He couldn't even stay in a room with the two of them together. He was a broken man.

I remember one day, Anna brought her baby daughter Carla to see us. I was doing all the usual things with her, trying to make her smile, playing with her feet, making funny faces. Mike sat at the other end of the long sofa, looking on. He had always been wonderful with babies before and could make them laugh quicker than me. But now he just watched from afar. I went off to put the kettle on, then Anna, bless her cotton socks, picked up Carla and plonked her down next to Mike.

'I've got to go to the loo,' she said as she left the room.

'Trisha,' he called me back urgently. I thought something was wrong.

'You can't leave me on my own with Carla.'

'She just wants picking up, love,' I reassured him, my heart aching, heavy with the sadness of what was lost.

'Stay in the room, won't you?'

'Yes, I want to take a photo of you with Carla, so you just hold her on your knee.'

'I can't hold her,' he protested, his face lined with anxiety.

'Just for the photo then,' I said. He picked her up gingerly and I pressed the button as Anna came back into the room.

'You shouldn't have left me with Carla,' Mike said to her. 'I had to call Trisha.'

Anna gave him a gentle smile. 'If I'd thought there was even an ounce of truth in that allegation, do you think I'd have brought my daughter to see you today?'

She was an angel and I was very moved by her loving gesture. I know that, deep down, Mike was too. But it didn't make the hurt go away.

We hadn't heard from Jamie for several weeks now and he didn't return my texts or calls. I hoped he was OK. There wasn't a day that went by without my thinking of him. I hoped he would come back to us one day, but I knew he might not and I feared what the future would bring for him. After all those years of looking after his younger siblings, he needed someone to care about him.

I know it sounds ridiculous, after all the harm she had done to us, both Mike and me, over the previous few months, but I never stopped worrying about Stacey, either. I couldn't shed the anger and resentment, but I didn't stop loving her. I couldn't talk about it with anyone. If I ever tried to broach the subject with any of the rest of the family, it was like a brick wall. I couldn't even mention her name.

'I'll never forgive her for what she did,' said Jane, and the others all agreed. I didn't feel I could forgive her either. It was such a malicious betrayal and the pain of it was still too raw. I just wanted to know where she was and whether she was safe.

One morning, when the postman came, I went to pick up the mail from the mat, and there was one with handwriting I recognised. I tore it open.

Alright Mum. It's Jamie. I just wanted to say sorry for not speaking to you since Christmas . . . It is just that I think

you and Dad want nothing to do with me . . . Did you have
a good birthday? How are the kids? I have stopped drinking
now and I am living with my girlfriend. She is lovely and
you would like her. She has put me on the right track again.
One of the reasons I am writing to you is to tell you that
you're going to have another grandchild. I am hoping you
don't take that in a bad way because I want my child to
know all his family, including you, and not have a life like
I did.

I am sorry Mum and I hope you and Dad can give me one
more chance because it hurts so much not having you and Dad
there for me. I love you Mum and Dad.

Please write back or call me as soon as possible.

Love you loads,

Jamie XXXXXXXXX

The tears came to my eyes as I reached for the phone, so
relieved that he had come back to us. It was wonderful to be
in regular contact with him again. He had a new life now,
gearing up to become a father for real, not just a big brother
acting as a father. This time he was confident he could love
and protect his child and meet his needs, without the dangers
he had battled in his own past. We all looked forward to the
birth, and when he arrived we welcomed Jordan with joy.
He was a gorgeous baby.

Sometimes I would call Jamie if I was going into town.

'Do you want to meet for a coffee, Jay?' He was doing
casual work, so he was often free during the day, and he

always wanted to know how the other three were getting on. Knowing Stacey so well, he was as worried as I was.

'I know she's been awful to you both, Mum. And you didn't deserve any of that. But she's not a hundred per cent bad.'

'Yes,' I said nodding. 'I know. Always the actress!' I stirred my coffee. 'Funny girl.'

Jamie gave me a quizzical look.

'No,' I assured him. 'I haven't forgiven her for what she did. I don't think I ever could. But she is one of us, one of the family. I've heard she is sleeping rough. I just want to know where she is and how she's coping.'

He looked down and shuffled his feet, then met my gaze. 'She's in Ashbridge, Mum. I saw one of her old friends a couple of weeks ago. She told me Stacey's having a hard time and she's been quite poorly.'

'Promiscuous?'

'Yes.' His shoulders drooped.

'Drugs?'

'I think so.'

'Thank you for being honest with me, Jay. It doesn't paint a pretty picture, does it?'

'But she's tough, Mum. She'll survive. I've been there, and look how I've turned my life around.'

'Yes, but it sounds like she's fallen lower than you did.'

'Maybe.'

'Well, at least now I know where she is, and I know she's alive. Maybe that will help me sleep a little better tonight.'

But, of course, it didn't. This news preyed on my mind almost as much as my constant anguish and fury with her for damn near destroying her father. Would either of us ever get beyond that?

27

Reaching Out

'I hope you get this and will respond.'

From my email to Stacey

After a restless night I woke before dawn with one word shouting in my head: 'Ashbridge'. That was where Jamie had said Stacey was. And I knew she was homeless, but where?

This was still going through my head as I parked the car in town that morning and walked up Weston Road. As I approached a hamburger place my gaze froze on a girl sitting on an old coat on the pavement, with a dog by her side. For one heart-stopping moment, I thought it was Stacey.

Jamie had told me that she was in Ashbridge, not here, and anyway I could see that this girl wasn't Stacey, but I couldn't stop staring. It could be her. She might be sitting just like this in a street in Ashbridge, begging like this girl.

The rest of the day I was mesmerised by this girl's image, but with Stacey's face. I couldn't get her out of my head. I knew what I would have to do.

* * *

The following morning, without telling anyone, I went over to Ashbridge, drove around a bit without seeing her, then parked the car, with the idea of just walking the streets, imagining that I would somehow come across her. As I walked, I remembered someone telling me they thought Stacey might be at the YMCA, so I turned the corner into that street and walked towards it.

I strained my eyes to see if she might be one of a group of young people smoking outside the front of the building. As soon as I recognised her, she looked in my direction, saw me coming and ran off, disappearing into the distant crowd. I'd caught only a glimpse of her, but my fears were realised when I saw her pasty face and her startled gaze in that moment when her eyes met mine.

Right, OK, I thought. She obviously doesn't want to see me. Or perhaps she daren't. I'll leave it. So I went back to the car and set off home again, going over and over those seconds of recognition and her running away.

Back home again, I just sat and thought . . . and the tears began to flow. Mike and I have always had one another, through thick and thin. Sally and Jane had both had bad starts in their lives, leaving their birth families within days of their births, but they've always had us. And Stacey, even though she was with us all those years, now had nobody.

If Mike had died, with all of this still unresolved between them . . . I took a long breath in. And if I'd died when they thought I had the stroke, there would have been a day when she would come out of it all and she'd have to live with that guilt. I sobbed uncontrollably. It felt like I was putting a nail in her coffin . . . and I couldn't do it.

I rang Jamie in the hope that he had a contact number for her. He was wary at first, but he gave it to me and I texted her. I just wanted to know why . . . why she'd done it.

But she didn't reply.

A few weeks later, I had a phone call from Lawrence, our new solicitor.

'Katy has sent me all the papers she compiled the first time around and, now that we have some new funding, I'm keen to restart work on the case against Social Services for you.'

'What are the chances, do you think?'

'I've read through quite a lot of what Katy sent me and I can already see you've got a case. You've definitely got a case.'

'Phew!' I was so relieved after the rock-bottom disappointment of Katy pulling out because the money had all gone. I still didn't understand that, but never mind.

'Have you read Dr Boteral's report?' I asked him.

'Oh my God!' he exclaimed. 'Not Dr Boteral!'

'You've heard of her then?'

'You could say that. I'd better have a look at it I suppose.'

'Well, I should put a large clove of garlic with that one.'

He laughed. 'Really, that bad?'

'She was awful. Confrontational to all the kids and especially hard on me.'

'So they didn't want to cooperate?'

'Did they hell? They were all in floods of tears and frustration by the time we left to go home. It was appalling.'

'Right. Well, we won't be using it. I want a fresh start, and we'll commission our own report. I want to specify the focus we need for the case, and I know just the right man for that, Dr Robson. He's a much more sympathetic character. I reckon you'll all get on fine with him.'

'Well, anybody has got to be better with children than that harridan!'

'Next,' he changed the subject, 'I need to see and speak to all of the children, to introduce myself, explain what will happen and ask them a few questions. Do you think that would be all right?'

'I'll check with them,' I said. 'Carrie and Sam still live at home. Jamie is in a place of his own, but I can talk to him. I'm sure it will be fine with all of them, once they realise it's not a Dr Boteral situation. Except maybe Stacey, because she's had a rift with the family and I'm not sure she will cooperate.'

'Well, I will need to include all of them.'

'I can give you Jamie's contact details if you like.'

'Thanks. I'll contact him direct,' said Lawrence. 'What about Stacey?'

I drew breath between my teeth. Then gave him a brief rundown on Stacey's allegation and its repercussions.

'I see,' he said. 'That must have been very difficult for you all.'

'Very difficult,' I agreed. 'It still is.'

'Do you have her contact details?'

'Just her phone number, if she still has it. But I think Jamie might be able to help you with that.'

I texted Jamie later that day and he texted me back an email address for Stacey. He said she'd lost her phone and that was all he had.

Being dyslexic, I'm not a great one for emails, so I waited a few days, till I was in the mood, then took a deep breath and gave it a try. I typed in her email address and checked it carefully. That bit was fine, but now the difficult part – what to write?

Hi Stace, are you aware the court case is continuing? This will be the last chance you will have to get yourself sorted. You really need to think that you could make new beginnings and get your life back on track. You have a brain and could make a difference to other lives. Perhaps it's time to take stock of your friendship group. They may not have your best interests at heart.

Dad found a memory stick with your photos on. Do you still have your memory box? Try not to lose it.

I hope you get this and will respond. Are you aware how ill Dad has been? He was glad to get out of hospital. We are still cooking brownies, but not as good as yours! Are you still cooking? Carrie is in a musical – 'Fame', and is driving us mad with her songs. Gina and Jamie's baby is just like Jamie and I have another granddaughter, Carla.

If you want to join us in the case, I will take you and treat you to something to wear. Please think about it. You

*can make a better life for yourself if you want it badly
enough.*

Mom

I clicked the send button and waited . . . Five days later,
Stacey replied. I opened it with trepidation.

Heya Mum.

*I am aware of the court case. Lawrence Chandler came to see
me to talk about it. I'm in Durvale now and have my own
place, yeah! I heard about Dad. I hope he's OK. Gina told me
over facebook. I had no idea. How is he coping? And the
family? To be honest, Mom, it's been so long since we've
talked. I'm a different person now. I know I made so many
mistakes Mom, but I wish you were there for me. I needed you
so much and Dad and the family. But I've done it, Mom. I've
walked away from the worst things of my life. I still am not
perfect. I still manage to make the wrong decisions and yeah,
I haven't sorted my life out entirely yet but I've got time and
I'm in the process. It's just difficult.*

*I'm glad to hear about Carrie and her musical talents. Is
she a good singer Mum? I miss her too and Sam and Jamie.
Wanna see the family again, but I don't think I'll ever be able
to look at you and Dad in the eyes after everything. Can't
believe you wrote to me. I didn't know if we'd ever talk again.
I got involved with the wrong people. It messed me up a bit.
How are you though? How are you coping with the kids and
after, well, you know, the stroke?*

I never had the courage to ask or rather speak to you. Are you still living at the farm? I've lost weight lol ☺ How are the dogs and cats doing? God, I forgot about those brownies. Haven't made them in years. Can't believe it's already been two years since I left home. I missed you tho Mum and I just wish so much me and you had that mother–daughter relationship we should have had . . . I've wanted to talk to you about so many things, and problems that I never thought I'd go through. One being that I had to walk away from someone that hurt me. It was hard, but I did it, and I've had to learn a lot.

I thank you so much for teaching me the important things in life, things that I thought back then were stupid, that are now there fixed inside me like a flippin marker pen, like I can't stand an untidy flat. Does Dad still play his keyboard???? I've seen a picture of little Jordan. He's so gorgeous and just by looking at the picture I can see Jamie in him so much. How old is he now? And Carla – is she Anna's little baby? That's a beautiful name . . .

Well, I have no children as of yet ☺ Waiting to find the right man. However in my last two years' experience, men are pigs and very few are decent. However, I met someone not long ago and we're doing well atm. He's 24 but works full time. A hard worker, Mum, and he has his head screwed on.

To be honest Mum, I'd love to see you again, but I won't lie. It will be hard for me as much as it will most likely for you. Hope things are well with the family and that you and Dad are doing OK. Please keep me updated about the family, but especially Dad. I love you Mum, and I don't think I've ever said it with as much meaning as I do now.

Please write back. Xxxxxxxx

*P.S. I would love to see those pictures . . . and yeah, I still
have my memory box. Lol xxx*

I scoured it through. Not a mention of an apology for the
allegation. But I was very relieved that things seemed to be
going better for her now, though it didn't quite match what
I'd heard from other people.

I wrote back straight away, only minutes after she had
sent her email to me.

*I hope you are impressed I can email. Are you going to do the
case? You should. I will ask Dad to sort out the photos. But he
is like a broken man . . . when you made the allegations, he
had the police and social workers all over him and he then had
the heart attack.*

*Cats and Dogs are fine. We are still living at the farm. I'm
glad you are now houseproud. So is Jamie. He can't cook
brownies though!!!!!! Carla is beautiful . . . Are you working
at college?*

*Glad you are settled as we're hearing all sorts of dreadful
things about you – drugs and sleeping around, but when
people are jealous of you they make up lies, don't they?
Rise above the rumours. It's nice you have someone in your
life who cares. Sam is just making me a drink. Got to go.
Speak soon. Mom.*

I wasn't surprised she didn't reply straight away. I had
worded my email carefully and it must have struck home.
Eleven days later, Stacey sent her reply.

*Mum, I would love to see you again and talk, but I can't do it
and you know why, deep down. How could me and you have a
relationship when you don't believe your own daughter and
you assume I'm lying . . . At the end of the day, I love Dad
and I'm not a manipulative cow, I'm not writing to you to
cause shit, I'm saying what is.*

*Yes, I am doing the court case, but separately, because
the allegations are gonna be brought up. Lawrence Chandler
explained this to me. Do you really think we could make it
work when all my family don't believe me? I'm sorry
Mum. I truly am. I would give anything to have you in my
life again, including Dad. But come on. It's not possible is
it? . . . Love you Mum. Never forget that what I say, I
mean it.*

Sad as it made me, and angry too, there wasn't anything else
to be said after that. I couldn't forgive her for what she did
to Mike. He was deeply scarred by her allegation and it was
all still so raw. I couldn't have her in the house. I couldn't.
It had deeply wounded me too, but there was still a hidden
part of me that couldn't stop loving her.

It had been a long time since we had exchanged those
emails. All I knew from Jamie was that Stacey had moved
to Durvale. All the family were still so angry with her,
that I could never talk about her, except to Mike. He
never said anything, but I knew he worried about her
too.

Would we be estranged from her forever? She was still
very young to cope without any family to fall back on. I

knew we couldn't do that for her, but maybe I should just reach out my hand to her. So I asked Jamie for her phone number and sent her a brief text, suggesting we meet for coffee the next morning.

I kept the phone by me, but there was no reply for several hours. Then finally it came. She agreed.

I was there early at the little bistro in the centre of Durvale, so I sat at a table and watched the world go by. Time passed slowly, very slowly, as my apprehension grew. This was a stupid idea. She wouldn't come. Why should she? How long should I wait before leaving? I might as well order a drink to fill the time.

Just then, she came through the door, looking better than last time I'd seen her, but that had been more than a year ago.

'Hi, Mum,' she said in a tentative voice and sat down opposite me.

'Hello, Stace. Thanks for coming. Do you want a coffee?' I ordered. Then we began a guarded conversation.

'How is life treating you now?' I asked.

'OK,' she said.

'How are you managing?'

'I've got a waitressing job.'

'Oh good. Do you ever see Jamie?'

'Not really, but he texts me sometimes.'

'It's good to see you, Stace,' I reached my hand out to her across the table.

She hesitated. 'You too, Mum,' she said, then put her hand in mine for a few seconds. 'How's Dad?'

'He's more or less recovered from the heart attack now.' I paused. 'But he's never been the same since your allegation.'

She took her hand away. 'I don't want to talk about it.'

'I didn't tell any of the family I was going to meet you.'

She said nothing, but her dark-brown eyes looked steadily into mine. 'How are Carrie and Sam?'

'They're fine. They miss us all being together. Dad and I do too, but that can't be, can it?'

'I suppose not.' She lowered her head, on the defensive now.

I let the silence lie between us.

'I'd like to come back,' she said in a small voice, looking up again, her eyes almost pleading.

'I don't think it could happen, Stace . . . unless you apologise for everything. The stealing and lying. But the worst thing was the allegation. It hurt your dad so badly, worse than you'll ever know. And me too. You owe us all an apology. If you want to come back, even for a visit, you would have to apologise. And you would have to retract your allegation.' I had meant to be cautious. Maybe I had said too much.

She said nothing as she finished her coffee and got up from the table. 'I've got to go now. Give my love to Dad . . . and everyone.'

I wanted to get up and give her a hug. It was instinctive I suppose, but before I could, she was gone, walking towards the door and out into the crowded street.

I stayed in my seat for a few minutes longer, going

through what we'd both said. Would I see her again? Could she ever apologise to any of us? I felt immensely sad, but there was a small flicker of hope, deep down. Was it misplaced?

28

A Wary Reconciliation

'Dear Mum, this letter has taken some time to write.'

'What on earth have you been doing in our bedroom?' asked Mike, when I came back from taking the kids somewhere.

'What do you mean?'

'When I came in and went upstairs, there was stuff all over the bed.'

'What stuff?'

'I don't know. I didn't go in and look. It was just a pile of papers, bits and pieces, and some cards stood up on the bed.'

'That wasn't me!'

We both went straight upstairs to have a look. As soon as I got into our room I could see there was a lot more that Mike hadn't noticed. We stood and stared.

In that short time when we were both out, someone had come into our bedroom, found my memory box and turned it out all over our bed, fished amongst the jumble of photos and souvenirs, and the children's notes to me, and stood up some of the cards on top of the duvet. Looking at which cards had been chosen, I had a good idea who this might have been. But if I'd had any doubts, they would have been dispelled by the awful mess they'd made on the mirrors and dressing table, all covered, the mirrors obliterated, with garish colours of metallic spray paint. What a mess!

The painting over of the mirror made me think of just one person. Not long after the children had arrived with us, Stacey, or Anita as she was then, at the age of six announced to us all that she was growing her fringe long enough to cover her face, so that nobody could recognise her as the girl she used to be.

As I inspected the damage and imagined Stacey making merry with the spray cans, Mike went off and phoned the police. There must have been a squad car nearby as they arrived minutes later.

One policeman stood in the doorway while the other came in to have a closer look at the mess.

'Somebody doesn't like you, dear,' he said.

'No,' I said. 'My daughter left under very difficult circumstances.'

'How did you know it was Stacey?' Mike asked me later, after they'd gone.

'Who else could it be? Who was the one who hated mirrors, who wanted to grow her fringe to hide her face so nobody would see it and recognise her?' I paused. 'It was the mirrors she sprayed in our bedroom. She completely covered them with paint.'

A few days later, the police called us and I answered.

'Hello, Mrs Merry. We've tracked down your daughter, Stacey, and we've questioned her about the break-in and the damage to your bedroom, but she's given us an alibi. We checked it out and it's a solid alibi, so we are not charging her with this.'

'Oh, I see.' I didn't know whether to be relieved or indignant that she'd managed to cover her tracks. It was a bizarre episode . . . maybe a sign of something. I just didn't know what.

Carrie and Sam were doing all right at their schools and Jamie kept in sporadic contact, when he felt like it. It was depressing texting him every week and hardly ever hearing back from him. But then I would think back to that first night, when they all arrived on our doorstep. It wasn't their fault. It's not their fault, I thought, and it's not my fault either. So instead of beating myself up about all the mistakes I'd made along the way, I just kept trying. I don't know how many times he rejected my attempts to keep in touch, how many times he let me down, and I was quite surprised at myself that every time I managed to pick myself up and think: This is the very last time, Jamie, that I'm giving you another chance. And of course it never was the last time.

One day, when it was coming up to his birthday, which is the same day as mine, I texted him.

'Your birthday's coming up. I'm going to Ashbridge. Would you like to come and have a coffee and I'll buy you a birthday present?'

'Yes,' he texted back straight away.

I picked him up and he was terribly polite. I leaned

forward a little to give him a kiss, but he wasn't having any of that. He just got in the car and off we went. We had a polite chat over coffee and went off to choose something new for him to wear. When we got back and I dropped him off, he turned back to face me and smiled.

'Thank you very much for the birthday present.'

The next day he texted me. 'Thank you for the present and hope you have a nice birthday as well.' And then I didn't hear from him again for a while. But I just had to keep texting him and hoping that one time he would text me back.

With Stacey it was different. Even though she hadn't contacted me, I did text her from time to time, just so that she knew I was thinking of her, and she wasn't abandoned. But it was up to her to respond, and she didn't.

We were approaching our golden wedding the following year, so I wondered if perhaps we should hold a big party at home.

'Yes, that would be lovely,' said Mike. 'A big party for all our family and friends.'

'And Stacey?' We hadn't talked much about her lately and all I knew about her was that she was all right, according to Jamie.

'What do you think?' he asked, looking at me rather warily.

'I'd like the whole family to be there.'

'Well, why not?' he shrugged. 'She's part of the family, but what do you think the others will say?'

'I don't think any of them would be happy with that. They're so protective of you, and still incensed about how much she hurt you.'

'Both of us.'

'Yes, but maybe if I talk to them . . . I don't know. I'll call a family meeting and see how it works out.'

'Good idea.'

Neither of us had mentioned the F word – forgive – but I felt it was still the big stumbling block. How could I expect any of us to forgive without an apology, some sign of remorse? I had said to Stacey about Dad deserving an apology, and the rest of us too, the last time we met. When we had coffee in that Durvale bistro. I had heard nothing from her since, unless you count the spray-paint episode.

'It's our golden wedding coming up next year,' I began to explain the following Sunday afternoon, when we all sat around the dining table for a family meeting. Whenever there was any important decision to be made, we had always gathered everyone together to ask for their opinions. I felt this was going to be one of the biggest decisions we would make for quite a long time.

'We've got to do something for that,' grinned Laura.

'Let's have a party,' added Brett.

'Yes, I could help Mum make some cakes,' suggested Carrie.

'Good idea, but I don't think Mum should have to make her own anniversary cake, though,' said Jamie.

'I agree,' said Sam with a nod.

'We could hire a big room in a hotel,' suggested Jane. 'And invite your and Dad's friends there as well. We could make it a special lunch party.'

'It's very kind of you, but that would be awfully expensive.'

'We could all club together,' Jane offered straight away.

'I know, and it's very generous, but I've talked about it with Dad and what we'd both really like is to put on a big party here, for everyone to come and share our special day. We could put on lots of food, and you could all bring things too. Everyone could help us decorate the house and get everything ready.'

'That sounds great!' Laura smiled. 'I can't wait. When is it?'

'Not for ages yet,' I said. 'I just hope we both last that long!'

'Of course you will,' said Anna, always the one to re-assure us.

'We want the whole family to be there,' I said pointedly. 'Everyone.'

There was a stunned silence as they all thought about that and began to realise what I meant. The whole atmosphere changed and even the air in the room seemed to cool.

'You don't mean Stacey? Surely you can't mean Stacey, after she nearly killed you both?' Jane was on a mission now. 'If you give Stacey another chance to come back to this house, I will not come. None of us will. You can't mean it.'

'Dad and I did have a talk about it and we would like to

have everyone there that day. I know she might not want to come, but we'd like to be able to invite her.'

'Do you want this family party or don't you?' insisted Jane. 'Because if Stacey comes, I won't. You cannot let her do this to Dad again.'

'I won't come either,' agreed Brett.

'Me neither,' added Laura. 'I'll never be able to forgive her for what she did to Grandad.'

And everyone else agreed that they could not forgive her. They could not have her in the house and she must not come. They made it very, very clear; they were absolutely vehement.

I wasn't surprised by the strength of their feelings. I hadn't forgiven her myself.

It was about a year since I had last seen or heard from Stacey when I received a letter through the post, addressed just to me, with what looked like her handwriting. I stared at it, as if that could tell me for sure. I felt I knew, but it was so long since I had seen her writing on anything . . . I turned the white envelope over and over in my hands, then put it down carefully on the table, address right way up, facing me.

I was alone in the house. Had Stacey come back into my life or was this some new bombshell about to drop on us? I felt almost afraid to open it, to break the spell. I put the kettle on and made a cup of coffee, then brought that back to the table and sat down in front of the letter.

Finally, I could wait no longer. I opened it and unfolded two neatly typed A4 pages. I began to read. One word leapt out at me, on the first line, and then again . . . and again. I didn't read far into Stacey's letter before the tears welled up and blurred my vision so much I had to go and get a tissue. As I read, so many parts of the letter stood out and hit me:

Dear Mum,

This letter has taken some time to write . . . Firstly, I would like to apologise for the behaviour that I portrayed in the time I was living with you. It has taken me this long to realise the mistakes I made and I am hoping to show you that I am a very different person now . . . I want to take this time to tell you the absolute honest truth. When I look back on how I was at home I cringe and hate the person I once was and if I could redo it again with the knowledge and understanding I have now I know I would do it better and me, you and our family wouldn't be so distant as it feels now. I wish that we could have had that mother–daughter relationship I now crave.

The first apology I would like to make is for all the lies and deceit I put you and our family through. Looking back now I realise I didn't need to lie about things . . . I realise that it was hard for you, especially when you thought of ways to teach me it was wrong and all I did was make it worse . . . When we sat down and talked about things as a family, I really did believe that I could change . . . but I was so wrapped up in myself and thinking that everything was unfair, I stopped myself from seeing the bigger picture . . . Back then I didn't think I was spoilt but not many children get what you and Dad gave me. Especially all those chances you used to give me. At home I would think you didn't care, but now I see you cared a great deal, otherwise why would you have put up with so much? Any other foster/adopted parent would of gave up I think but you kept pushing me to be a better person and even though it felt like I threw it all back without a single gratitude I want you to know that I am very grateful for it now and I know Im so lucky that even now you still are trying and I want so much to prove to you Im very different now.

The second apology is for the stealing . . . I cannot explain why I stole. You and Dad gave me everything and yet I still stole from you and I am especially ashamed about the money from your purse and your credit card . . . However with the rings my memory is so fuzzy about whether I stole the original sets . . . I was such a kleptomaniac that I can't remember whether I did . . .

I would like to pay you back for the rings to reimburse you of your loss. I know how sentimental those rings were to you and . . . I want to say I am sorry for causing you the discomfort . . .

. . . even though I caused so much trouble and animosity at home . . . if it wasn't for you believing in me I wouldn't be the person I am today. You made me believe if I put my mind to it I could do and be anything I wanted. I also remember the little quote you gave me, 'if I always do what I have always done, I will always get what I have always got.' It is a very good saying because I see that if I change a simple pattern of behaviour it can make a small difference. But then if I was to change a big act of behaviour I would get a completely different outlet. And Im hoping that with this letter me and you can get back on track to how things should of been a long time ago. I hope this letter has

helped and would love to be able to start being a proper family
again. I would like to thank you as well mum for never giving up
on me and I will always thank you for that I am grateful.

Love Stacey xx

I was stunned, and full of emotion too. Some of the things she wrote in her letter really heartened me, that maybe I had done some things right after all, and a few of the things I had said had stayed with her. The apologies struck me as genuine, though she didn't directly mention what she did to Mike. Maybe that was too much to hope for.

Straight away I texted the only number I had for Stacey to thank her for the letter, to let her know I appreciated how hard it must have been for her to write, and to tell her I appreciated the apologies and I sent her my love.

Only a few days later, two more letters arrived, this time to Carrie and Sam. Stacey had handwritten these. I never saw Sam's. I don't know what he did with it and he didn't ever talk about it. But Carrie was very pleased to have a letter to herself and showed it to me. Stacey had taken care to write a really chatty letter, remembering back to some funny times together and, in between some affectionate phrases, she apologised to Carrie too.

'I've never had a letter from Stacey before,' said Carrie with a beaming smile. 'Do you think she will come and live back home again?'

'No, I don't think so, love. She has her own life now, but maybe she will come back to visit. Let's wait and see.'

Jamie had a letter as well. So now Stacey had apologised to me and to the other three. Mike was pleased for them especially, and he had read my letter a couple of times.

'I'm glad she admitted the thefts,' he said. But it's what he didn't say that upset me. He must have felt that we had heard from her and he hadn't. We had all had apologies, but nothing for him, and he was the one who was hurt most.

Finally one day, when I logged on to my emails, there was one from Stacey starting 'Dear Dad . . .'. I went out onto the landing to call him, but of course he couldn't hear me, so I had to go and find him.

'There's an email for you from Stacey,' I said.

'Really? What does it say?'

'I don't know,' I laughed. 'I don't read letters addressed to you, well not unless you want me to.'

'OK, let's have a look and see. Perhaps she's after all the pocket money she would have had since she left!' He grinned. 'Why don't you sit down with me and we'll read it together?'

So I brought in another chair.

Dear Dad

I know this letter has took some time to write and you may believe it was because i didnt care but that isnt the reason.

What i did to you was the worst thing any daughter could ever do to their father and i know its been extremely difficult, hard and very upsetting for you. This letter has taken so long partly because although i can say im sorry about everything i did and especially for what i put you through with the allegations i made against you. But for me sorry doesn't condole enough and it never will as what i did is unforgivable and sorry doesn't even come near. Ive found it hard to write to you as i wasnt sure if this would upset you more or make it harder as this is very hard for me to write as it brings it all up.

If i could go back and change the way things turned out i would. Belive me when i say that you were always on my side at home backing me up even when i was in the wrong. We used to be so close and i miss that so much and i know we will never be the same. I am sorry dad and if i could honestly tell you why i did it i would and i dont know if i ever will know. My head is just so messed up . . .

I also want to apologise for all the stress i put you through at home. It wasnt fair to expect you to intervene all the time when i was in the wrong and it certainly wasnt fair to keep putting you into awkward positions with mum. I know it caused a lot of arguments and stress between you and mum and for that i really do want to say sorry . . . Back then i was selfish and spoilt and only really cared about myself. I did and still do care and love you dad, as my dad you will always be. No one else will ever replace you. When I was upset you were my shoulder to cry on. You picked up all the pieces. You made me feel special like mum but you especially. I Love You Dad and im so sorry i really am. I hate myself for what i did to you. It hurts because i made you even more vulnerable and ive ruined the best things that i had was a father. You didnt care that i wasnt yours through blood you loved me for me and i was callous, stupid, irresponsible and blind not to see it.

I hope that one day, i know i could never be properly forgiven but i hope one day we would be able to sit down and talk about it and maybe be able to start some form of a relationship because to be honest i would really like that dad. I miss your hugs i miss the way we used to talk. I could always turn to you when i had a problem and i wish so much i still had that. I hope this letter has helped you a little bit i already feel a little bit better writing it but i know it won't be enough but i just want you to know that i never stopped loving you. Your my dad and always will be to me.

　　Love Stacey

We both sat back in silence, overwhelmed. After all this time, three long years, she had finally admitted how malicious she had been with her terrible allegation and apologised direct to him.

'Phew,' said Mike. 'She's done it. A bit late, but she's done it.'

On the following Saturday, I went to pick up Stacey in Durvale and bring her back to the city with me. She had asked me to go with her to the police station to retract her allegation.

The journey into town was tense and silent. I could see she was petrified. I was petrified! I thought they might want to put her away for wasting police time.

It was a strange feeling, sitting with her, listening to what she told them as she took it all back, everything she had accused Mike of.

'It was all lies,' she admitted, and they wrote down what she said. Then I watched her sign the retraction with a flourish.

'There!' she sighed.

'Well done, Stace.' I gave her hand a squeeze as we left the interview room and went back to the car.

'To be honest, Mum, it's a great relief,' she said. 'Social Services next.'

So off we went and we walked in together. I let her hand over the second signed copy of her retraction at the desk. 'Put that on file,' she said in a steady voice.

I could see she felt good about herself, having done it.

'Now let's go back to the house for a cup of tea,' I said. 'And Dad is waiting to see you.'

Just for a moment, she looked uncertain. A wounded look, as if she might change her mind about seeing him, but then she seemed to compose herself.

'Yes, I'd like to see the old place again, and especially Dad. But I'm frightened he might not want to see me.'

'He does, Stace. He's waiting for you now.'

When we walked in through the front door, Mike came into the hall, walked straight over to Stacey and put both his arms around her. She was as rigid as a board. I felt so moved that he had done that and so sad that she had not been able to reciprocate.

We didn't really talk about the letters she had sent or where things might or might not go from there. She told us about where she was living and some of the people she worked with. I felt she had been through it enough for one day, so we kept the conversation light, almost as if she had never been away. Finally I drove her back home.

'Dad is looking older,' she said in the car. 'It's all my fault, isn't it?'

'Well, yes it is your fault in a way, because of the allegation especially, but you know it's not *all* your fault. You didn't choose the birth parents you had or the terrible life you lived when you were little. You can rise above all that and be the different person you always wanted to be. But you have to tell the truth. No matter how bad things are, you have to tell the truth, because with the truth we can fight the demons.'

'Yes, Mum. You're right. You always know the right thing to say. I wish I could do that.'

'It took courage for you to go to the police station today and to admit you had lied.' I paused to let that sink in. 'And I think it probably took even more courage to come home and see Dad this afternoon. I know he was very glad you did.'

29

Golden Wedding

'Stacey is trying to mend fences.'
Extract from psychologist's report

Our golden wedding anniversary was only weeks away now and I really wanted to have the whole family together, including Stacey. I didn't know whether inviting her would do her any favours, especially if she thought everybody was going to forgive her. I knew that wasn't going to be possible.

'If she could be on her best behaviour,' suggested Mike, 'that might help.'

'Yes, but it would be hard for her to cope with anyone's disapproval.'

'Time for another family powwow?'

'Yes.'

So we invited them all for lunch one summer Sunday and I broached the subject in the afternoon.

'Now that we've got the party planned for our golden wedding,' I said, 'let's talk about the guest list.'

'How many people do you want, Mum?' asked Jane.

'Well I'd like to come,' grinned Mike, who had joined us for the discussion this time.

'We could hardly do it without you, love.' I put my arm round his shoulders.

'Let's have as many as we can squeeze in,' said Laura, who always loves a big party.

'Have we got that many friends?' joked Mike.

'Yes, let's invite as many friends as we can. I'll make a list. We'll hire a marquee so there will be lots of space. It can be a day and evening do. And, of course we want all of the family to be there.'

'Except for Stacey,' added Jane.

'No, including Stacey, if she will come. I've talked about it a lot with Dad and we both want to invite her, then it's up to her.'

'That's right,' agreed Mike.

They all looked shocked, dismayed.

'It will be hard for her to come and face you all, but she has written apology letters, as you know. And I went to the police station with her so I heard her telling the police-woman that her allegation had been all lies.'

'But none of that really matters,' protested Jane. 'The damage was done, and it was the most terrible damage she could have inflicted.'

'She realises that now,' I said.

'Well I'm not coming if Stacey comes,' announced Laura, who had always been Stacey's friend before all this had happened.

'Me neither,' said Brett, and all of the family joined in.

'We just can't have her in the house, stealing our things like she always did,' said Sam, who obviously felt strongly about this.

'Yes,' agreed Carrie. 'She mustn't go upstairs to my bedroom.'

'It's OK to keep in touch. We text each other sometimes,' said Jamie. 'But having Stacey here would be much harder for everyone.'

'Especially with so many of your friends here,' agreed Laura. 'Knowing what she did to you both.'

'I can't ever forgive her for that,' stressed Jane.

'Phhh . . .' I let out a long breath, disappointed, but hopefully not completely defeated. 'Look, it's just one day. If we haven't brought you up well enough for you all to just . . . I'm not asking you all to throw your arms around her. But it's an important day in our lives, Dad and me. It's an achievement, fifty years . . .'

'You can say that again,' laughed Mike.

I gave his arm a slap.

'Did I tell you about the domestic violence?' he asked everyone. It broke the ice a bit, which helped me continue with what I wanted to say.

'It's something we should celebrate, and I really would like us to celebrate as a whole family.'

'Well, I'm not speaking to her if she comes.'

'She can stay away from me too.'

The responses had changed just slightly, but was I asking too much?

'Right,' said Jane. 'I think I'm speaking for all of us?' She looked round and everyone nodded, so she carried on. 'I accept that it's your party, so you should invite who you want to. We can all understand that. But it doesn't mean we have to accept Stacey if she dares to come. It doesn't mean we have to speak to her, and it certainly doesn't mean, and won't ever mean, that we forgive her.'

'I agree,' said Anna, with little Carla sitting on her knee.

So I sent an invitation to Stacey, with a note saying that Dad and I would love her to come, but she must be sober and she must be on her best behaviour. She must try not to upset anyone and she must agree not to go upstairs, under any circumstances. We wanted it to be a happy day, and we wanted very much to include her.

It was a few days before I received her reply, by text. Yes, she would like to come and she agreed to be a good girl.

The day came, the weather was dry, the marquee had been set up the day before and decorated by the family. We did all the last-minute things and then got dressed up ready for the fray. It was amazing.

The whole long drive was like a procession of vehicles, stretching all the way uphill from the road. Soon the marquee was buzzing and it was wonderful seeing so many of our old friends together, especially for us. If we'd had time, I think we would have felt quite overwhelmed by people's kindness and generosity, some coming very long distances, just to spend a few precious hours with us.

I can't remember what time of the day Stacey arrived, but I remember she was driven over by two male friends in their battered car, and all three of them got out and came to say hello to us in the marquee, then left in the direction of the house. I knew there were several people in there, including Carrie and Sam, so I didn't worry too much. Perhaps Stacey just wanted to show the house to her friends. But quite a few people had noticed her arrival and none of them had spoken to her as she passed.

'Mum . . .' Jane waved to attract my attention and pointed to the house.

'I'm just going to see if the people in the house are all right,' I said to Mike.

As I walked into the hall, both Carrie and Sam made panicky faces at me and looked pointedly at Stacey and the two lads who were halfway up the stairs.

'See, Mum?' wailed Carrie.

'You've got to stop her,' added Sam.

Just then some good friends of ours stopped Stacey and the lads.

I went to the bottom of the stairs in time to hear what they were saying to her.

'I think you'd better go back down, Stacey, and your friends too. Your mum wants us to guard the landing and make sure nobody goes upstairs today.'

'But I'm family,' protested Stacey.

'Yes, but she didn't say there were any exceptions, even for family. Look' – she pointed at the two younger ones in the hall – 'even Carrie and Sam who live here are not going upstairs today.'

Phew, I thought. What great friends we have. Stacey and the boys reluctantly turned and came down again.

'Look, Stacey, I'm so glad you came, but remember our agreement?' I said. 'Why don't you come back to the marquee with me and have something to eat. We can give some food to your friends too for them to eat in the car as they leave. They can always come back for you later if you like.'

Stacey hesitated for two or three seconds and I crossed my fingers.

'OK,' she said, with a defeated expression.

As we walked back and I pointed people out to her, I was relieved that she had come smartly dressed, with shining clean hair. But from her eyes, the way she moved and the slur in her voice, I could tell she was as high as a kite. I just hoped she wouldn't cause any trouble. I dreaded a scene, especially a family confrontation, but that didn't look likely as everyone gave her a wide berth and shunned her if she approached them. No one in the family spoke to her at all, except for Mike and me. She just walked around like a spare part and all our friends were very polite to her, greeting her when she came near. But she didn't fit in – not surprising I suppose, but she made very little effort.

I don't recall how long she stayed, but it didn't seem more than an hour or so, perhaps two. We were all back in the house in the lull between lunch and dinner when she came to say goodbye to me.

'Thanks for having me,' she said, like a little kid. I gave her a hug, but she pulled away, then turned to leave. I watched her walking through the groups of people, who parted to let her pass. She looked so vulnerable and my heart went out to her. I followed her out, ready to wave her off.

We had put a couple of tables out in the courtyard. Anna was sitting there when Stacey went out of the door. Then the most astonishing thing happened. With several of our family and friends looking on, Anna stood up, stepped forward, threw her arms round Stacey and gave her a kiss.

'I forgive you,' she said in a voice loud enough for us all to hear.

Time stopped for a moment as the tears clouded my eyes. I held my breath and my heart really did seem to miss a beat. What a remarkable thing to do. I was so moved that I was speechless, which is very rare for me. The emotional tension held me like a vice.

As Stacey strode off down the drive, I stood arm in arm with Anna, watching her leave, ready to wave if she turned back, but she didn't.

'Thank you,' I said, unable to utter any more words than that.

'I felt I owed it to you, Mum,' said Anna.

I shall never forget that.

After it was all over in the late evening that Sunday, I gathered the kids together before they left.

'Thank you for giving us a wonderful day and making it so happy for us. And thank you for being civil to Stacey when she came. I know it was difficult for everybody, but it all went OK in the end, didn't it?'

And when I went to bed that night, exhausted but elated, I thought of Anna's amazing gesture and the way that none of the family openly rejected Stacey. I can build on this, I thought. Maybe things will improve . . .

* * *

A couple of months later, Stacey was in hospital after her then boyfriend attacked her. Then Social Services put her into a B & B to recuperate, as she had nowhere else to go. Jamie came round to tell me while Laura was with us.

'That's awful,' I said. 'Maybe we should have her here.'

'Don't talk to me about her, Nan,' said Laura.

'Don't give her any more chances, Mum.'

'Well, how many chances have you got then, Jay, if we're counting them?' I said to him. 'Is there a finite number which we won't go beyond?'

I went to visit Stacey in the B & B and asked her to come back to our house to recover properly.

'No, Mum. I'm OK here. I don't want to upset any of the family.'

'Well, can I do anything for you? Do you need anything?'

She gave me a rueful smile and looked across the room at a full black bag behind the door. 'You couldn't take my washing, could you?' she asked, with a twinkle in her eyes.

Over the next few days, I took her washing back and brought home some forms that needed filling in for her to apply for a flat. Being dyslexic, I had to ask Jane to help.

'Oh, you're no good at anything like that, Mum! Who is this for, anyway?' asked Jane.

'It's for Stacey.'

'Well, I could have filled this form in for her . . . if I was speaking to the bitch.'

'I don't trust her,' said Laura. 'I don't trust her. Don't let her hurt Grandad again.'

This form-filling went back and forth for two or three

weeks and all the time Jane was muttering about Stacey. But in the end she and Laura came over again one day.

'Laura and I have been talking about it. We'll give Stacey another chance. But if she lies or steals, that will be it.'

So the next day I went to pick up Stacey and I told her what Jane said. She had a panic attack in the car and I thought I was going to have to take her straight to the hospital.

'I don't deserve this. I don't deserve this!' she kept saying.

Gradually, over the next few weeks, the relationship grew, with Jane and Laura and her boyfriend going over to Stacey's new flat, painting and putting things up for her.

Things were definitely looking up at last.

30

Nemesis

'It is in their best interests for the litigation to be completed as soon as possible.'

Extract from psychiatrist's report, 2013

The court case against Social Services for neglect was coming closer now and Lawrence, our solicitor, was organising for us all to go and see Dr Robson, the new psychiatrist he knew who was apparently at least as good as the accursed Dr Boteral was bad. It was time I had a meeting with all four children so that everyone knew what was happening.

I told the two younger ones that Stacey would need to be included and they responded predictably.

'She mustn't tell lies or steal anything,' said Sam.

'And I don't want her going in my bedroom,' added Carrie.

When I phoned and asked Jamie, his main condition was: 'She's got to let everyone have a turn to speak.'

So, for the first time in years, the four of them came together round the table for a family meeting.

We started with a discussion of the purpose of the

case not being just to get their own back on Social Services, but also to obtain the therapy they all agreed they would really like. 'When the case stopped the first time, they must have thought they'd got away with it,' said Jamie. 'But won't it be harder to win the case now that we're all grown up?'

'Yes, Lawrence did say that it weakened the case a bit that you were no longer small children, but it doesn't change the fact that the local authority were totally at fault.'

'Do you think we will win, Mum?' asked Carrie.

'I can't see how anyone can deny the damage they let you suffer, so yes, I do think you will win. And if it gets in the papers, as it should, then it will be a finger in the air to them, to put it crudely.'

Stacey smiled. 'That's what I love about you, Mum. You always say it like it is.'

'You four are still alive, you survived it, just.'

'Only because Jamie found us food, and saved me from the canal,' said Stacey.

'I want to put Social Services to shame really. That's what should happen. So they don't do it to anyone else,' said Jamie.

'Carrie, do you have any worries about the court case?'

'I don't really know what will happen.'

'Right, well I'm going to ask Lawrence to explain all of that to us before it starts, because I don't think any of us know exactly how it will work.'

'I think it will be good to tell our stories to the judge in court, because at least people will believe us,' said Stacey. I had my doubts about that, with her record, but I'd try and have a word with Lawrence privately about Stacey's history of lying and her compulsion to embroider the truth.

'What about you, Sam? Any questions?'

'You know when they have trials on television? There's always a guy who tries to make you look like a liar. Will that happen to us?'

'We can ask Lawrence whether it will be like that or not.'

'I don't want to speak if that happens,' said Carrie.

'I definitely don't want them asking difficult questions about when we were abused,' added Stacey.

'Lawrence said he thought you would be able to give your evidence by video, from another room.'

A few weeks later, we all trooped off together to see Dr Robson, the child psychiatrist. When we got there, he was very friendly and welcoming. I could see him watching us all perceptively, gauging our relationships and how we reacted to each other. He sussed out Jamie very quickly.

'Is it all right if I go to the toilet?' Jamie asked him.

'Yes, of course.'

'And is it all right if I go and have a cigarette after that?'

'Yes, that's fine, Jamie. Any time. Just say and you can go.'

It was Jamie to go in for his session first.

'All right?' he said, looking at me.

'Shall I just sit here then, Jay?'

'Yes, OK, Mum. You won't go out and leave?'

'No, I'll sit here in the corner.' So that's what I did, quietly reading my book while the other three played a board game and constantly squabbled about whose turn it was, with somebody always cheating. Nothing had changed since they were children.

After half an hour, Dr Robson's door opened.

'Mrs Merry. Could you pop in and join us for a few minutes?'

'Yes.' I followed him back into his room to find Jamie with his head in his hands, sobbing quietly, breaking his heart.

I sat next to him on the sofa and put my arm round him.

'I've not told you, Mum, because you'll think it's awful, but . . .' He couldn't go on.

'You can tell me,' I coaxed him with a gentle voice.

'There were certain things that Jill's boyfriends used to want me to do.' He paused for several seconds. 'I did some of it.' He sobbed again, more loudly than before.

'But, Jamie . . .' I soothed him, reaching up my hand to stroke his hair. 'You weren't even seven.'

'Well, I need to tell you now. You'll think I'm terrible . . .'

'Come on then, but I don't think I will.'

Dr Robson gave me a look and I knew what he needed me to do.

'Come on, love, you need to move away from that now. Dr Robson wants to ask you some more questions,' I said. 'I'm going to go out and have a coffee. And when you come out to have a cigarette, we can have a cuddle.'

'Really?'

'Yep. You're never too old for a cuddle.'

When Jamie finished his session, he came out and sat with me. 'You don't think that was bad of me then, Mum.'

'No. None of it was your fault, Jay.'

The rest of the day went well, much better than with the last psychiatrist, and I was on hand for the moments when I was needed, which weren't many this time.

On the way back in the train, I sat next to Jamie, away from the other three.

'Can I just tell you something?' I began. 'There's nothing on this earth that I've not heard. There is nothing on this earth that I would hold a little boy responsible for. It doesn't matter what it is.' I paused. 'As a child, you can only do what you can do, and like as a parent, you know I can only try my best to improve things as much as I can, by agreeing with you that you need therapy, and that's why we're doing all this.'

Lawrence rang me up a couple of weeks later and asked me to meet him and the barrister at his office, so off I went.

George, the barrister, explained why he wanted me to come on my own.

'I sent for all the Social Services paperwork,' he said.

'It's not very detailed, is it?'

'No, you could say that,' he said with a smile. 'And I've seen the notes you sent to Lawrence about the children's problems at school.'

'Yes?' I wondered where this was going. Lawrence

seemed to be as much the audience as I was, though I'm sure they must have talked to each other beforehand.

'It all looks a bit tricky to me, Mrs Merry,' he continued. 'It's Stacey I'm concerned about. You see, the other side are bound to have access to these case notes and maybe other information that we don't know about.'

'So what is it about Stacey?'

'Unfortunately, some of these incidents that have taken place . . . well, there seems to be a lot of lying going on, especially at school, and when she's not lying, she's exaggerating. Would you agree?'

'Yes, that's a fair assessment.'

'Well, I'm afraid that may be our stumbling block,' he said. 'The other side will go to town on her. They'll push her and push her until even she doesn't know whether something actually happened or not.'

'Oh, I see.'

'And being the one who seems to have suffered the most sexual abuse . . .'

'Yes, I think that's right. And it makes her more fragile than the others.'

'That's what I thought,' added Lawrence. 'When I first met her at the place where she was staying, she seemed very vulnerable, though she was putting on a brave face.'

'Yes, she does that, she can be quite gutsy – she's had to be, but she can't usually keep it up for very long.'

'There has been an important change in the court proceedings for this case,' said George.

'Yes, Trisha,' explained Lawrence. 'That's the main

reason why we wanted to talk to you without the children. Of course, we all know that this is the children's action, but I think you will need to break it to them and see how they react.'

'How do you mean?' This sounded a bit alarming.

'Well . . .' George continued, 'the defence have apparently got hold of all the children's school records, so they must have seen their chance with Stacey.'

'So now,' explained Lawrence, 'they have applied for the case to be heard in open court, with a longer duration allocated for the trial. And their request was granted.'

'What does that mean?'

'It means that each of the children will be interviewed in public, in the courtroom itself, and the defence intend to cross-examine the children much more closely, for up to three days each.'

'Oh no!'

'And the other impact of that,' continued Lawrence, 'is that if Stacey is shown to be lying about even one little detail of her evidence – they will be able to prove that she was an inveterate liar throughout her schooling – so everything she says might be lies. I think we can say goodbye to the huge compensation the judge might have awarded them.'

I was angry now, at the thought that they would crucify Stacey. 'So, what do you suggest?'

'I think it would be better to settle out of court, Trisha. But you'll need to discuss that with all four of them.'

* * *

I drove back fuming, mulling it all over. How could they do this? Hadn't the children had enough to cope with already in their short lives, without having to expose every nasty little detail for public consumption? I was furious. They had stitched up my kids all over again.

Stacey was the one who had said she was looking forward to being believed, and now that didn't seem likely. They would destroy her, and I didn't think I could have stood it, watching them tear her apart. How could I let her be exposed to that? It could destroy her. It would destroy them all.

We had another family meeting and they were all appalled.

'I couldn't face it,' said Stacey. 'It makes me tremble just to think about it. It would be terrible. I would fall apart.'

They all agreed they could not go through with this public cross-examination about the intimate details of all the abuse they had suffered.

'So, the only other thing you can do,' I explained to them, 'is to instruct Lawrence to negotiate an out-of-court settlement. It may not be as much money, but it will be a lot less painful for you all.'

'Yes, let's do that,' said Jamie, and they all nodded their agreement, relieved that they could avoid the public ordeal.

'You've made the right decision,' I told them. 'Now we'll just have to wait and see what compensation they offer you for settling out of court.'

We didn't have long to wait. Lawrence rang.

'They're offering £2,000 for Sam, £4,000 for Carrie, £6,500 for Stacey and £7,000 for Jamie,' he said.

'What?' I was shocked and furious. 'These offers are derisory, insulting. Is that really all they think my kids are worth?'

'It is very low,' Lawrence agreed.

As I expected, when I told the four of them what they'd been offered, they were disgusted and insulted by the paltry amounts.

'Is that supposed to make up for everything those evil paedophiles did to us?' exclaimed Stacey. 'The abuses that have blighted our lives.'

A few days later Lawrence rang with new offers, hardly any better than the first lot. Again the kids felt humiliated, and they refused.

'Why did they offer me more than Stacey?' asked Jamie in a rage. 'She should get more than any of us – she was the one who suffered the most.'

The two younger ones agreed, so they asked Lawrence to get the highest amount he could for Stacey.

This time, we had to wait two weeks for them to reach a decision. OK, so all the amounts had gone up a bit further again, and they had at least bumped Stacey's up higher than the rest. But it still wasn't great. Nowhere near what other comparable cases had been.

'Can't we go back to them again?' I asked Lawrence.

'No, I don't think it would be any good. If we push them any further they said they would insist on going ahead with the court case and take their chances.'

'That's like blackmail.'

'They say that's the highest they can possibly go, so I suppose the trial would be the only alternative, unless you want to back out altogether.'

'So Social Services cheated my kids out of their childhoods, and now they want to cheat them again!'

'But you have won, Trisha. The kids have won. Settling out of court is like an admission of guilt.'

'It's a hollow victory.'

So the children had no choice. They agreed to settle on the third offers and we all went to the judges' chambers on the final day. We were in one big room, with Lawrence and George, the barrister, and the other side were in another room down the corridor. There was a bit of toing and froing between the lawyers to finalise the settlement agreement.

Then the barrister checked one final time with my four. 'Are you happy to accept these amounts of compensation?'

'Yes,' they all said.

'Right, can you each sign this page, next to your names?'

The kids all trooped across to the desk with serious expressions and took turns to sign.

Then I noticed the surprise in the barrister's face as he pointed something out to Lawrence on the contract. Lawrence picked it up and read it, leafing through the pages before and after as well. They whispered a few words between them, then came over to us, all smiles.

'What's happened?' I asked.

'They've made a fundamental cock-up,' said Lawrence.

What? I thought, oh no, don't tell me we've got to go through all this again. But then I saw they were still smiling.

'Well, you won't believe this, Trisha,' he continued, 'but they have forgotten to put in a gagging clause.'

'And they can't bring it in now,' added George. 'It's too late.'

'What do you mean, gagging clause?'

'Whenever there is an out-of-court settlement,' explained Lawrence, 'the agreement includes some wording that prohibits any of the signatories from revealing the details of the settlement to anybody, which basically means, no publicity. That's what we call a gagging clause.'

'But there's no gagging clause here,' explained George, holding up the agreement. 'Nothing at all. I've checked it all through.'

'So what does that mean?' I asked, warily.

They looked at each other then grinned back at us.

'It means you are all free to tell the world that the local authority have agreed an out-of-court settlement with you in your case of negligence against them. In other words, you won, and you can tell whoever you like.'

'You could call the newspapers,' said George. 'They'd love that story.'

'Or,' suggested Lawrence with a triumphant flourish, 'you could even write a book about it if you want!'

'Who, me?' I laughed. 'I'm dyslexic!'

But when I thought about it later on, that wasn't such a bad idea.

It took a while for the kids' money to come through, and they each opened a savings account. It would have bought them the therapy they still so badly needed, but they were all grown up by now, so it was their choice.

The first one to spend any of it was Stacey.

'I want to pay you back for everything I stole from you,' she said to me.

'It's your money, Stace. I'm not forcing you to pay me back anything.'

'I know. But I want to, and that's that.' She was adamant.

'Well, only what we are sure about,' I said. 'Only pay back what we have proof of. Like you admitted to stealing those two rings, but you have told me you don't remember taking any other jewellery, so that other ring that disappeared could have been stolen or lost by someone else.'

'I'll pay you back for that one as well.'

'Thank you for the offer, but no. I couldn't stand up in court and say you stole it.'

But she was so insistent that I had to accept it in the end. I knew there were another two rings that disappeared at some time, but I didn't even mention them in case she tried to pay for those too.

I think Stacey paying me back like that, as soon as her money came, went a long way with Jane and Laura. They had been the ones with the least faith in her before things started to improve between them. Now, they felt I'd been properly compensated; they could see that she had kept her word. It was the commitment they wanted to see. We were all relieved to have that.

Slowly, slowly, Stacey was coming back to us . . . part of the family again.

It's like she said to me one day recently, when it was just the two of us.

'I'm really, really lucky, Mum. I wouldn't have been saying this to you four years ago. I couldn't wait to get out. But I felt everyone was against me then, being a teenager. Now I feel really lucky, because of what I've experienced in the last four years. I'm so grateful that you didn't give up, because I thought at one point that you actually, finally did. And I thought crap. That was my initial reaction. But now I'm glad, because if I hadn't been put into care with you, I'd have most likely been on the streets, stealing food. I probably would have got pregnant young, children . . . everything. Because I wouldn't have had all that background – all that safety around me that you and Dad gave me, so I would have been left to my own devices, and we all know what I'm like when I'm left to my own devices!'

We both laughed.

'I didn't have the best start in life. I probably had one of the worst. But I've been given an olive branch. And I didn't take that olive branch. Well . . . yes I did, I took it with four hands and four feet, but I took it and overused it, then chucked it, right?'

I nodded. She certainly did chuck everything away.

'But now I've been given this other olive branch and I

just feel like, I just sit there and think "Why have I been given another olive branch?" I'd never let it go now.'

'Good job, Stace,' I said, putting my hand on hers.

'Just think, Mum,' she said. 'I'll be here for Christmas this year.'

'I haven't invited you.'

Her face fell. 'Oh, sorry . . .'

'Of course you'll be here,' I laughed, and gave her hand a squeeze.

'Oh, Mum!' she giggled.

Has Stacey been forgiven? Yeah. Everyone has forgiven her now, and that makes me feel full of hope for them all.

One Saturday morning, Jamie popped in with little Jordan, and Stacey had come over to see Laura, who was staying with us that weekend. Carrie made us all cups of coffee and Sam joined us for an impromptu chat. It was maybe the first time that there was no bad feeling or wariness between any of them. Laura went off with her boyfriend and it was just us. Mike, me and our four waifs grown up.

'It's great to be a proper family again, the six of us,' I said with a huge smile.

'Yes,' said Stacey. 'Do you remember, Mum? You used to say all the time when we were young: "Friends come and go, family stay the rest of your life." As I grew up, friends were the most important thing to me. I had to be liked. I had to fit in. Then as I started to grow up, I came to realise. Friends can be with you only for a short time, but family will always be there.'

'I agree,' said Jamie. 'I did the same as you, but now I'm a dad myself, I really appreciate being part of the family again. Looking after all of you when we were little has helped me to be a good dad to Jordan.'

'You all ought to be proud of how far you've come,' I said. 'Even just over the past three or four years. It's massive.'

'I don't know where all those years went,' said Mike. 'Since that night when you arrived on our doorstep. It's all a blur to me!'

We all laughed. 'It was a very eventful blur,' I said. 'That's for sure. I wish I'd written it all down!'

'Do you remember what Lawrence said?' asked Sam. 'About writing a book?'

'Yes, I've been thinking about that quite a lot.' I looked around at them all. 'Do you think I should?'

They all agreed. Mike nodded too.

'Well,' I continued, 'at first, when I was so angry about your low compensation amounts, compared with the scars Social Services had left you all with, I thought yes, I'd do it to spite them. But that's not a good enough reason. What I'm most sorry for was that you didn't get your day in court and the knowledge that the judge had listened to you. Do you remember, Stacey? You said you wanted to be believed.'

'Yes. I always wanted to be believed, and mostly people were quite right not to believe me. I can see that now. But that was one time when I should have been believed.'

'Well, I'm hoping people who read the book will be

disgusted that the Social Services could do this,' said Jamie. 'And let down children so badly. They let us all down.'

'I agree,' nodded Carrie.

'I think it should have our adoption in it,' said Stacey. 'I love the fact that I've been adopted. I love it. I love it! I often sit and think "Thank God. I was lucky." I would never change it at all.'

'Yeah,' agreed Jamie. 'That was the best thing.'

'Well . . .' I smiled at the synergy of what they'd said with what I was thinking. 'If I do this book, and I do want to do it, I'm hoping just one foster carer, just one adopter, one social worker, perhaps one social-work manager, one psychiatrist, one teacher, one whatever, will pick it up and read it and sit and think. But most of all, I would like a child who's been in the care system, perhaps who's just been kicked out at sixteen, to pick up our book and read it, and be inspired by how you've turned your lives around. I would like it to help them. And I would like somebody who perhaps isn't sure about adoption to think "Yes, I'm going to adopt." That alone would be a reason for writing this book.'

'That's great, Mum,' said Stacey. 'You're inspirational. That's what your book should be.'

'Yes, I want people who read this book to know that even when things are as black as black, there is usually a rainbow somewhere. And at times when you think things are so dire that there's no way out, just hang in there and that rainbow will appear.'

* * *

After the family had all dispersed, Mike and I were sitting, just the two of us, reminiscing.

'Would you do it all again?' I said.

He looked at me for several seconds, then broke into a smile. 'Yeah.'

'Even the bad bits?'

'Yeah. Even the bits that were worse than the bad bits,' he laughed.

Laughter is what's kept us going through it all. Laughter . . . and love.

Where Are They Now?

'Go ahead, judge me, but remember to be perfect for the rest of your life.'

Anonymous

A lot of people who hardly knew me, and a few who did, were only too keen to judge me in the bad times. Each of our children, when they ran away, did so not because of anything we did, but to avoid the consequences of what they did. They are all now back in our lives, not because we got it wrong, but because we got it right. They are in our lives because they *want* to be . . . and they're really lovely people. I'm proud of them all. I really am. We both are.

JAMIE is twenty-four and has his own flat, which he's just decorated, and it's looking absolutely the bee's knees. He split up with five-year-old Jordan's mother and is now in a new relationship. His girlfriend has her own baby girl and they are now expecting their first baby together. Jamie works long hours in a well-known pub, honing his cooking skills and taking a break from his college catering course. He loves Jordan to bits and sees him whenever he can. Jamie has long wanted to have his own car and to learn to drive, so he recently bought a second-hand car with some of his compensation money and is hoping to take his driving test soon. Jamie still suffers a lot from anxiety, and was able to have a course of cognitive behavioural therapy on the NHS. He is also paying out of his compensation for some additional counselling and is optimistic about his future with his own family.

STACEY is twenty-three and also has her own flat, which she decorated herself. She is in a steady relationship with a boyfriend she went out with quite seriously a few years ago and they are now back together. She loves him, she always has, and he's very good for her, so fingers crossed, but I won't buy a hat just yet! Stacey is currently volunteering as a play-ranger in a children's holiday scheme, working double shifts, prior to starting her degree at university, hoping to achieve her long-held ambition to become a social worker. She certainly has enough experience of social work, from the other side, and wants to be the kind of social worker she never had, the kind who cares, and the kind who looks out first and foremost for the children's best interests, rather than the adults'.

CARRIE is twenty-two this year and still lives at home with us. With her learning difficulties and special needs, she couldn't do any full-time job, but she did voluntary work in a play scheme for quite a while and loved that. I helped her to set up her own little cleaning business, just within the family, and Jamie was her first client. She said his flat was very tidy and he complimented her on how well she had cleaned it. She has recently started part-time work as a washer-up in the kitchen of a little country pub near where we live. Mike or I take her down there and collect her again at the end of her shift. She does voluntary work one day a week in a children's nursery and they are very pleased with her. She has now got a place at college for a three-year child-care course and has the offer of a paid job at the nursery if she passes. Carrie has been going out with the same boyfriend for two years now and they seem very happy together.

SAM is nearly twenty and did very well at school, so he rebelled later than Jamie and Stacey, but he has had his own 'time out', running away and staying with friends or in a squat, living, but not very well, on social security. Sam was the one who was awarded the least compensation money and he has now used it all up on drinking and drugs. But after a few months he came back and since then has been living at home again. He was hoping to join the Territorial Army, and he wondered whether his autistic difficulties with emotions and social skills would stop him getting a place. The sergeant said, 'No, I don't want to fall in love with you!' Sadly he didn't pass his test to get in and is now helping out in a play scheme, whilst preparing to start his Forensic Science studies at technical college.

MIKE and I live with Carrie and Sam, four rescued dogs, two rescued cats and three 'talking' goldfish in a lovely old farmhouse, surrounded by beautiful countryside. Over the past fifty years we have taken into our home and our hearts nearly seven hundred children, most of whom have experienced the most difficult and traumatic childhoods before arriving on our doorstep, including many emergency placements and large sibling groups. Along the way, we adopted seven of these children and have another semi-adopted daughter. We now have seven wonderful grandchildren and we love spending time with them all.

Acknowledgements

To my dearest husband Mike, I want to thank you for being the best father, grandfather and husband. Your endless support, patience and humour have enabled me to play all my life.

To all my family who have been a part of this monumental journey, from the bottom of my heart, I would like to thank each and every one of you. Without your strength, courage and spirit, this family would not be how it is today. You are all a patchwork of personalities, and I love you all dearly.

To Jacquie, thank you for finally making my dream come true. You have allowed what has been a very traumatic journey to be turned into a chapter of positivity and finally closure. To me you will always be somebody very special.

To all carers and adopters, never give up.

To Lawrence, thank you for finally giving my children justice.

To Clare, thank you for believing in not only me, but my four children.

To Simon & Schuster, thank you for finally giving my children a voice.

Lastly, I would like to thank Jamie, Stacey, Carrie and Sam. While times have indeed been challenging at best, I would like to express how proud I am of the four young people you have become. All four of you have helped me in my own personal journey in which you have filled my life with laughter, happiness, tears, frustration and most of all love.